THE SLANGMAN GUIDE TO

DIRTY ENGLISH

DANGEROUS EXPRESSIONS AMERICANS USE EVERY DAY

ON THE FRONT COVER
Flasher
A person who enjoys showing people his or her genitals in public.

SLANGMAN DAVID BURKE

Editor-in-Chief . . . . . . David Burke

Main contributors . . . . . John Antonino
Jason Reese
Kenny Smith
Janis Tantric

Translators . . . . Sylvia Pabón Andraca (Spanish)
David Burke & Noémie Ducourau (French)
Hyejin Chun (Korean)
Haruka Funase (Japanese)
Qian Jiang (Chinese)

Book Layout & Design . . . Jenn Reese

Illustrators . . . . Ty Semaka (Cover)
Janis Tantric (Interior)

ISBN 1891888-234
Printed in the United States of America
10 9 8 7 6 5 4 3 2 1

CONTENTS

ABOUT THIS BOOK (English) **X5**
   Chinese X5
   French X6
   Japanese X6
   Korean X7
   Spanish X7

HOW TO USE THIS BOOK. **X8**

A **1**
   Dialogue: "Let's haul ass out of here!" 3
   At the Movies: *American Pie* 5

B **8**
   In Other Words... "Breasts" 11
   Dialogue: "Trish has big boobs". 15
   In Other Words... "Butt" 21
   Dialogue: "Mike makes a booty call" 25

C **28**
   In Other Words... "Coward" 33
   In Other Words... "Crazy" 39
   Dialogue: "Dickie and the boys" 41

D **43**
   In Other Words... "Defecate" 45
   Dialogue: "Wanted: Dominatrix" 49
   In Other Words... "Drunk" 53
   Dialogue: "Ray delivers street pizza" 55

E **57**
   At the Movies: *Erin Brockovich* 59

F **61**
   Learn More: "Fuck" in a Sentence. 63
   At the Movies: *Fight Club*. 67
   Learn More: Five Naughty Numbers. 69
   Dialogue: "The fucked up floozy" 73
   At the Movies: *Full Metal Jacket* 75

G **79**
   In Other Words... "Gay Men" 81
   Dialogue: "Get your gaydar fixed!" 83
   Dialogue: "Don't barf in the car" 87

H **90**
   In Other Words... "Surprise" 93
   Dialogue: "Hooking up with a hot chick". . . . 95
   At the Movies: *Home Alone*. 99
   Learn More: Tricky Technical Terms 103

I **106**

J **108**
   At the Movies: *Jaws*. 111

K **112**
   Dialogue: "Harris needs to kiss ass" 113

L **115**
   In Other Words... "Lesbians" 117
   Dialogue: "Married to a low-life". 119

M **122**
   In Other Words... "Masturbate" 125
   At the Movies: *My Cousin Vinny* 129

N **132**
   Dialogue: "Nadine's no nymphomaniac" 135

O **137**
   In Other Words... "Orgasm". 139

P **141**
   Dialogue: "What a pain in the ass". 143
   In Other Words... "Penis" 147
   At the Movies: *Pulp Fiction* 151
   In Other Words... "Prostitution" 153

Q **157**

R **159**
   Dialogue: "The rat-bastard" 161
   At the Movies: *Risky Business* 163

S **166**
   In Other Words... "Have Sex" 169
   Dialogue: "Cindy swallows!". 173
   Dialogue: "John got shit-faced" 181
   In Other Words... "Stupid" 187
   At the Movies: *Scent of a Woman* 191

T **193**
   Dialogue: "Tommy wants tits" 197
   At the Movies: *Titanic*. 199
   In Other Words... "Toilet" 203

U **205**
   In Other Words... "Ugly" 206
   In Other Words... "Urinate" 207

V **208**
   In Other Words... "Vomit". 209
   In Other Words... "Vagina" 210

W **211**
   Dialogue: "Raoul was a wuss" 213
   At the Movies: *What Women Want*. 215

X **217**

Y **218**

Z **220**

MAIN INDEX **221**

INDEX BY USE **226**

DEDICATION

This book is dedicated to **Haruka Funase,** an amazing woman who gifted the Slangman team with her intelligence, insight, sense of humor, and hard work. We miss you, Haruka, and wish you the best of luck for the future.

We would also like to thank our translators who, in the spirit of world-wide communication, volunteered to help us with this book. Sylvia Pabón Andraca, Hyejin Chun, Noémie Ducourau, Haruka Funase, and Qian Jiang, you have our deepest thanks.

And, as always, we'd like to thank Slangman's Mom, without whom Slangman would not have been possible.

DISCLAIMER
(SO WE DON'T GET OUR BUTTS KICKED)

The terms and expressions contained in this book may be objectionable to some people. If you are looking to be offended, you will be offended. If you are looking to laugh, you may *still* be offended...but hopefully laugh.

The terms, expressions, and sample sentences used in this book were taken directly from the demographic which uses this type of language, and are presented in this book as they would actually be heard. The authors do not endorse the usage of this type of language, or the meaning conveyed in the example sentences, as much of it may be considered vulgar, obscene, rude, offensive, and pejorative. The purpose of this book is solely to explain how and where this type of language is used. To help demonstrate this, references to movies, songs, and TV shows are used throughout the book to emphasis the frequency of this type of language in American entertainment and culture.

Further, this book includes textual and visual depictions of nudity in addition to heterosexual, bi-sexual, and homosexual situations. The illustrations are presented to make the book more interesting to use and are not meant to offend. Persons under eighteen (18) years of age and persons who may be offended by such depictions and language are advised not to purchase this material.

This book was created with the intention of creating a more harmonious global community by minimizing misinterpretations through better communication and understanding. In reporting this type of language and its usage, Slangman Publishing is in no way advocating or condoning, directly or indirectly, racism, sexism, ageism, homophobia, hate, violence, or any other form of intolerance.

ABOUT OUR CONTRIBUTORS
(NICE PEOPLE WITH DIRTY MOUTHS)

John Antonino
John has worked various jobs in the entertainment industry during his time in Los Angeles. His contributions to "The Slangman Guide to Dirty English" remain one of his favorite projects to date. "The book really was a labor of love. I feel it is very important for those learning English as a second language to have a complete command of the language. That includes, above all, the ability to swear like a sailor." Currently, John is pursuing his career in stand-up comedy.

Jason Reese
Jason started working with Slangman David Burke in 2000, determined to help people around the world communicate better with each other. He moved to Japan for 8 months in 2001 to explore the culture, teach English, and experience the difficulties of learning another language. As a person who uses the words in this book in almost every sentence he speaks, Jason wants to share the joy and responsibility of using "dirty English" with the world.

Kenny Smith
Kenny is a 1998 graduate of the University of Southern California and a devout listener of rap music. A native Californian, Kenny has grown up with access to "dangerous English" spoken by a variety of ethnic groups. He studies a Korean martial art called Hwa Rang Do and will be testing for his black sash in Korea very soon.

Janis Tantric
Janis has worked as a graphic designer, an editor, a programmer, a writer, and a Web designer. She's also a science fiction and fantasy writer, a martial artist, and a student of humor behavior. "Dirty words are just another way people choose to express themselves and their individuality. The more words you know, the easier it is to communicate your thoughts with others."

ABOUT THIS BOOK

Who is this book for?
Anyone who wants to communicate with Americans. Both beginning and advanced students will understand the definitions and example sentences.

Who uses these words?
All Americans. Some Americans use one or two of these expressions every day, and others use four or five expressions in every sentence! Once you learn these phrases, you'll start hearing them in American conversations, movies, music, businesses, etc.

Why did you write a book about rude and offensive expressions?
Because Americans do use rude and offensive expressions every day. They're an important part of American English.

Is it ok to use the expressions in this book with anyone?
No! Many of the expressions in the book are extremely offensive... but not all. That's why we tell you when each can be used. When the expression is shown in a light gray box, below it you will see the words "used with anyone." When the expression is shown in a gray box, you will see the words "used with friends" below. But, if the expression is shown in a dark gray box with the words "used with extreme caution," don't use it unless you are with very close friends, or you want to start a fight! These are some of the worst words in the English language.

Do you have any products on conversational American English that aren't offensive?
Absolutely! Slangman has many other products on conversational American English using everyday, non-offensive, slang and idioms. For more information, please see the listing of products in the back of this book, or visit our website at www.slangman.com.

Who is Slangman David Burke?
Author Slangman David Burke wrote his first slang and idioms book at the age of 15 after an embarrassing summer homestay in France. He had studied French for years and was fluent in French (or so he thought!), but he could not understand the family he was living with. David discovered that slang and idioms are so common in everyday conversations that most people do not even realize they are using them. Since then, author Slangman David Burke has dedicated his life to writing books on conversational language — the real language. Now with over 24 books on slang and idioms in 5 different languages, Slangman David Burke has no plans to stop writing.

关于本书...

本书适合哪些读者使用?
本书适合英语学习和美语会话学习使用。书中各短语的解释和例句适合所有初级和高级学员阅读。

哪些人使用这些短语?
所有美国人都使用这些短语。这些短语频繁出现在美语日常会话、娱乐活动和商业交流中。

为什么要写书专门介绍这些粗鲁、冒犯的语言?
因为这些语言出现在在美语会话,是美国英语的重要组成部分。

这些短语在任何场合下都可以使用吗?
不是。书中的部分短语非常没有礼貌。因此,我们对书中的各个短语加了标注,区分它们的使用场合。所有用浅灰色框表示的短语适合在任何场合下使用。所有用灰色框表示的短语适合朋友间使用。所有用深灰色框表示的短语必须谨慎使用;这些语言粗鲁、容易冒犯人,只有在很熟悉的朋友之间才可以使用。

除了本书外,Slangman 公司还有其他美语会话类书籍和音像磁带或 CD 吗?
有。Slangman 公司出版、发行了大量美语会话类书籍和音像磁带及 CD,介绍美语日常会话、礼貌用语,俚语及俗语。详见本书封页或访问本公司网站 www.slangman.com。

Slangman David Burke 是谁?
Slangman David Burke 是本书作者。David 在 15 岁那年写了自己第一本介绍美国俚语和俗语的书。一年暑假,David 住在一户法国人家里,虽然他之前已经学了好几年法语,而且口语也很流利(至少他自己这样认为),可是他却听不懂那户法国人说话。David 发现,人们在日常会话中不经意地会使用很多俚语和俗语,因而有了这本介绍俚语和俗语的书。David 决心将毕生致力于口语书籍的编写工作。David 认为口语才是真正的语言。目前,David 已经用 5 种语言写了约 24 本介绍俚语和俗语的书,并决心要将自己的事业继续下去。

A propos du livre...

A qui s'adresse ce livre?
A ceux qui veulent communiquer avec les américains. Les débutants et les étudiants confirmés comprendront facilement les définitions et les exemples.

Qui emploie ces mots?
Tous les américains. Quelques américains emploient une ou deux de ces expressions quotidiennement, et d'autres en emploient quatre ou cinq dans chaque phrase! Après avoir appris ces expressions, vous commencerez à les reconnaître dans les conversations, les films, les entreprises, la musique, etc.

Pourquoi avoir écrit un livre sur les expressions familières et grossières?
Parce qu'en effet, les américains emploient ce type d'expressions tous les jours. Elles jouent un rôle important dans la langue américaine.

Est-il convenable d'employer les expressions de ce livre avec n'importe qui?
Non! Plusieurs expressions de ce livre sont extrêmement grossières... mais pas toutes. C'est pour cela que l'on vous indique clairement à quel type de conversation elles sont destinées: Si l'expression est présentée dans une boîte grise-claire, en-dessous vous verrez les mots «used with anyone.» Si l'expression est présentée dans une boîte grise, vous verrez «used with friends» en-dessous. Mais si l'expression est présentée dans une boîte grise-foncée avec les mots «used with extreme caution» en-dessous, ne les employez pas à moins que vous soyez entre très bons amis. Sinon, vous risquez d'en arriver aux mains! Ce sont les pires mots de la langue américaine.

Avez-vous des produits sur l'anglais américain conversationnel qui ne contiennent pas des mots grossiers?
Absolument! Slangman a beaucoup d'autres produits sur l'anglais américain conversationnel qui comprennent l'argot populaire et des expressions idiomatiques quotidiennes. Pour plus d'information, veuillez jeter un coup d'œil sur la liste des produits au dos de ce livre, ou bien, visitez notre website sur www.slangman.com.

Qui est Slangman David Burke?
L'auteur Slangman David Burke a écrit son premier livre d'argot et d'expressions familières à l'âge de 15 ans après avoir passé un été en France. Il avait étudié la langue du pays pendant des années et n'avait aucun problème à comprendre le français (pensait-il!), mais il ne pouvait pas comprendre la famille qui l'hébergeait. David découvrit que les natifs parlaient en code et que cette langue apparaissait dans les conversations quotidiennes. Depuis lors, l'auteur Slangman David Burke a consacré sa vie aux livres sur la langue conversationnelle. C'est-à-dire, la vraie langue du peuple. Maintenant, avec plus de 24 livres sur l'argot et les expressions populaires dans 5 différentes langues, Slangman David Burke ne compte surtout pas s'arrêter là!

この本について...

この本はどんな読者にぴったり？
アメリカ人とコミュニケートしたいという、どんな方にもお奨めします。それぞれの表現について、ある程度話せる人にもビギナーにもわかりやすく明確に説明されています。

誰がこの本にのっている言葉を使っているの？
すべてのアメリカ人が使っています。この本にでてくる言葉を毎日1、2個使う人もいれば、一言話すたびに5、6個使う人もいます！一度表現を学べば、アメリカ人の会話、映画、音楽、ビジネスで頻繁に使われていることに気づくでしょう。

なぜ、よりによって無礼で攻撃的な表現ばかりを集めた本を書いたの？
私たちアメリカ人は無礼で攻撃的な表現を毎日使っているからです。これらの表現は、アメリカ英語の重要な一部分なのです。

この本に出てくる表現は、誰に対して使っても大丈夫？
いいえ！全てではありませんが、この本に含まれる多くは非常に無礼な表現です。そのため、「使ってもいい状況」がわかるように説明されています。薄いグレーで囲まれた表現の下には「誰に対しても使って良い」、グレーで囲まれた表現には「友達同士なら使ってよい」と書いてあります。しかし、濃いグレーで囲まれた表現には「非常に気をつけて使うこと」と書いてあります。その表現は、とても仲のいい友達以外の人には使わないで下さい。ケンカになってしまうかもしれません！これらは英語表現の中で最も下品なものです。

無礼ではない表現や会話集がのっている本はないの？
あります！スラングマン出版社には、アメリカ人が毎日使う表現、無礼ではないスラングやイディオムを満載した本が沢山あります。詳しくは、この本の後ろにあるリストをご覧下さい。ウェブサイトwww.slangman.comでもご覧頂けます。

著者のSlangman David Burkeって、どんな人？
著者であるSlangman David Burke は15歳の夏にフランスでのホームステイで体験したあるショックをきっかけに、15歳で最初の本を出版しました。ホームステイに行前に何年もフランス語を学んでいたので、彼は流暢にフランス語を話せました。（と、本人は思っていた）ところが、ホームステイファミリーの話す内容が理解できなかったのです。教科書や辞書には無かった言葉—スラングやイディオム—が日常会話であまりにも多用されていて、話している人たちはスラングを使っていることすら気づいていません。この「スラングとイディオムがわからなければ、会話を理解することはできない」という経験以来、Davidはスラングやイディオムの本、すなわちリアルな会話の本を書き続けています。これまでに英語を含む5ヶ国語、24冊を出版しています。そして、今後も書き続ける予定です。

책에 관하여...

이 책은 누구를 위해 지어졌습니까?
미국인과의 대화를 원하시는 모든 사람들을 위해 지어졌습니다. 책에 있는 뜻풀이와 예문을 통해서 영어를 많이 아시는 분이나 이제 시작하시는 분들도 쉽게 이해하실 수 있을 것입니다.

이 표현들은 누구에 의해 쓰여집니까?
모든 미국인들에 의해 쓰여집니다. 어떤 사람들은 하루에 한 두개 정도의 표현들을 쓰지만 어떤 사람들은 네 다섯 개의 표현을 한꺼번에 쓰기도 합니다. 이 표현들을 배우고 나면 미국인들의 대화, 영화나 음악 등에서 많이 듣게 될 것입니다.

왜 이렇게 무례하고 공격적인 표현들에 대한 책을 쓰셨나요?
왜냐하면 이런 표현들을 미국인들이 일상에서 흔히 쓰고 있기 때문입니다. 이런 표현들이 이제는 미국 영어에 있어서 빼 놓을 수 없는 중요한 부분입니다.

이런 표현들은 아무에게나 사용이 가능한가요?
아니오. 다는 아니지만 이 책에 있는 많은 표현들이 상당히 무례합니다. 그래서 저희가 어떤 때에 각각의 표현을 쓸 수 있는지 가르쳐 드리는 것입니다. 옅은 회색상자에 있는 표현 밑을 보시면 "아무 때나 사용 가능함"이라고 적혀 있는 것을 보실 수 있을 것입니다. 회색 상자에 있는 표현 밑에는 "친구와 사용 가능함"이라고 적혀있을 것입니다. 하지만, 짙은 회색 상자에 있는 것은 "아주 조심스럽게 사용해야함"으로써 아주 친한 친구 사이이거나 싸움을 원하는 게 아니라면 피해야 하는 표현들입니다. 이것들은 미국 영어에 있어서 제일 나쁜 표현들에 속합니다.

무례한 영어가 아닌 일반 미국 회화에 관한 제품도 있습니까?
물론이죠! 미국인들이 일상에서 흔히 쓰는 무례하지 않은, 속어나 숙어에 관한 제품들도 많이 있습니다. 더 자세한 정보는 이 책의 뒤에 있는 목록을 보시가나 저희웹사이트 www.slangman.com을 이용해 주시면 감사하겠습니다.

슬랭맨 데이빗 버크는 누구인가?
이 책의 저자 슬랭맨 데이빗 버크는 만 15살에 프랑스를 다녀온 뒤 속어와 숙어에관한 책을 처음 지었습니다. 그는 불어를 몇년간 배웠고 불어는 완벽하게 한다고 생각했음에도 불구하고 프랑스 하숙집 가족들을 알아듣고 이해하기 가힘들었습니다. 그래서 그는 사람들이 무의식중에 얼마나 많은 속어와 숙어를 일상의 대화 속에서 쓰고 있는지 깨닫게 되었습니다. 그 후부터 그는 회화에 관한 책을 쓰기 시작했고 지금까지 속어와 숙어에 관한 책을 다섯 개의 언어로 24권의 책을 썼습니다. 그리고, 앞으로도 그 노력은 계속될 것입니다.

Sobre este libro...

¿Para quién es este libro?
Para todo el que quiere comunicarse con americanos Estudiantes pricipiantes y avanzados podrán entender las definiciones y oraciones que se darán de ejemplo.

¿Quiénes usan estas palabras?
Todos los americanos las usan. Algunos una o dos veces al día, mientras ¡otros los usan 4 o 5 en una misma oración! Una vez aprenda estas frases empezará a oirlas en conversaciones, películas y negocios americanos, etc.

¿Por qué escribieron el libro con frases tan rudas y ofensivas?
Porque los americanos usan estas expresiones rudas y ofensivas todos los días. Son una parte importante del inglés americano.

¿Es apropiado usar las expresiones de este libro con cualquier persona?
¡No! Muchas de las expresiones en este libro son extremadamente ofensivas... pero no todas lo son. Por eso le indicamos cuándo se debe usar cada una. Cuando la expresión esté rodeada por un cuadrado gris claro, verá debajo de la misma las palabras "Use con cualquier persona." Cuando la frase esté en un cuadrado gris verá las palabras "Use con amigos." Pero cuando la frase está rodeada por un cuadrado gris oscuro con las palabras "Use con extrema precaución" debajo de la misma, ¡no la use a menos que esté con amigos muy cercanos o a menos que quiera empezar una pelea!

¿Tiene algún producto de inglés coversacional americano que no tenga lenguaje ofensivo?
¡Absolutamente! Slangman tiene muchos otros productos tratando del inglés conversacional americano los cuales usan frases y dichos común y corrientes y no ofensivos. Para más información, favor de ver la lista de productos que se encuentra en la parte de atrás del libro, o visite nuestra página de internet en: www.slangman.com.

¿Quién es Slangman David Burke?
El autor Slangman David Burke escribió su primer libro de frases populares a los 15 años después de una vergonzosa visita un verano a Francia. Había estudiado francés por varios años y lo hablaba con fluidez (¡o así pensó!), pero no pudo entender a familia con quien se estaba quedando. David descubrió que palabrerías y frases callejeras se usaban tan comunmente en conversaciones cotidianas que la mayoría de la gente ni se daba cuenta que las estaba usando. Desde ese entonces, el autor Slangman David Burke ha dedicado su vida a escribir libros que tratan sobre el uso del lenguaje conversacional- el lenguaje de verdad. Ahora, con 24 libros sobre frases callejeras y dichos populares escritos en 5 leguajes diferentes, Slangman David Burke no tiene ningún deseo de parar de escribirlos.

HOW TO USE THIS BOOK

The expressions in this book are arranged alphabetically. Read the book from front to back, or jump directly to the expression you want.

SAMPLE

Used with anyone*

Expressions in a light gray box are considered safe to use with anyone by most Americans.

Blockhead
USED WITH ANYONE

A stupid person.

EXAMPLE 1

"Joe is a blockhead. He never understands my jokes."

EXAMPLE 2

"Jan is wearing shorts in the snow. What a blockhead!"

○ **Learn more...**

• Men are called "blockheads" more often than women.

Definition

Under each main word or expression, you will see a definition in bold.

Learn More

This section contains information such as the origin of the word or expression, variations, and examples used in American television, movies, music, or other media.

Used with friends*

Expressions in a medium gray box are considered offensive by many Americans, and are only used with close friends.

Blow Chunks
USED WITH FRIENDS

To vomit.

EXAMPLE 1

"I blow chunks every time I eat your mother's cooking."

EXAMPLE 2

"I ruined Amanda's dress. I blew chunks all over it."

Examples

Two example sentences are presented for each definition, written as Americans really speak.

Used with extreme caution*

Expressions in a black box are considered very offensive by most Americans. In fact, some Americans will never use them at all.

Blow Job
USED WITH EXTREME CAUTION

Oral sex performed on a man.

EXAMPLE 1

"I just saw Tim getting a blow job in his car!"

EXAMPLE 2

"Lisa says I'm too big for her to give me blow jobs."

* Note that our rating system is completely subjective, as different people may rate the terms and expressions differently.

A IS FOR ASSHOLE

A Face Only A Mother Could Love

USED WITH FRIENDS

An ugly face.

EXAMPLE 1

"Did you see that guy? Now that's a face only a mother could love."

EXAMPLE 2

"I asked Lucy for a date, but she said I had a face only a mother could love. How rude!"

○ Learn more...

- You may also hear "a face that could stop a clock" or "a face that could crack a mirror."

A Few Sandwiches Short Of A Picnic

USED WITH ANYONE

To be crazy or strange.

EXAMPLE 1

"Larry plays tennis in the rain. He's a few sandwiches short of a picnic."

EXAMPLE 2

"Janet is a few sandwiches short of a picnic if she thinks I'll pay that much for her car."

A Talker
USED WITH ANYONE

A person who talks a lot.

EXAMPLE 1
"I used to be a talker, but now I try to listen more."

EXAMPLE 2
"Jeff's a talker. I didn't say anything all night!"

Abso-fucking-lutely
USED WITH EXTREME CAUTION

"Yes, absolutely."

EXAMPLE 1
DINA: "Do you want to get lunch?"

CHET: "Abso-fucking-lutely! I'm starving!"

EXAMPLE 2
NED: "Did you like the movie?"

GRETTA: "Abso-fucking-lutely! It was great!"

o **Learn more...**

- In this phrase, "fucking" is placed inside the word "absolutely" to intensify it.

- Mr. Big on HBO's television series "Sex and the City" often used this phrase.

AC/DC
USED WITH FRIENDS

Bisexual.

EXAMPLE 1
"Ginger is AC/DC. She's attracted to both men and women."

EXAMPLE 2
"I wish I was AC/DC, then I would have more people to date."

o **Learn more...**

- This phrase refers to the two types of electrical current: "alternating current" and "direct current."

- There is a famous rock band called *AC/DC* but as far as we know, they're not bisexual.

AIDS
USED WITH ANYONE

A disease that slowly destroys a person's immune system.

EXAMPLE 1
"I would never have sex without a condom because I'm afraid of getting AIDS."

EXAMPLE 2
"My father died from AIDS last year. That disease has killed so many people."

Airhead
USED WITH ANYONE

A stupid person.

EXAMPLE 1
"Heather can't do math. What an airhead!"

EXAMPLE 2
"Margaret is an airhead. Guys like her because she's pretty, but she's really dumb."

o **Learn more...**

- Women are called "airheads" more often than men.

- There is a 1994 movie called *Airheads* in which three stupid guys take control of a radio station using fake guns. The movie starred Brendan Fraser, Steve Buscemi, and Adam Sandler.

All Over Each Other
USED WITH ANYONE

To touch each other constantly in a sexual way.

EXAMPLE 1
"When we first started dating, we were all over each other. Now I'm lucky if we have sex once a month."

EXAMPLE 2
"My mother and father are all over each other! I hate it when they touch each other in front of me."

Androgynous
USED WITH ANYONE

Having both male and female characteristics.

EXAMPLE 1
"That man is androgynous. He has a feminine face, but a masculine body."

EXAMPLE 2
"Sam wears men's clothes. She wants to appear androgynous."

Andy Gump
USED WITH FRIENDS

Toilet or bathroom.

EXAMPLE 1
"Andy Gump always has a line. Next time, I'll urinate behind a tree instead of waiting."

EXAMPLE 2
"I love going to outdoor concerts, but I can never find Andy Gump."

o **Learn more...**

• "Andy Gump" is the name of a company that makes portable toilets.

Anorexic
USED WITH ANYONE

Too thin.

EXAMPLE 1
"Is Carrie okay? She looks anorexic!"

EXAMPLE 2
"Since Tom went to college, he looks anorexic. Is he eating anything?"

o **Learn more...**

• "Anorexia" is a shortened form of the medical condition *anorexia nervosa*. People with this problem stop eating in order to lose weight, even when they are already dangerously thin.

Apeshit
USED WITH FRIENDS

Angry or crazy.

EXAMPLE 1
"Connie went apeshit when I hit her with the football. She tried to pull all my hair out!"

EXAMPLE 2
"My father goes apeshit if I don't clean my room every night. He yelled for almost an hour last time."

Aphrodisiac
USED WITH ANYONE

Anything which increases the desire for, or the enjoyment of, sex.

EXAMPLE 1
"I've never found an aphrodisiac that really works. I tried eating oysters once, but nothing happened."

EXAMPLE 2
"Rollercoasters were an aphrodisiac for my last girlfriend. She always wanted to have sex after riding them."

DIALOGUE
"LET'S HAUL ASS OUT OF HERE!"

Here is a short dialogue between two Americans.

BRET
Fucking A! Some asshole just floated an air biscuit in here. It smells terrible!

PETER
No shit! Let's haul ass out of here before I puke.

Fucking A! (p. 77)
Asshole (p. 6)
Float an air biscuit (p. 68)

No shit! (p. 134)
Haul ass (p. 92)
Puke (p. 155)

o Learn more...

- Some people think chocolate, cinnamon, and oysters are "aphrodisiacs."

Around The World
USED WITH FRIENDS

The act of kissing the entire body before sex.

EXAMPLE 1

"Jeremy loves to go around the world before we have sex."

EXAMPLE 2

"I want to go around the world before we have sex. I love your body!"

Arse
USED WITH FRIENDS

❶ Butt.

EXAMPLE 1

"If Jeff tries to touch me, I'll kick him in the arse!"

EXAMPLE 2

"Nancy slipped and fell on her arse. It's lucky for her that her butt is so big!"

❷ A rude, mean, or irritating person.

EXAMPLE 1

"When I drink too much alcohol, I'm an arse. I always insult my friends."

EXAMPLE 2

"Don't be an arse! Leave those woman alone."

o Learn more...

- This is a nicer way to say "ass" (p. 4).

- We took this word from the British. It's not used as often as "ass."

As Shit
USED WITH FRIENDS

To the extreme.

EXAMPLE 1

"You're funny as shit! Are you a comedian?"

EXAMPLE 2

"This test is easy as shit! I'm glad I didn't study last night!"

Asexual
USED WITH ANYONE

Having no interest in, or desire for, sex.

EXAMPLE 1

"I thought Toby was asexual until I saw him kiss a girl yesterday."

EXAMPLE 2

"I wish I was asexual. It's so difficult to have sexual relationships these days."

Ass
USED WITH FRIENDS

❶ Butt.

EXAMPLE 1

"Carson has a great ass! I love to watch him walk."

EXAMPLE 2

"My ass is huge! I need to exercise and stop eating ice cream."

❷ A rude, mean, or irritating person.

EXAMPLE 1

"Gloria is an ass when she's drunk. She always tries to kiss my boyfriend."

EXAMPLE 2

"Zak was an ass before he got married. He insulted women all the time. Now he's really nice!"

Ass Backwards
USED WITH FRIENDS

In the wrong order; incorrect.

EXAMPLE 1

"You asked for a raise before you did the work? That's ass backwards!"

EXAMPLE 2

"Anne did an ass backwards job of writing the report. She'll have to write it again."

o Learn more...

- Some people say "bass ackwards" instead of "ass backwards" as a joke.

Ass Clown
USED WITH FRIENDS

A stupid person.

EXAMPLE 1

"You spilled wine on my shirt. You ass clown!"

EXAMPLE 2

"Ernie is an ass clown. No one wants to be friends with him."

o Learn more...

- In the 1999 movie *Office Space*, starring Ron Livingston and Jennifer Aniston, the singer Michael Bolton is called a "no-talent ass clown."

Ass-fuck
USED WITH EXTREME CAUTION

To have anal sex.

EXAMPLE 1

"I ass-fucked Sheila last night. I like it better than regular sex, but she doesn't."

EXAMPLE 2

"I heard that Thomas ass-fucked Carl in the park last night. I didn't know he was gay!"

AT THE MOVIES
"AMERICAN PIE" (1999)

American Pie is a great example of the American "teen movie" — a movie about teenagers and their sexual relationships. In *American Pie*, four high school seniors make a deal that they'll each have sex (for the first time) before the end of the school year.

STIFLER

"I say, why don't you guys locate your dicks, remove the shrink wrap, and fucking *use* them!"

—

Dick (p. 46)
Fucking (p. 77)

MICHELLE

"And this one time, at band camp, I stuck a flute in my pussy."

Pussy (p. 155)

JIM

"Excuse me?"

MICHELLE

"What, you don't think I know how to get myself off? Hell, that's what half of band camp is—sex-ed! So, are we gonna screw soon?"

—

Get off (p. 82)
Hell (p. 97)
Screw (p. 169)

[Oz is singing with a choir.]

STIFLER

"What did you cocks do to him?"

Cock (p. 34)

OZ

"You came to see me in action?"

STIFLER

"Yeah, man. I think you need your balls reattached!"

Balls (p. 10)

Ass-kisser
USED WITH FRIENDS

A person who will do anything to make other people like him or her.

EXAMPLE 1
"Kara baked a cake for her teacher again. She's such an ass-kisser!"

EXAMPLE 2
"Don't be an ass-kisser! You'll get the promotion if you deserve it. Buying lunch for the boss won't make a difference."

○ **Learn more...**

- You may also hear "ass-licker" as in "Jerry has been an ass-licker for years, but he still hasn't gotten a raise."

Ass Man
USED WITH FRIENDS

A man who is primarily attracted to women's or men's butts.

EXAMPLE 1
"Earl is an ass man. He always looks at a woman's butt before he looks at her face."

EXAMPLE 2
"I love the shape, the feel, and the size of a good butt. I'm definitely an ass man."

Ass-peddler
USED WITH FRIENDS

A woman who trades sex for money; a prostitute.

EXAMPLE 1
"Be careful! Someone will think you're an ass-peddler if you wear that cheap dress!"

EXAMPLE 2
"If I don't get money soon, I'll have to become an ass-peddler!"

○ **Learn more...**

- You may also hear "peddle some ass" as in "I saw Tina peddling some ass last night."

Ass-ream
USED WITH FRIENDS

To punish.

EXAMPLE 1
"I ass-reamed Joanne this morning. She forgot to buy the plane ticket for my flight!"

EXAMPLE 2
"Patty will ass-ream us for losing her ring. I hope we find it soon!"

○ **Learn more...**

- You may also hear "ream someone's ass" as in "Charlie's going to ream my ass if he sees me with his girlfriend!"

Asshead
USED WITH FRIENDS

A stupid person.

EXAMPLE 1
"Hey, asshead! You can't park there!"

EXAMPLE 2
"Neal punched my father last night. What an asshead!"

Asshole
USED WITH FRIENDS

❶ **Rectum.**

EXAMPLE 1
"Gareth put a bottle in his asshole, and now he can't get it out!"

EXAMPLE 2
"No, you can't put your penis in my asshole!"

❷ **A rude, mean, or irritating person.**

EXAMPLE 1
"You asshole! Stop yelling at me!"

EXAMPLE 2
"Nate is an asshole. He tried to have sex with my mother!"

○ **Learn more...**

- You may also hear "A-hole." This is said on the radio where you can't say "asshole."

Asswipe

USED WITH FRIENDS

A stupid, rude, or irritating person.

EXAMPLE 1

"Don't invite Paulie to the party. He's an asswipe!"

EXAMPLE 2

"You asswipe! You forgot the beer again!"

o Learn more...

- Some people use "asswipe" to mean "toilet paper," but it's not common.

Au Natural

USED WITH ANYONE

Totally naked.

EXAMPLE 1

"Tori sleeps au natural. She hates wearing clothes in bed."

EXAMPLE 2

"I'm coming to your room au natural. Be ready for sex!"

o Learn more...

- This phrase comes from the French phrase "au naturel," meaning "in a natural way."

Aunt Flo Is Visiting

USED WITH FRIENDS

Said of a woman who is menstruating.

EXAMPLE 1

"Samantha and I wanted to have sex, but Aunt Flo is visiting."

EXAMPLE 2

"You should never wear white pants when you think Aunt Flo might visit."

B IS FOR BITCH

B. And D.
USED WITH FRIENDS

Bondage (physical restraint) and discipline (punishment and reward).

EXAMPLE 1
"I'm nervous to go home. My husband bought a book about B. and D., and he wants to tie me to the bed tonight!"

EXAMPLE 2
"My boyfriend was really upset when I suggested a little B. and D. to make our sex life more interesting."

o Learn more...

• You may also hear "B. but no D." meaning "bondage, but not discipline," or any other variation.

B.M.
USED WITH ANYONE

❶ To defecate.

EXAMPLE 1
"Mommy, I went B.M. in my pants again."

EXAMPLE 2
"My stomach really hurts. Maybe I need to B.M."

❷ Excrement.

EXAMPLE 1

"There's a B.M. on the bathroom floor! How could you miss the toilet?"

EXAMPLE 2

"Paul left a B.M. in the toilet. He never remembers to flush."

❍ Learn more...

- This is a shortened version of "bowel movement," a medical term often used to describe waste being passed out of the body.

Back
USED WITH FRIENDS

Butt.

EXAMPLE 1

"My girl's got back! I love her butt."

EXAMPLE 2

"Look at the back on that girl by the door. Nice!"

❍ Learn more...

- The rapper Sir Mix-A-Lot won a Grammy in 1992 for his song "Baby Got Back" about his attraction to women with large butts.

Badass
USED WITH FRIENDS

❶ A dangerous person.

EXAMPLE 1

"Kenny studies karate. He's a total badass!"

EXAMPLE 2

"Don't pick a fight with Haruka. I heard she's a badass and carries a knife!"

❷ Great; wonderful.

EXAMPLE 1

"That's a badass car! I wish I could buy one like that."

EXAMPLE 2

"What a badass movie! I want to see it again tomorrow."

Bag It
USED WITH FRIENDS

To wear a condom.

EXAMPLE 1

"Sharon makes me bag it every time we have sex."

EXAMPLE 2

"You should bag it if you want to have sex with a sheep."

Ball
USED WITH EXTREME CAUTION

To have sex.

EXAMPLE 1

"I balled Valerie last night, but it was nothing special. She's not as good as she says."

EXAMPLE 2

"Megan and I haven't seen each other in three months. We're going to ball all night long the next time she visits."

Ball And Chain
USED WITH ANYONE

❶ One's spouse.

EXAMPLE 1

"Marty can't go to the football game because the ball and chain said he has to stay home."

EXAMPLE 2

"I'd love to go to the bar, but my husband wants me to cook dinner. I have to listen to the ball and chain."

❷ Marriage.

EXAMPLE 1

"I've been avoiding the ball and chain for twenty-five years, and now I'm finally going to get married."

EXAMPLE 2

"Is Jesse really ready for the ball and chain? I thought he'd be single forever!"

o **Learn more...**

- You may also hear "the old ball and chain" to mean one's husband or wife.

- This is often said as a joke.

- In the old days, prisoners had a heavy ball and chain attached to their ankles so they couldn't escape.

Ball-buster
USED WITH FRIENDS

❶ **A hard task; something difficult.**

EXAMPLE 1

"This project is a ball-buster! We'll be working all night."

EXAMPLE 2

"I hope the test isn't a ball-buster. I didn't have time to study last night."

❷ **A demanding boss.**

EXAMPLE 1

"Are you working for Edna? She's a real ball-buster. You'll have to work hard."

EXAMPLE 2

"I'm a ball-buster. If you can't do the job, I'll fire you."

o **Learn more...**

- You may also hear "ball-breaker."

Balloons
USED WITH FRIENDS

Breasts.

EXAMPLE 1

"Look at the balloons on the woman across the street! They're really big."

EXAMPLE 2

"I like it when a woman rubs her balloons in my face."

o **Learn more...**

- You may also hear "bazongas," "bazookas," or "bazooms."

Balls
USED WITH FRIENDS

❶ **Testicles.**

EXAMPLE 1

"There's nothing worse than getting hit in the balls with a baseball bat."

EXAMPLE 2

"I can't stop scratching my balls. They're really itchy today."

❷ **Courage.**

EXAMPLE 1

"You need balls to go sky-diving!"

EXAMPLE 2

"Nan doesn't have the balls to argue with me."

Balls Deep
USED WITH FRIENDS

In trouble.

EXAMPLE 1

"The police found marijuana in my car. I'm really balls deep this time!"

EXAMPLE 2

"Hank is going to be balls deep if his mother sees his tattoo."

Ballsy
USED WITH FRIENDS

Courageous.

EXAMPLE 1

"Garret is really ballsy. He told the boss to change his suit because it looked bad."

EXAMPLE 2

"It was ballsy to move the company to Japan, but the company is even more successful now."

o **Learn more...**

- Women don't have "balls" (testicles), but they can still be "ballsy."

Baloney
USED WITH ANYONE

Stupid; nonsense.

EXAMPLE 1

"Americans are always nice? That's baloney!"

EXAMPLE 2

"Sam always lies. Don't believe his baloney."

o **Learn more...**

- This is a nicer way to say "bullshit" (p. 24).

Bang
USED WITH EXTREME CAUTION

To have sex.

EXAMPLE 1

"Chet likes to bang as many woman as he can when he gets drunk. I wonder if he tells his wife?"

EXAMPLE 2

"I really want to bang Melissa. She has great breasts."

Bare-assed
USED WITH FRIENDS

Totally naked.

EXAMPLE 1

"Daron is sitting in the street bare-assed. He must be drunk!"

EXAMPLE 2

"I dare you to go to the store bare-assed."

o **Learn more...**

- You may also hear "bare-assed naked."

Barf
USED WITH FRIENDS

To vomit.

EXAMPLE 1

"When I was sick, I barfed every day for two weeks."

EXAMPLE 2

"The taste of uncooked meat makes me barf."

Bastard
USED WITH FRIENDS

A very mean person.

EXAMPLE 1

"Professor Grant likes to fail his students. He's a real bastard!"

EXAMPLE 2

"Bobbie is a total bastard! He's my boyfriend, but I saw him kissing my best friend last night."

o **Learn more...**

- Literally, a bastard is a person whose father is not known.

IN OTHER WORDS...
"BREASTS"

Anything shaped like a ball or a cone can be compared to a woman's breasts. See those mountains? They look like breasts. See those sea shells? Breasts again. You get the idea.

USED WITH ANYONE

Bust (p. 26)

USED WITH FRIENDS

Balloons (p. 10)

Boobs (p. 20)

Cans (p. 30)

Guns (p. 89)

Headlights (p. 97)

Highbeams (p. 100)

Hooters (p. 103)

Jugs (p. 110)

Knockers (p. 114)

Maracas (p. 124)

Melons (p. 126)

Milk Bottles (p. 127)

Rack (p. 159)

Ta-tas (p. 193)

Yabbos (p. 218)

USED WITH EXTREME CAUTION

Tits (p. 201)

- In the Austin Powers series of movies starring Mike Myers, there is a character named "Fat Bastard."

Battering Ram
USED WITH FRIENDS

Penis.

EXAMPLE 1
"Josh is always showing his battering ram to other people. Everyone has seen it!"

EXAMPLE 2
"Molly promised to touch my battering ram tonight. I can't wait!"

o **Learn more...**

- A traditional "battering ram" is a large tree trunk used to break down doors and castle gates.

Batty
USED WITH ANYONE

Crazy or strange.

EXAMPLE 1
"Joe gets batty when anyone touches his hair."

EXAMPLE 2
"Professor Mathews was dancing in class today. He's batty!"

Bazooka
USED WITH FRIENDS

Penis.

EXAMPLE 1
"Gary's bazooka is really big! We had some great sex last night."

EXAMPLE 2
SASHA: "Where's Joel?"

MARK: "He's probably playing with his bazooka in the bathroom again."

o **Learn more...**

- A "bazooka" is a portable rocket launcher.

- Men can refer to their penises as almost any long, hard weapon: "bazooka," "gun," "sword," etc.

Be On The Rag
USED WITH FRIENDS

To menstruate.

EXAMPLE 1
"Sally doesn't like to play tennis when she's on the rag."

EXAMPLE 2
"I always want to eat chocolate when I'm on the rag."

o **Learn more...**

- You may also hear "O-T-R."

Be Regular
USED WITH ANYONE

To defecate with healthy frequency.

EXAMPLE 1
"My doctor says if I eat a lot of bran, I'll be more regular."

EXAMPLE 2
"Randal is always eating bananas. He says they keep him regular."

Be Sick
USED WITH ANYONE

To vomit.

EXAMPLE 1
"Please stop the car. I think I'm going to be sick."

EXAMPLE 2
"I was on the boat all day, and I didn't get sick once."

Bean Pole
USED WITH ANYONE

A skinny person.

EXAMPLE 1
"Ned is a bean pole. He should try to eat more."

EXAMPLE 2
"I like thin women, but Wanda is a bean pole!"

Beard Burn
USED WITH FRIENDS

When a man's facial hair scratches a woman's inner leg during oral sex.

EXAMPLE 1
"Amber has beard burn on her legs from two hours of oral sex last night."

EXAMPLE 2
"Hitomi complained that I gave her beard burn this morning, so I have to shave my face before I can perform oral sex on her again."

Beat Off
USED WITH FRIENDS

To masturbate.

EXAMPLE 1
"I don't need a girlfriend. I just need some swimsuit catalogs, so I can beat off six or seven times each day."

EXAMPLE 2
"My parents told me that if I beat off too much, I'd become blind."

Beat One's Meat
USED WITH FRIENDS

To masturbate.

EXAMPLE 1
"When I was nine years old, my mother found me beating my meat in the closet."

EXAMPLE 2
"I think that man is beating his meat while he's driving! He's going to have an accident."

Beat The Shit Out Of Someone
USED WITH FRIENDS

To defeat someone, often physically.

EXAMPLE 1
"I beat the shit out of Bernie for stealing my bike."

EXAMPLE 2
"You beat the shit out of me on this test! How did you do so well?"

Beatch
USED WITH FRIENDS

A nasty person.

EXAMPLE 1
"Listen, you beatch. This is my house and I want you to leave!"

EXAMPLE 2
LIL: "Tomas kicked my dog!"

JILL: "That beatch! You should punch him in the face!"

o Learn more...

- This is a nicer way to say "bitch" (p. 16).

- This word is pronounced "B-atch," and you might see it written "bi-atch."

Beaten With The Ugly Stick
USED WITH FRIENDS

To be very ugly.

EXAMPLE 1
"That man looks like he was beaten with the ugly stick. Twice!"

EXAMPLE 2
"I think Betty was beaten with the ugly stick. I'll never date her."

"Beats the shit out of me."
USED WITH FRIENDS

"I don't know."

EXAMPLE 1
GREG: "What's for dinner?"

ANNA: "Beats the shit out of me. You want to order something?"

EXAMPLE 2
JEFF: "Where's the car?"

EDITH: "Beats the shit out of me! I wasn't here when you parked it."

Beaver
USED WITH EXTREME CAUTION

Vagina.

EXAMPLE 1

"Eddie is always bragging that his girlfriend has the tightest beaver. I'm jealous!"

EXAMPLE 2

"I like it when Kelly rubs her beaver all over my face."

o Learn more...

- A "beaver" is also a cute furry animal, so be careful of the context!

Beaver-eater
USED WITH EXTREME CAUTION

Lesbian.

EXAMPLE 1

"Janice won't date guys. She must be a beaver-eater."

EXAMPLE 2

"That beaver-eater has two girlfriends. She must be very happy."

Behind
USED WITH ANYONE

Butt.

EXAMPLE 1

"Suzie fell on her behind while she was ice skating. It looked very painful!"

EXAMPLE 2

"Martin has a really cute behind. It looks great when he wears tight jeans!"

Bestiality
USED WITH FRIENDS

Sex with animals.

EXAMPLE 1

"Donald enjoys bestiality, but I doubt his dog does!"

EXAMPLE 2

"Joe should try bestiality. Sheep can't say no when he asks them for sex."

Between The Sheets
USED WITH ANYONE

In bed, having sex.

EXAMPLE 1

"Laura and I were between the sheets all night and all day."

EXAMPLE 2

"Chiara is really beautiful. I would love to get her between the sheets."

Bi
USED WITH ANYONE

Bisexual (someone who is attracted to both men and women).

EXAMPLE 1

"Lisa is bi. She dated Tommy last year, but she's dating Lucy now."

EXAMPLE 2

"I don't think I could date someone who is bi. There's too much competition!"

o Learn more...

- You may also hear "bicycle" or "convertible."

Big Backyard
USED WITH FRIENDS

Big butt.

EXAMPLE 1

"My last husband had a big backyard. You could land a plane on his butt."

EXAMPLE 2

"I love having sex with a girl who has a big backyard. There's more to hold on to."

Big-boned
USED WITH ANYONE

Large; fat.

EXAMPLE 1

"I love big-boned women. They're more fun to have sex with than really thin women."

EXAMPLE 2

"My husband is big-boned, so he eats more than most people."

o **Learn more...**

- This is a nicer way to say "fat."

- Today, many people joke "I'm not fat, I'm just big-boned!"

"Big fucking deal."

USED WITH EXTREME CAUTION

A nasty way of saying that something isn't important.

EXAMPLE 1

"Sharon got tickets for the concert? Big fucking deal! Anyone can get those."

EXAMPLE 2

"Willy won the contest? Big fucking deal. He probably cheated."

o **Learn more...**

- You may also hear "B-F-D."

Big Red Dropped In

USED WITH FRIENDS

To start menstruating.

EXAMPLE 1

"Mellisa had to leave the party early because big red dropped in."

EXAMPLE 2

"We were having a great time at the museum until big red dropped in."

Bimbo

USED WITH ANYONE

An attractive but very stupid woman.

EXAMPLE 1

"Stop dating bimbos and find a woman you can talk to intelligently!"

EXAMPLE 2

"I wanted to date Adel, but I heard she's a bimbo."

o **Learn more...**

- Women are called "bimbos" more often than men.

Birdbrain

USED WITH ANYONE

Very stupid.

EXAMPLE 1

"Grace is a birdbrain. She forgot to do her homework again!"

EXAMPLE 2

"Mark failed the test, and it was very easy. He's a birdbrain!"

o **Learn more...**

- A "birdbrained" person is very stupid because he or she has a brain the same size as a bird's — very small!

DIALOGUE
"TRISH HAS BIG BOOBS"

Here is a short dialogue between two Americans.

BRENT
"Look at the size of Trish's boobs! I'd like to get her between the sheets."

PAMELA
"Her boyfriend would beat the shit out of you. Hitting on her would be ballsy."

BRENT
"I'll risk it. I'm tired of beating off every night. I have to find someone to bang."

Boob (p. 20)
Between the sheets (p. 14)

Beat the shit out of someone (p. 13)
Hit on (p. 101)
Ballsy (p. 10)

Beat off (p. 13)
Bang (p. 11)

- Women are called "birdbrains" more often than men.

Birth Control
USED WITH ANYONE

Methods used to avoid pregnancy.

EXAMPLE 1

"My wife doesn't believe in birth control, so I think we'll have a large family."

EXAMPLE 2

"The best form of birth control is not to have sex, but who is crazy enough to do that?"

B-I-T-C-H
USED WITH FRIENDS

A nasty woman.

EXAMPLE 1

"Anne is mean to her friends. She's a B-I-T-C-H."

EXAMPLE 2

"I don't want to be a B-I-T-C-H, but you owe me money, and I want it now!"

○ **Learn more...**

- This is a nicer way to say "bitch" (see next entry).

- Bad words are often spelled instead of spoken to make them less rude. Many people spell bad words when they are around children who are too young to understand.

- Literally, a "bitch" is a female dog.

Bitch
USED WITH FRIENDS

❶ **A nasty woman.**

EXAMPLE 1

"I hate working with Lynne. She is such a bitch!"

EXAMPLE 2

"Trudy is a bitch today. I asked her a simple question, and she yelled at me!"

❷ **A nasty homosexual man.**

EXAMPLE 1

"Peter has been a bitch to everyone since he wasn't promoted."

EXAMPLE 2

"Alexander forgot our anniversary, the bitch!"

❸ **Something very difficult.**

EXAMPLE 1

"This test is a bitch! I should have studied more."

EXAMPLE 2

"Life's a bitch, and then you die."

❹ **To complain.**

EXAMPLE 1

"I don't want to bitch about the movie, but the acting was terrible!"

EXAMPLE 2

"Lydia has been bitching at me all morning! I need to leave now."

○ **Learn more...**

- Literally, a "bitch" is a female dog.

Bitch On Wheels
USED WITH FRIENDS

A very nasty woman.

EXAMPLE 1

"Tracey is a bitch on wheels today! She's yelling at everyone."

EXAMPLE 2

"Maggie ruined my shirt and didn't tell me. She's a bitch on wheels!"

Bitch Session
USED WITH FRIENDS

A meeting where people complain about someone or something.

EXAMPLE 1

"We need a bitch session to talk about the new boss. I hate her!"

EXAMPLE 2

"We had a bitch session about Ronald last night. He's been so mean lately."

Bitch Slap
USED WITH EXTREME CAUTION

To slap someone as if he or she is less important.

EXAMPLE 1

"If you insult me again, I'll bitch slap you."

EXAMPLE 2

"Jenny bitch slapped her husband. I don't understand why he doesn't leave her."

○ **Learn more...**

- Traditionally, a "bitch slap" described the way a "pimp" (p. 145) hit his prostitutes.

Bitchin'
USED WITH FRIENDS

Great; wonderful.

EXAMPLE 1

"That's a bitchin' new computer. How much did it cost?"

EXAMPLE 2

"You won the lottery? Bitchin'!"

○ **Learn more...**

- "Bitchin'" was very popular in the 1980s and is still said as a joke.

Blabbermouth
USED WITH ANYONE

A person who talks too much, even about secret things.

EXAMPLE 1

"Cheryl is such a blabbermouth! I told her that I like Jason, and she told him!"

EXAMPLE 2

MARTIN: "I told everyone that you got fired."

SUSIE: "You blabbermouth! Why did you do that?"

○ **Learn more...**

- "To blabber" is to talk too much.

Bleed The Weasel
USED WITH FRIENDS

To masturbate.

EXAMPLE 1

"I really need some privacy so I can bleed the weasel. I haven't masturbated in three hours."

EXAMPLE 2

"I walked into my brother's bedroom and saw him bleeding the weasel. He should lock his door if he's going to do that!"

Bleeping
USED WITH ANYONE

Stupid, terrible, irritating, or anything bad.

EXAMPLE 1

"That bleeping cashier gave me the wrong change!"

EXAMPLE 2

"I forgot the bleeping tickets to the show!"

○ **Learn more...**

- This is a nicer way to say "fucking" (p. 77).

- On radio and television, bad words are replaced by a "bleep" sound. Now people say "bleeping" when they want to say "fucking," but don't want to be that rude.

Blimp
USED WITH FRIENDS

A fat person.

EXAMPLE 1

"Look at that blimp eating that big dessert! That's the fattest man I have ever seen."

EXAMPLE 2

"Donna ate too much food during her first year of college. She's a real blimp now."

Blitzed
USED WITH ANYONE

Drunk.

EXAMPLE 1

"We got totally blitzed last night on vodka. My head hurts today!"

EXAMPLE 2

"I'm tired of getting blitzed every night at the bar. I want to stay home and watch T.V.!"

Blockhead
USED WITH ANYONE

A stupid person.

EXAMPLE 1

"Joe is a blockhead. He never understands my jokes."

EXAMPLE 2

"Kathy wore shorts to the wedding instead of a dress. What a blockhead!"

○ **Learn more...**

- Men are called "blockheads" more often than women.

- In Charles Schultz' "Peanuts" cartoon, Lucy always called Charlie Brown a "blockhead."

Blow
USED WITH EXTREME CAUTION

❶ **To perform oral sex on a man.**

EXAMPLE 1

"My girlfriend won't have sex with me, and she won't blow me either. I think I am going to date someone else."

EXAMPLE 2

"Ed wants me to blow him, but I would hate to have his penis in my mouth. What should I do?"

❷ **To ejaculate.**

EXAMPLE 1

"Keep sucking my penis. I'm almost ready to blow!"

EXAMPLE 2

"Don't blow near my hair. I have to go to work in ten minutes, and it takes a long time to wash semen out!"

○ **Learn more...**

- You may also hear "blow one's load," "blow one's wad," or "shoot" to mean "ejaculate."

Blow Chunks
USED WITH FRIENDS

To vomit.

EXAMPLE 1

"I blow chunks every time I eat your mother's cooking."

EXAMPLE 2

"I ruined Amanda's dress. I blew chunks all over it."

Blow Job
USED WITH EXTREME CAUTION

Oral sex performed on a man.

EXAMPLE 1

"I know a prostitute who is having a sale for the holidays. All blow jobs are $5!"

EXAMPLE 2

"Lisa won't have real sex with me, but she gives me amazing blow jobs!"

Blowhard
USED WITH ANYONE

A person who talks too much, usually about something he or she will never do.

EXAMPLE 1

"Neal always talks about visiting Japan, but I don't think he ever will. What a blowhard."

EXAMPLE 2

"Janet is a blowhard. She keeps promising to give me more money, but never does."

Blue Balls
USED WITH FRIENDS

Pain in the testicles caused by a man's need to have an orgasm.

EXAMPLE 1

"Donna had to leave just before I could have an orgasm, so now I have blue balls again."

EXAMPLE 2

"Fred says I have to perform oral sex on him, or he'll get blue balls."

○ **Learn more...**

- "Blue balls" is the slang name for the medical term "vasocongestion."

- Most people don't know this, but women can suffer from "vasocongestion," too.

- Some men complain of "blue balls" in order to get sex from their partners.

Blue-veined Throbber
USED WITH FRIENDS

An erect penis.

EXAMPLE 1

"Sally loves to touch my blue-veined throbber."

EXAMPLE 2

"Howard calls his penis his blue-veined throbber. I'm not surprised that he can't find a girlfriend!"

B.O.
USED WITH ANYONE

Offensive body smell ("body odor").

EXAMPLE 1

"I can't go on another date with Gerald because of his B.O."

EXAMPLE 2

"I smell B.O. I bet the guy behind me hasn't showered in a week."

○ **Learn more...**

- Pronounced "B-O."

Boink
USED WITH FRIENDS

To have sex.

EXAMPLE 1

"I'm getting boinked tonight. Roger is finally coming back from vacation."

EXAMPLE 2

"I'll boink any woman who will boink me. I don't care what she looks like, smells like, or tastes like."

○ **Learn more...**

- You may also hear "bonk."

Bombed
USED WITH ANYONE

Drunk.

EXAMPLE 1

"I've never seen Chris so bombed! He shouldn't drink whiskey."

EXAMPLE 2

"I was so bombed after the champagne that I took off all my clothes and jumped off a bridge."

○ **Learn more...**

- You may also hear "bombed out of one's tree."

- In school, "to bomb" is slang for "to fail" as in "I bombed the test yesterday. My parents are going to be so angry!"

Bone
USED WITH FRIENDS

❶ **To have sex.**

EXAMPLE 1

"Marc boned that girl three times, and he still doesn't know her name."

EXAMPLE 2

"If I don't bone someone soon, I'm going to cry. I need sex!"

❷ **Penis.**

EXAMPLE 1

"Lilly was disappointed when she saw my bone. I guess she thought it would be bigger."

EXAMPLE 2

"Ian gives his boyfriend a bone every night."

Bonehead
USED WITH ANYONE

A stupid person.

EXAMPLE 1

"Pete drove his car into the lake. What a bonehead!"

EXAMPLE 2

"I forgot about your birthday! I'm such a bonehead."

o Learn more...

- Men are called "boneheads" more often than women.

Boner
USED WITH FRIENDS

Erect penis.

EXAMPLE 1

"Kelso's boner was so big, everyone in class knew he was sexually aroused."

EXAMPLE 2

"When I was dancing with Steve, I could feel his boner. I guess he likes me!"

Bonkers
USED WITH ANYONE

Crazy or strange.

EXAMPLE 1

"Too much studying makes me bonkers. I need to rest."

EXAMPLE 2

"You're bonkers if you think goldfish are better than cats. You can't pet a goldfish!"

o Learn more...

- You may also hear "go bonkers" as in "Megan will go bonkers if you don't get her some chocolate soon."

Boob
USED WITH FRIENDS

❶ A woman's breast.

EXAMPLE 1

"I hurt my boob when I was playing soccer."

EXAMPLE 2

"I touched Emily's boob last night! It was soft, but firm."

❷ A stupid person.

EXAMPLE 1

"Chuck's socks are different colors. What a boob!"

EXAMPLE 2

"I insulted Rita by accident. I'm such a boob!"

o Learn more...

- Only women can *have* "boobs" (breasts) and only men can *be* "boobs" (stupid people).

- You may also hear "boobies" to mean "breasts."

Booger
USED WITH FRIENDS

❶ A piece of nasal mucus.

EXAMPLE 1

"Roger sneezed and three big boogers came out of his nose."

EXAMPLE 2

"My best friend likes to pick his nose and eat the boogers."

❷ A stupid or unpopular person.

EXAMPLE 1

"You booger! Stop kissing my sister."

EXAMPLE 2

"I'll fight you any time, you big booger."

o Learn more...

- There is a character named "Booger" in the movie series *Revenge of the Nerds*. "Booger" is the most crude and disgusting "nerd" (p. 133).

Boot
USED WITH FRIENDS

To vomit.

EXAMPLE 1

"We should take Roy home. He looks like he's going to boot."

EXAMPLE 2

"My stomach feels strange. I think I'm going to boot."

Booty
USED WITH FRIENDS

Butt.

EXAMPLE 1
"Her booty is so nice! She always has guys asking for her phone number."

EXAMPLE 2
"She wears tight pants to show everyone her booty."

o Learn more...

- In 1976, the musical group *KC and the Sunshine Band* released the popular song "Shake Your Booty."

Booty Call
USED WITH FRIENDS

To contact someone for sex.

EXAMPLE 1
"I made my Friday night booty call to all the women I know, but none of them wanted to have sex with me."

EXAMPLE 2
"The only time Jeff contacts me is when he's making a booty call."

Bordello
USED WITH ANYONE

A place of prostitution.

EXAMPLE 1
"I saw Adrian leaving the bordello last night. He finally had sex!"

EXAMPLE 2
"If Petunia won't have sex with you, you can go to the bordello and pay for it."

o Learn more...

- The 1996 movie *Bordello of Blood*, starring comedian Dennis Miller, features vampire prostitutes!

Bottom
USED WITH FRIENDS

❶ The person who is penetrated by the other person during homosexual sex.

EXAMPLE 1
"Luke likes bottoms. He enjoys taking a more aggressive role during sex."

EXAMPLE 2
"If I could find a bottom who is sexy, I would be really happy."

❷ Butt.

EXAMPLE 1
"Danny is crying because he fell on his bottom."

EXAMPLE 2
"Uncle Keith touched my bottom when I was six years old. Now he's in jail."

o Learn more...

- "Bottom" is a polite way to say "butt" and may be used with anyone.

IN OTHER WORDS...
"BUTT"

Although most people use "butt" or "ass" to talk about their bodies, you'll probably hear a lot of these other words, too.

USED WITH ANYONE

Behind (p. 14)

Bottom (p. 21)

Bum (p. 24)

Caboose (p. 28)

Derriere (p. 46)

Duff (p. 55)

Fanny (p. 62)

Heinie (p. 97)

Keester (p. 112)

Rear end (p. 160)

Rump (p. 164)

Seat (p. 172)

Tush (p. 204)

USED WITH FRIENDS

Arse (p. 4)

Ass (p. 4)

Booty (p. 21)

Buns (p. 25)

Can (p. 29)

Dumper (p. 56)

Tail (p. 193)

- Among homosexuals, "bottom" and "top" (p. 201) are very common terms to describe sexual preferences.

Box
USED WITH EXTREME CAUTION

Vagina.

EXAMPLE 1

"Bill says that Suzanne has a big box and that he can't feel anything during sex."

EXAMPLE 2

"I love my girlfriend's box. I can't stop touching her."

Box Lunch
USED WITH EXTREME CAUTION

Oral sex performed on a woman.

EXAMPLE 1

"Andrea and I are going on a picnic. Instead of chicken, I'm hoping for a box lunch."

EXAMPLE 2

"I know that girl makes a great box lunch. I've tried it before and it was great."

Boytoy
USED WITH FRIENDS

A younger male lover.

EXAMPLE 1

"My mom has a new boytoy. She'll have sex with him for a few months then find someone new."

EXAMPLE 2

"Is that Will's new boytoy? He's cute!"

o Learn more...

- You may also hear "toyboy."

Break Wind
USED WITH FRIENDS

To expel gas from the anus; to flatulate.

EXAMPLE 1

"I heard Mrs. Jones break wind at church today. I was very surprised."

EXAMPLE 2

"Did one of you girls break wind? Something smells strange in here."

Breast Fuck
USED WITH EXTREME CAUTION

To have sex by rubbing a man's penis between a woman's breasts.

EXAMPLE 1

"We need oil if we want to breast fuck. Lubrication is important!"

EXAMPLE 2

"When we breast fuck, I can see Rod's penis as he ejaculates."

Breast Man
USED WITH FRIENDS

A man who is primarily attracted to women's breasts.

EXAMPLE 1

"I'm a breast man. I always look at a woman's breasts first, then look at the rest of her."

EXAMPLE 2

"Larry is a breast man, so his wife just got her breasts enlarged."

Breeder
USED WITH FRIENDS

A heterosexual.

EXAMPLE 1

"See all the women? This looks like a breeder bar. Let's go to the gay bar next door."

EXAMPLE 2

"Most breeders get divorced, but you never see any homosexuals getting divorced."

o Learn more...

- This word is used by homosexuals more than heterosexuals.

Broad
USED WITH FRIENDS

A woman.

EXAMPLE 1

"Your wife is one sexy broad."

EXAMPLE 2

"See that broad over there? I'm going to have sex with her tonight."

o Learn more...

- Generally, a person who uses this word does not think well of women.

- This is an old phrase still used today.

Brothel
USED WITH ANYONE

A place of prostitution.

EXAMPLE 1

"I love sex. Maybe I should work in a brothel!"

EXAMPLE 2

"If you have sex with any more men, you'll belong in a brothel!"

Buck Naked
USED WITH ANYONE

Totally naked.

EXAMPLE 1

"When I found Travis, he was buck naked and sleeping on the street!"

EXAMPLE 2

"Meg has a pretty face, but when she's buck naked, she's ugly!"

o Learn more...

- You may also hear "butt naked."

Buffalo Chips
USED WITH FRIENDS

Buffalo excrement.

EXAMPLE 1

"Be careful not to step in any buffalo chips."

EXAMPLE 2

"My brother threw buffalo chips at me when we were young. He's so disgusting!"

o Learn more...

- "Buffalo chips" got their name from buffalo excrement which usually becomes flat and hard like a potato chip.

Buick
USED WITH FRIENDS

To vomit.

EXAMPLE 1

"Be careful! Sam just buicked, and I think he's going to do it again soon."

EXAMPLE 2

"Don't drink too much wine or you might buick."

Bulldyke
USED WITH EXTREME CAUTION

A masculine lesbian (female homosexual).

EXAMPLE 1

"My gym teacher is a bulldyke, and she wants all the girls to know it."

EXAMPLE 2

"That bulldyke just asked me where I bought my motorcycle."

o Learn more...

- You may also hear "diesel dyke."

Bullshit
USED WITH FRIENDS

❶ Nonsense.

EXAMPLE 1
"Laurie has three cars?
That's bullshit! She only has
one."

EXAMPLE 2
GARY: "The boss said we
have to work on Saturday."

JAY: "That's bullshit! We
worked last Saturday!"

**❷ To lie to or deceive
someone.**

EXAMPLE 1
"Jessica is bullshitting me.
She said she's not dating
anyone, but I saw her with
Ross last night."

EXAMPLE 2
"If you bullshit me, I'm going
to get very angry!"

o Learn more...

- A person who "bullshits" a
lot is a "bullshitter."

- You may also hear "horse
shit" as in "That's horse
shit, Michael. You know I
don't like bananas!"

- You may also hear "B-S."

Bum
USED WITH ANYONE

Butt.

EXAMPLE 1
"My bum looks great in my
new leather pants!"

EXAMPLE 2
"I think most English girls
have big bums."

o Learn more...

- A "bum" also means "a
homeless person" as in
"Give that bum some
money. He needs a good
meal."

- We took this word from the
British.

Bum-fuck
USED WITH EXTREME CAUTION

**The countryside; very far
away.**

EXAMPLE 1
"Kelly wants us to drive all
the way to bum-fuck Iowa."

EXAMPLE 2
"Jonah lives in bum-fuck
nowhere. It will take us
hours to get there!"

o Learn more...

- You may also hear
"bumble-fuck" or "East
bum-fuck." Almost any
variation will work!

Bump And Grind
USED WITH FRIENDS

❶ To have sex.

EXAMPLE 1
"I'm hoping to bump and
grind with Amanda tonight
while my parents are at the
movies."

EXAMPLE 2
"It's hard for me to walk
today because of all the
bumping and grinding I did
last night."

**❷ To rub one's body against
someone else's body in a
sexual way while dancing.**

EXAMPLE 1
"Jack and Brenda were
bumping and grinding on the
dance floor all night."

EXAMPLE 2
"Of course I can dance! I can
bump and grind until the sun
comes up."

Bump Pussy
USED WITH EXTREME CAUTION

To have lesbian sex.

EXAMPLE 1
"I have pictures of my sister
and her girlfriend bumping
pussies. Ten dollars if you
want to look!"

EXAMPLE 2
"Susanne and Maki were
bumping pussies all night.
They're in love!"

Bump Uglies
USED WITH FRIENDS

To have sex.

EXAMPLE 1
"That guy is really handsome! I would bump uglies with him any day."

EXAMPLE 2
"I don't know how to stop my dog from interrupting when my boyfriend and I are bumping uglies."

Bung Hole
USED WITH FRIENDS

❶ **Rectum.**

EXAMPLE 1
"Don't stick a bottle up your bung hole. It might get stuck."

EXAMPLE 2
"My bung hole hurts. I should see a doctor before it gets worse."

❷ **A stupid person.**

EXAMPLE 1
"What kind of a bung hole would urinate in a car?"

EXAMPLE 2
"Some bung hole tried to put a box of condoms down the toilet."

❍ **Learn more...**

- We took this phrase from the British.

Buns
USED WITH FRIENDS

Butt.

EXAMPLE 1
"That woman has a great pair of buns."

EXAMPLE 2
"I just bought a workout video for my buns. My butt is too big!"

Bush
USED WITH EXTREME CAUTION

A woman's pubic area.

EXAMPLE 1
"I saw Victoria's bush last night. Very nice!"

EXAMPLE 2
"I shaved my bush. Sam likes it smooth."

DIALOGUE
"MIKE MAKES A BOOTY CALL"

Here is a short dialogue between two Americans.

SAMANTHA
"I just heard that Mike and Professor Lane have been doing the nasty all year!"

Do the nasty (p. 48)

AUSTIN
"Are you shitting me? No wonder that fuckstick Mike always gets the best grades in class. Are they in love?"

Shit someone (p. 176)
Fuckstick (p. 78)

SAMANTHA
"No, it's just a booty call."

Booty call (p. 21)

AUSTIN
"They're both so fugly! The idea of them bumping uglies makes me want to retch."

Fugly (p. 78)
Bump uglies (p. 25)
Retch (p. 161)

Bust

USED WITH ANYONE

The area of the chest containing the breasts.

EXAMPLE 1

"Ingrid's bust is huge! She must look great in a bathing suit."

EXAMPLE 2

"You have to measure your bust if you want to order the dress in the right size."

Bust A Nut

USED WITH EXTREME CAUTION

To orgasm.

EXAMPLE 1

"I'm so sexually excited that I'm ready to bust a nut!"

EXAMPLE 2

"I busted my nut inside Melody during sex."

Bust Ass

USED WITH FRIENDS

❶ To expel gas from the anus; to flatulate.

EXAMPLE 1

"When I find out which one of you busted ass in my car, I'm going to kill you!"

EXAMPLE 2

"Every time I eat green peppers, I bust ass all night."

❷ To work hard.

EXAMPLE 1

"If we don't bust ass on this project, the company will lose money."

EXAMPLE 2

"Charlotte really busted ass on this report. It looks great!"

❸ To move quickly.

EXAMPLE 1

"We have to bust ass to class or we'll be late."

EXAMPLE 2

"I busted ass to the train station but I still missed my train."

❍ Learn more...

- You may also hear "rip ass" as in "I hate Rick because he ripped ass in my face last week."

- You may also hear "tear ass" as in "I ate too many beans and now I have to tear ass. You better open the windows."

Butch

USED WITH FRIENDS

Masculine.

EXAMPLE 1

"Nadine is really cute, but she's butch. I think she's a lesbian."

EXAMPLE 2

"The first girl I kissed was really butch, but now I like to be with more feminine women."

❍ Learn more...

- "Butch" is often considered an insult when used with women.

Butt Fuck

USED WITH EXTREME CAUTION

❶ To have anal sex.

EXAMPLE 1

"I really want to butt fuck my girlfriend, but she's scared that it will hurt."

EXAMPLE 2

"Dina never wants to have regular sex anymore. She always wants to butt fuck."

❷ A stupid person.

EXAMPLE 1

"That butt fuck almost killed my dog!"

EXAMPLE 2

"Look at those butt fucks trying to fight with that police officer!"

Butt Pirate
USED WITH EXTREME CAUTION

A homosexual man.

EXAMPLE 1
SANDY: "Is John gay?"

PETER: "Yeah, he's a butt pirate."

EXAMPLE 2
"A lot of butt pirates live in San Francisco. My brother met his lover there."

o **Learn more...**

- To most homosexuals, a "butt pirate" is a man who takes the active role in anal sex.

Butt Plug
USED WITH FRIENDS

An object inserted into the butt to increase sexual pleasure.

EXAMPLE 1
"I have better orgasms when I use a butt plug during sex."

EXAMPLE 2
"Greg has the biggest butt plug I've ever seen. It must hurt!"

Butt Ugly
USED WITH FRIENDS

Very ugly.

EXAMPLE 1
"That guy has a great body, but his face is butt ugly."

EXAMPLE 2
"Kendra is so butt ugly! Was she in a car accident?"

Butthead
USED WITH FRIENDS

A rude, mean, or irritating person.

EXAMPLE 1
"Jack insulted my mother. What a butthead!"

EXAMPLE 2
"Allan is a butthead. He never came to my party last night!"

o **Learn more...**

- Men are called "buttheads" more often than women.

Button
USED WITH FRIENDS

Clitoris.

EXAMPLE 1
"Megan goes crazy when I suck on her button."

EXAMPLE 2
"I put the vibrator on my button and in one minute, I had an orgasm."

o **Learn more...**

- You may also hear "love button."

Buzzed
USED WITH ANYONE

A little drunk.

EXAMPLE 1
"I'm not drunk, I'm just buzzed. I can drive myself home."

EXAMPLE 2
"I got buzzed at Larry's house last night. He offered us expensive alcohol, and I couldn't say no."

C IS FOR CREEP

C-U-Next-Tuesday
USED WITH FRIENDS

❶ Vagina.

EXAMPLE 1
"Mary stuck a cucumber in her C-U-Next-Tuesday, and she can't get it out!"

EXAMPLE 2
"I need to see a doctor. My C-U-Next-Tuesday is itching a lot."

❷ A nasty woman.

EXAMPLE 1
"She took my soda! What a C-U-Next-Tuesday!"

EXAMPLE 2
"That man called me a C-U-Next-Tuesday! How rude!"

○ Learn more...

- This is a nicer way to say "cunt" (p. 42).

Caboose
USED WITH ANYONE

Butt.

EXAMPLE 1
"My brother has a big caboose. He has to buy special pants."

EXAMPLE 2
"I like a woman with a big caboose."

○ Learn more...

- A "caboose" is the last car on a freight train.

Cajones
USED WITH FRIENDS

❶ Testicles.

EXAMPLE 1

"I like girls who play with my cajones."

EXAMPLE 2

"That guy has a big pair of cajones. Look at his pants."

❷ Courage or strength.

EXAMPLE 1

"I know why you won't fight me. You don't have the cajones."

EXAMPLE 2

"That little guy doesn't have the cajones for the army."

○ Learn more...

- This Spanish word meaning "testicles" is pronounced "cah-ho-nes."

Call Boy
USED WITH FRIENDS

A male prostitute.

EXAMPLE 1

"George made a lot of money as a call boy. Gay men love him."

EXAMPLE 2

"Call boys don't need to be cute, they just need to be ready for sex all the time."

○ Learn more...

- You may also hear "rent boy."

Call Girl
USED WITH FRIENDS

A female prostitute.

EXAMPLE 1

"Ted hired some call girls for the party. It should be fun!"

EXAMPLE 2

"I got a call girl when I was in Denver. I really needed sex!"

Camel Toe
USED WITH EXTREME CAUTION

The appearance of a woman's groin when the seam of her pants is pulled tightly against her vagina.

EXAMPLE 1

"Naomi's pants are so tight you can see her camel toe."

EXAMPLE 2

"Fred goes to aerobics class just to see all the camel toes."

○ Learn more...

- This expression refers to the V-shaped space between the two toes on a camel's foot.

Can
USED WITH FRIENDS

❶ Butt.

EXAMPLE 1

"I really like Bonny, but her can is too big for me."

EXAMPLE 2

"My wife has the best can."

❷ Toilet or bathroom.

EXAMPLE 1

"Hey, where is the can? I have to urinate."

EXAMPLE 2

"I saw $5 on the floor in the can, but I didn't want to touch it. That place is so dirty!"

Candy-ass
USED WITH FRIENDS

A coward.

EXAMPLE 1

"Jacob screamed during the movie. What a candy-ass!"

EXAMPLE 2

"You candy-ass! I'm not going to hurt you."

Canned Fruit
USED WITH FRIENDS

A homosexual man who has not publicly admitted to being homosexual.

EXAMPLE 1

"I used to be a canned fruit, but now everyone knows I'm gay!"

EXAMPLE 2

"I touched Jeff's butt and he ran away. That canned fruit! He needs to admit that he likes it!"

○ Learn more...

- "Fruit" (p. 72) is a rude way to say "gay."

Cans
USED WITH FRIENDS

Breasts.

EXAMPLE 1

"I wish my girlfriend had cans like that girl over there."

EXAMPLE 2

"My friend Joyce showed me her cans after I gave her $10."

Castrate
USED WITH ANYONE

To remove a male's testicles, making sex impossible.

EXAMPLE 1

"I heard the government is thinking about castrating men who rape women."

EXAMPLE 2

"George was castrated in a strange coffee-maker explosion."

Catch Shit
USED WITH FRIENDS

To be in trouble.

EXAMPLE 1

"We're going to catch shit if we don't get home before eleven!"

EXAMPLE 2

"Did you catch shit for forgetting your mom's birthday?"

Catcher
USED WITH FRIENDS

For homosexual men, the man who is penetrated by the other man during anal sex.

EXAMPLE 1

"I found a great gay website that lists who is a catcher, and who isn't."

EXAMPLE 2

"Jed told me he's a catcher. I'd love to penetrate him!"

o **Learn more...**

• In baseball, the "catcher" catches the balls thrown by the "pitcher" (p. 148).

Cathouse
USED WITH FRIENDS

A place of prostitution.

EXAMPLE 1

"I'm spending all of my money at the cathouse. I need a girlfriend!"

EXAMPLE 2

"My girlfriend saw me leaving the cathouse. I'm in trouble!"

o **Learn more...**

• In Canada, the 1982 movie *The Best Little Whorehouse In Texas* was renamed *The Best Little Cathouse In Texas*.

Cha-cha
USED WITH FRIENDS

Vagina.

EXAMPLE 1

"Matilda hid the drugs in her cha-cha during the inspection."

EXAMPLE 2

"I can put my penis in Debbie's cha-cha whenever I want, and she can use my credit card."

o **Learn more...**

• In Comedy Central's T.V. show "South Park," Cartman's mom often uses "cha-cha" instead of vagina, as in "He put his ho-ho-dilly ["penis"] in her cha-cha."

Change Of Life
USED WITH ANYONE

Menopause.

EXAMPLE 1

"My mother is acting a little strange because of her change of life."

EXAMPLE 2

"After her change of life, Monica couldn't have any more children."

Cheapskate
USED WITH ANYONE

A person who hates spending money.

EXAMPLE 1

"Don't be a cheapskate, Jose. You owe me five more dollars!"

EXAMPLE 2

"My mother is a cheapskate. She never buys me new clothes!"

Cherry
USED WITH EXTREME CAUTION

A woman's virginity.

EXAMPLE 1

"Debbie won't have sex with you. She's 23 years old and still has her cherry."

EXAMPLE 2

"I've tried everything, but Kathy won't give me her cherry."

o **Learn more...**

- The blood that comes out of a woman's vagina when she has sex for the first time is red like a cherry.

Chick
USED WITH FRIENDS

A girl or a woman.

EXAMPLE 1

"Look at that sexy chick over there! I wonder if she will have sex with me."

EXAMPLE 2

"Hey, chicks. Are we going shopping today?"

o **Learn more...**

- Many women find this phrase offensive, and others do not. If you're male, it's safer not to use it.

- You may also hear "chickie."

Chicken Hawk
USED WITH FRIENDS

An adult male homosexual who is attracted to younger men.

EXAMPLE 1

"He's a chicken hawk. He only likes men half his age."

EXAMPLE 2

"Most men think I'm a chicken hawk because my boyfriends are usually young, but I like older guys, too."

Chicken Ranch
USED WITH FRIENDS

A place of prostitution.

EXAMPLE 1

"That chicken ranch has great prices. Just $200 for sex!"

EXAMPLE 2

"I hate chicken ranches. The women are always dirty and ugly."

o **Learn more...**

- A 1983 documentary movie called *Chicken Ranch* is about a house of prostitution in Nevada. (Prostitution is legal in parts of Nevada, but not in most other states.)

Chicken-shit
USED WITH FRIENDS

A person who is easily scared.

EXAMPLE 1

"Do you want to climb this mountain, or are you a chicken-shit?"

EXAMPLE 2

"Joan is a chicken-shit. She won't leave her house at night!"

o **Learn more...**

- You may also hear the polite version "chicken."

Chocolate Speedway
USED WITH EXTREME CAUTION

To have anal sex.

EXAMPLE 1

"Some homosexual men ride the chocolate speedway all the time."

EXAMPLE 2

"Susan likes when I ride the chocolate speedway. We have anal sex every week."

Choke The Chicken
USED WITH FRIENDS

To masturbate.

EXAMPLE 1

"Mary still won't have sex with me, so I'm going to the bedroom to choke the chicken."

EXAMPLE 2

"I can choke the chicken in less than five minutes. How long do you need to masturbate?"

Chubby-chaser
USED WITH FRIENDS

A person who is attracted to fat people.

EXAMPLE 1

"My brother is a chubby-chaser. He only dates large women."

EXAMPLE 2

"Michael must be a chubby-chaser because his boyfriend is so fat."

o **Learn more...**

- "Chubby" is another way to say "fat."

Chucklefuck
USED WITH EXTREME CAUTION

A stupid person.

EXAMPLE 1

"That chucklefuck Ryan can't do anything right!"

EXAMPLE 2

"You are such a chucklefuck, Quinn. Why did you lie to the teacher?"

Chum
USED WITH FRIENDS

To vomit.

EXAMPLE 1

"I went sailing yesterday, but I was chumming most of the day."

EXAMPLE 2

"I get sick so quickly, I usually chum just seeing a boat on the water."

o **Learn more...**

- "Chum" is fish bait made from pieces of other fish. When you use "chum" to fish, you are "chumming."

- A "chum" is also a polite word for "a good friend" and can be used with anyone.

Chump
USED WITH ANYONE

A person who believes everything he or she is told.

EXAMPLE 1

"I thought Frank loved me! I'm such a chump."

EXAMPLE 2

"Brad is such a chump! Sheila promised him a raise if he worked harder, but she's going to fire him instead."

Chunder
USED WITH FRIENDS

To vomit.

EXAMPLE 1

"I'm going to chunder. If you need me, I'll be in the bathroom."

EXAMPLE 2

"Mr. Sato was surprised when I chundered on his wife after the party."

Circle Jerk
USED WITH FRIENDS

Men who masturbate themselves or each other in a group.

EXAMPLE 1

"My football coach says a circle jerk will help us be a better team, but I don't want to touch another guy's penis!"

EXAMPLE 2

"Some guys I knew in college got really drunk and had a circle jerk. I thought it was strange because they all had girlfriends."

Clean
USED WITH ANYONE

Sober.

EXAMPLE 1

"I've been clean for three weeks, but I really want a beer."

EXAMPLE 2

"Kyle is trying to stay clean, so we don't go to bars or any places that serve alcohol."

Climax
USED WITH ANYONE

❶ Orgasm.

EXAMPLE 1

"That was the best climax I ever had. Let's do it again!"

EXAMPLE 2

"William says he can give a woman three climaxes in one hour. I don't believe him!"

❷ To orgasm.

EXAMPLE 1

"Are you going to climax soon? My favorite T.V. show will be on in five minutes."

EXAMPLE 2

"I couldn't climax when I had sex with Ed's sister, but I really wanted to!"

Clit
USED WITH EXTREME CAUTION

Clitoris.

EXAMPLE 1

"I loved it when Jacob touched my clit with a feather! It felt amazing."

EXAMPLE 2

"My clit vibrates so much on Bill's motorcycle that I usually have an orgasm just riding downtown."

IN OTHER WORDS...
"COWARD"

Most Americans are insulted when they're called a "coward," especially men.

USED WITH ANYONE

Don't have a backbone (p. 51)

Fraidy-cat (p. 70)

Gutless (p. 89)

Scaredy-cat (p. 168)

Spineless (p. 185)

Wuss (p. 216)

Yellow (p. 219)

USED WITH FRIENDS

Candy-ass (p. 29)

Chicken-shit (p. 32)

USED WITH EXTREME CAUTION

Pussy (p. 155)

Sissy (p. 178)

---

o Learn more...

- Although "clit" is a shortened version of the medical term "clitoris," it's considered very vulgar.

Closet Case
USED WITH FRIENDS

A homosexual man who has not publicly admitted to being homosexual.

EXAMPLE 1

"Albert is a closet case. He's afraid he'll lose his job if anyone knows that he's gay."

EXAMPLE 2

"I was a closet case until college. Now my family and friends all know I'm gay."

Closet Queen
USED WITH EXTREME CAUTION

A homosexual man who has not publicly admitted to being homosexual.

EXAMPLE 1

"Richard is married to a beautiful woman, but I know he's really a closet queen."

EXAMPLE 2

"Most of my friends think Ricky Martin is a closet queen."

o Learn more...

- You may also hear "closet queer."

Clusterfuck
USED WITH EXTREME CAUTION

A disaster.

EXAMPLE 1

"Jill didn't plan enough. This meeting is a clusterfuck!"

EXAMPLE 2

"The basketball game was a clusterfuck! We didn't work as a team."

Cock
USED WITH EXTREME CAUTION

o Penis.

EXAMPLE 1

"Gerald's cock isn't very big, so I have trouble orgasming during sex."

EXAMPLE 2

"I don't think Manny's very cute, but he has a big cock. Good sex is more important than good looks!"

❷ A nasty person.

EXAMPLE 1

"Nathan kicked my dog! My dog is okay, but Nathan's a cock!"

EXAMPLE 2

"My ex-husband is a cock. He took all the furniture when he left me."

o Learn more...

- Be careful! A "cock" is also a male chicken.

Cock-block
USED WITH EXTREME CAUTION

To interfere with another man's attempts to get sex or sexual contact.

EXAMPLE 1

"If you cock-block me with Heather, I'll hurt you! I need sex."

EXAMPLE 2

"Are you trying to cock-block Allan? I saw you flirting with his date."

o Learn more...

- You may also hear "cock-blocking" as in "Oliver said I was cock-blocking him with Amelia. It's true! I want to have sex with her first."

- In this phrase, "cock" (see previous entry) means "penis."

Cock Ring
USED WITH EXTREME CAUTION

A rubber ring used to restrict the flow of fluid through the penis to give extra pleasure during orgasm.

EXAMPLE 1
"Every time I use a cock ring during sex, I have amazing orgasms."

EXAMPLE 2
"My girlfriend bought me my first cock ring. Now I don't want to have sex without it."

Cocksucker
USED WITH EXTREME CAUTION

❶ A nasty person.

EXAMPLE 1
"Patrick stole $100 from me. What a cocksucker!"

EXAMPLE 2
"My last boyfriend was a cocksucker. He made me pay for all our dates!"

❷ A person who enjoys performing oral sex on men.

EXAMPLE 1
"Cordelia's a great cocksucker, so I asked her to perform oral sex on me every night."

EXAMPLE 2
"Rina is a great cocksucker! She can do it underwater."

Cocktease
USED WITH EXTREME CAUTION

A person who gets a man sexually excited, but will not allow him a way to have an orgasm.

EXAMPLE 1
"Don't waste your time with Kimberly. She's a big cocktease and will never have sex with you."

EXAMPLE 2
"Cindy kisses everyone, but she's really just a cocktease. She won't have sex until she's married."

o Learn more...
- You may also hear "dicktease."

Cold Fish
USED WITH ANYONE

❶ An unfriendly person.

EXAMPLE 1
"Roger never says hello to me. He's a cold fish."

EXAMPLE 2
"I'm not a cold fish, but I don't like to hug people I just met."

❷ A person who doesn't get very excited during sex.

EXAMPLE 1
"I had sex with Janet last night. What a cold fish! She never moved."

EXAMPLE 2
"I heard that Bill is a cold fish in bed!"

o Learn more...
- People say good sex is "hot." A person who is a "cold fish" doesn't get "hot" during sex, so the sex isn't exciting.

Collar The Cock
USED WITH FRIENDS

To masturbate.

EXAMPLE 1
"I try to collar the cock at least four times a day to stay relaxed."

EXAMPLE 2
"I need to get a girlfriend, so I can stop collaring the cock and have some real sex!"

Come Hell Or High Water

USED WITH FRIENDS

Regardless.

EXAMPLE 1
"I'm going to finish reading this book tonight, come hell or high water!"

EXAMPLE 2
"I'm your mother! You will listen to me, come hell or high water. I don't care what your friends say."

o **Learn more...**

• If you do something "come hell or high water," you'll do it even if you're faced with the fires of hell or a flood.

Come On To Someone

USED WITH ANYONE

To flirt or try to attract another person.

EXAMPLE 1
"I think my History professor is coming on to me. He always stares at me in class."

EXAMPLE 2
"I know Devon has a girlfriend, but he was coming on to me all night."

Come Out Of The Closet

USED WITH ANYONE

To admit openly to being homosexual.

EXAMPLE 1
"Jerry talks about having a girlfriend, but I know he's just afraid to come out of the closet."

EXAMPLE 2
"Patricia came out of the closet last year. Her mom thinks it's fine, but her dad won't talk to her anymore."

o **Learn more...**

• You may also hear "closeted" or "in the closet."

• Today, a person can be "closeted" about any uncommon sexual preference. For example: "Gene is a closet masochist. He finally told me about it last night."

Cooch

USED WITH EXTREME CAUTION

Vagina; sex with a woman.

EXAMPLE 1
"Natalie's cooch hurt after we had sex last night. I guess I was too rough for her."

EXAMPLE 2
"Did you get any cooch last night? Your date looked eager for sex."

Cooter

USED WITH EXTREME CAUTION

Vagina.

EXAMPLE 1
"Last night was terrific! Rachel showed me her cooter."

EXAMPLE 2
"The first time I saw a girl's cooter was when I accidently walked into the girls' bathroom at school."

Cop A Feel

USED WITH ANYONE

To touch someone sexually without permission, usually while pretending it's an accident.

EXAMPLE 1
"Lynn copped a feel when the subway stopped. I felt her hand on my butt!"

EXAMPLE 2

"I tried to cop a feel when the teacher bent over my desk this morning. She has great breasts!"

Cornhole
USED WITH EXTREME CAUTION

❶ Anus.

EXAMPLE 1

"I like to lick my boyfriend's cornhole to get him really excited for sex."

EXAMPLE 2

"Jake was having sex in the cornhole last night, and now he can't sit down because his butt hurts."

❷ To have anal sex.

EXAMPLE 1

"Did you and Andy cornhole last night?"

EXAMPLE 2

"Don't open that door! Quinn and Stacy are cornholing in there."

Cover Your Ass
USED WITH FRIENDS

To protect yourself from possible blame.

EXAMPLE 1

"Rick tells his boss whenever he leaves the office. He likes to cover his ass."

EXAMPLE 2

"Save that letter! If someone blames you, you can use the letter to cover your ass."

○ Learn more...

- You may also hear "C-Y-A."

Cow
USED WITH FRIENDS

A fat person.

EXAMPLE 1

"What a cow! I would never date a man that big."

EXAMPLE 2

"You cow! You ate all the ice cream!"

○ Learn more...

- You may also hear "fat cow."

Cow Patty
USED WITH ANYONE

Cow excrement.

EXAMPLE 1

"I think Bill will be surprised when he realizes I gave him a cow patty instead of a hamburger."

EXAMPLE 2

"I have never seen a cow patty this big before. I hope the cow is okay."

○ Learn more...

- "Cow patty" got its name from cow excrement which usually becomes flat and round like a hamburger patty.

Coyote Ugly
USED WITH FRIENDS

Very ugly.

EXAMPLE 1

"Gary is too drunk to realize that the girl he's dancing with is coyote ugly."

EXAMPLE 2

"Wow, I was really drunk last night. I woke up next to a girl who was coyote ugly."

○ Learn more...

- "Coyote ugly" refers to the belief that coyotes will chew off their own legs to escape a trap. Likewise, a man would rather chew off his own arm than stay in bed with a very ugly woman.

- There was a movie released in 2000 called *Coyote Ugly* that took place at a bar.

Crabs
USED WITH FRIENDS

Genital lice.

EXAMPLE 1

"My testicles itch all the time because of these crabs."

EXAMPLE 2

"Grant gave me crabs, so I broke his television by pouring beer on it."

Crack
USED WITH EXTREME CAUTION

❶ Vagina.

EXAMPLE 1

"Amber has beautiful breasts and a great crack. I love to have sex with her."

EXAMPLE 2

"I put my penis in her crack and she started to scream with pleasure."

❷ The line between one's butt cheeks.

EXAMPLE 1

"Jeremy's pants are so low that I can see his crack!"

EXAMPLE 2

"If the plumber is coming here, I'm leaving. His crack is always showing while he works."

○ Learn more...

- "Crack" is also a low-quality form of the drug cocaine.

Cracked
USED WITH ANYONE

Crazy.

EXAMPLE 1

"That guy is cracked! He just keeps walking in circles."

EXAMPLE 2

"You're cracked if you think I'll kiss you. We just met."

Crackhead
USED WITH FRIENDS

❶ A stupid or crazy person.

EXAMPLE 1

"Jacob is a crackhead. He thinks Melissa is cute, but she's really ugly!"

EXAMPLE 2

"Rick failed the test again. What a crackhead!"

❷ A person addicted to the drug "crack," a low-quality form of cocaine.

EXAMPLE 1

"My mom's new boyfriend is a crackhead. I found a lot of white powder in bags by his clothes."

EXAMPLE 2

"Emily looks great! She used to be a crackhead, but she's made a full recovery."

○ Learn more...

- A person who uses the drug "crack" a lot becomes more and more stupid.

- You may also hear "crackpipe."

Crackpot
USED WITH ANYONE

A crazy person.

EXAMPLE 1

"Wendel is a crackpot. He thinks he knows more than Einstein."

EXAMPLE 2

"Ben jumped off a bridge wearing paper wings and broke both of his arms. What a crackpot!"

Crap
USED WITH FRIENDS

❶ Worthless.

EXAMPLE 1

"Gary always lies. Everything he says is crap."

EXAMPLE 2

"I yelled at Sarah for no reason. I feel like crap."

❷ Indicates frustration or surprise.

EXAMPLE 1

"Crap! I lost my wallet!"

EXAMPLE 2

MARY: "Tony was fired from his job today."

PAUL: "Crap! I hope he finds a new job soon."

❸ To defecate.

EXAMPLE 1

"Something smells like bad in here. Did the dog crap?"

EXAMPLE 2

"I'll be back in five minutes. I have to crap."

○ Learn more...

- This is a nicer way to say "shit" (p. 174).

- A "piece of crap" is something worthless.

- You may also hear "Holy crap!" to indicate surprise.

Crapper
USED WITH FRIENDS

Toilet or bathroom.

EXAMPLE 1

"The line for the crapper is too long. Let's go somewhere else."

EXAMPLE 2

"When is the last time they cleaned the crapper? It's a real mess in there."

○ Learn more...

- Many people believe that the toilet was invented by a man named Thomas Crapper, but they're wrong!

IN OTHER WORDS...
"CRAZY"

Many Americans call each other "crazy" on a regular basis, often as a joke. Many of these expressions are meant to be funny.

USED WITH ANYONE

A few sandwiches short of a picnic (p. 1)

Batty (p. 12)

Bonkers (p. 20)

Cracked (p. 38)

Crackpot (p. 38)

Cuckoo (p. 41)

Freak (p. 71)

Have a screw loose (p. 93)

Have bats in the belfry (p. 94)

Headcase (p. 97)

Kook (p. 114)

Loon (p. 120)

Not cooking on all four burners (p. 134)

Not playing with a full deck (p. 135)

Nut case (p. 136)

Nuts (p. 136)

Off one's rocker (p. 137)

Out of it (p. 139)

Out of one's mind (p. 139)

Out there (p. 139)

Out to lunch (p. 140)

Psycho (p. 154)

Screwed up (p. 172)

Whacko (p. 212)

USED WITH FRIENDS

Crackhead (p. 38)

Fruitcake (p. 72)

Schizo (p. 168)

Screwed in the head (p. 171)

USED WITH EXTREME CAUTION

Fucked in the head (p. 77)

Crater-face
USED WITH FRIENDS

A person with a lot of acne or acne scars on his or her face.

EXAMPLE 1

"Look at that crater-face over there! She needs to wash her face more."

EXAMPLE 2

"My brother is a crater-face. He's tried everything, but his acne is just getting worse."

Cream
USED WITH EXTREME CAUTION

To orgasm.

EXAMPLE 1

"I don't know how she did it, but she made me cream just by licking my foot."

EXAMPLE 2

"Larry said he made Lynne cream five times last night. Is that possible?"

Cream One's Jeans
USED WITH EXTREME CAUTION

To orgasm.

EXAMPLE 1

"Evan's motorcycle was vibrating so much, I almost creamed my jeans when he drove me around town."

EXAMPLE 2

"That girl is so sexy! I'm going to cream my jeans just looking at her."

Creep
USED WITH ANYONE

An unpleasantly strange person.

EXAMPLE 1

"Jake tried to kiss me at the funeral. What a creep!"

EXAMPLE 2

"Vince is a creep. He tried to steal my wallet at the party!"

o **Learn more...**

- Men are called "creeps" more often than women.

- In 1993, the band *Radiohead* released a very successful song called "Creep" containing the lyrics "But I'm a creep, I'm a weirdo." A "weirdo" (p. 212) is a "strange person."

Crock Of Shit
USED WITH FRIENDS

Nonsense.

EXAMPLE 1

"You love me? That's a crock of shit. You don't love me at all!"

EXAMPLE 2

"Caleb said he would pay rent this month, but I think that's a crock of shit. He doesn't have any money."

Crocked
USED WITH ANYONE

Drunk.

EXAMPLE 1

"Denise was so crocked that she had sex with the limosine driver."

EXAMPLE 2

"Lyle was so sad, he got crocked to forget about his problems."

Crop-Dusting
USED WITH FRIENDS

To expel gas from the anus; to flatulate.

EXAMPLE 1

"This room smells terrible! Who's been crop-dusting in here?"

EXAMPLE 2

"Luke has been crop-dusting for three hours! That's why we have the fan on and all the windows open."

o **Learn more...**

- Real "crop-dusting" involves dropping pesticides (powders that kill insects) on fields from an airplane.

Crybaby
USED WITH ANYONE

A person who complains a lot.

EXAMPLE 1
"When I turned out the lights, Monica screamed. What a crybaby!"

EXAMPLE 2
"The boss asked us to work late tonight, and Trevor won't stop complaining about it. What a crybaby!"

o Learn more...

- You may also hear the shortened version "baby."

Cuckoo
USED WITH ANYONE

Crazy.

EXAMPLE 1
"Matt is cuckoo. I saw him looking at the sun for ten minutes!"

EXAMPLE 2
"I know I acted strange, but I'm not cuckoo!"

o Learn more...

- "Cuckoo" comes from the "cuckoo bird," a bird that makes a "coo coo" sound.

Cucumber
USED WITH FRIENDS

Penis.

EXAMPLE 1
"I don't know what happened last night, but my cucumber would not get hard."

EXAMPLE 2
"I love to touch Rick's cucumber. It's so smooth!"

o Learn more...

- There are many ways to say "penis" that involve food. This connection between the penis and mouth implies oral sex.

Cum
USED WITH EXTREME CAUTION

❶ To orgasm.

EXAMPLE 1
"I love having sex with Janice, but I always have to stop right before I cum. She doesn't want to get pregnant."

EXAMPLE 2
"Don't stop, Henry! I'm going to cum! Don't stop! Don't stop! Don't Stop! I'm cumming! Okay, stop."

DIALOGUE
"DICKIE AND THE BOYS"

Here is a short dialogue between two Americans.

DYLAN
"Look at the jugs on that woman! I'd like to introduce her to Dickie and the boys."

JAMES
"Don't cream your jeans just yet. I heard she's boinked every guy on the football team. She's a total slut."

DYLAN
"Even better!"

Jugs (p. 110)
Dickie and the boys (p. 46)

Cream one's jeans (p. 40)
Boink (p. 19)
Slut (p. 181)

❷ Fluids released during orgasm.

EXAMPLE 1

"Monica Lewinsky's blue dress got stained with the president's cum!"

EXAMPLE 2

"Wendy loves to lick the cum from her fingers after she masturbates."

○ Learn more...

- Because "cum" sounds just like the word "come," Americans make a lot of jokes by switching the two words. For example: Joan says "I'm coming!" and Phil says "Then go to the bathroom! I just had the carpets cleaned."

- The past tense of "cum" is "came."

Cunnilingus
USED WITH FRIENDS

Oral sex performed on a woman.

EXAMPLE 1

"I didn't think I would like cunnilingus, but Kenny's tongue feels fantastic!"

EXAMPLE 2

"A lot of woman don't like cunnilingus, but I wish they did. I love the way women taste!"

Cunt
USED WITH EXTREME CAUTION

❶ Vagina.

EXAMPLE 1

"John stuck his fingers in my cunt without asking first!"

EXAMPLE 2

"Heidi has a sweet cunt. I love to lick it!"

❷ A nasty woman.

EXAMPLE 1

"Beatrice fired Ted for no reason. She's such a cunt!"

EXAMPLE 2

"Your sister is a cunt. She won't have sex with me!"

○ Learn more...

- You may also hear "the C-word" instead of "cunt," because many people won't say the word "cunt"!

Cuss
USED WITH ANYONE

To use bad words.

EXAMPLE 1

"Nina's mom was really angry and cussed at all of us for breaking the lamp."

EXAMPLE 2

"My dad says that if you cuss, you'll go to hell."

○ Learn more...

- "Cuss" is the slang word for "curse."

Cut One
USED WITH FRIENDS

To expel gas from the anus; to flatulate.

EXAMPLE 1

"If I don't cut one soon, I think my butt will explode."

EXAMPLE 2

"I heard my teacher cut one today when she walked into class. She was really embarrassed."

Cut The Cheese
USED WITH FRIENDS

To expel gas from the anus; to flatulate.

EXAMPLE 1

"Dad, Billy cut the cheese in my face again! Make him stop!"

EXAMPLE 2

"Oh, that smells awful! Who cut the cheese?"

Cyclops
USED WITH FRIENDS

Penis.

EXAMPLE 1

"Be careful, ladies. The cyclops is looking for love!"

EXAMPLE 2

"We were ready to have sex, and then she looked at my cyclops and stopped."

D IS FOR DILDO

"D'oh!"

USED WITH ANYONE

Indicates surprise or frustration.

EXAMPLE 1
AMELIA: "You just sat on your glasses!"

JERRY: "D'oh!"

EXAMPLE 2
PAM: "The boss saw you sleeping in your office."

MIKE: "D'oh! I'm in big trouble."

o Learn more...

- This phrase was made popular by Homer Simpson of Fox's animated television show "The Simpsons."

Daddy

USED WITH FRIENDS

The older, wealthier, or more dominant male in a homosexual relationship.

EXAMPLE 1
"Bill is the daddy in our relationship. He pays for everything we do."

EXAMPLE 2
"Phillip is a great daddy. He's only two years older than me, but I do everything he says."

o Learn more...

- A "sugar daddy" is a rich man who gives his lover (a man or a woman) gifts and money.

Daisy Chain
USED WITH EXTREME CAUTION

Group oral sex in a chain (or line) of people.

EXAMPLE 1

"I'm going to organize a daisy chain at Larry's birthday party. I know he'll love it!"

EXAMPLE 2

"Any good sex party should have a daisy chain."

Damn
USED WITH FRIENDS

❶ Indicates frustration or surprise.

EXAMPLE 1

"Damn! I hit my finger with the hammer again. That really hurts!"

EXAMPLE 2

"Damn! You got a date with that model?"

❷ Used to intensify an emotion.

EXAMPLE 1

"She has some damn fine breasts on her."

EXAMPLE 2

"That man is just too damn handsome!"

❸ Stupid, terrible, irritating, or anything bad.

EXAMPLE 1

"I got the answer wrong on the damn test!"

EXAMPLE 2

"The damn mailman gave me the wrong mail!"

○ Learn more...

• You may also hear "dammit."

Darn
USED WITH ANYONE

❶ Stupid, terrible, irritating, or anything bad.

EXAMPLE 1

"Do you have to play that darn music so loud?"

EXAMPLE 2

"The darn dog ate my sneaker!"

❷ Indicates frustration.

EXAMPLE 1

"Darn! I forgot to call my mother yesterday."

EXAMPLE 2

"Darn! I locked my keys inside the car!"

○ Learn more...

• This is a nicer way to say "damn" (see previous entry).

Date Rape
USED WITH ANYONE

To rape someone while on a date.

EXAMPLE 1

"My last boyfriend tried to date rape me. I broke up with him, but I was too scared to tell the police."

EXAMPLE 2

"Nicolas tried to date rape Kim after the dance, but she kicked him between his legs and ran."

Date Rosy Palm And Her Five Sisters
USED WITH FRIENDS

To masturbate.

EXAMPLE 1

"You need to find a girlfriend, so you can stop dating Rosy palm and her five sisters."

EXAMPLE 2

"I may be alone, but I can have a date with Rosy palm and her five sisters any time I want."

Decorate The Pavement
USED WITH FRIENDS

To vomit.

EXAMPLE 1

"Rita was so drunk, she decorated the pavement as she walked home."

EXAMPLE 2

"Don't vomit in the sink! Go decorate the pavement outside."

Deep Throat
USED WITH EXTREME CAUTION

To put the entire penis into one's mouth during oral sex.

EXAMPLE 1

"All I want for my birthday is a girlfriend who can deep throat."

EXAMPLE 2

"I would never marry a woman who couldn't deep throat me."

Deliver Street Pizza
USED WITH FRIENDS

To vomit.

EXAMPLE 1

"Bill looks sick. He should go home before he starts to deliver street pizza."

EXAMPLE 2

"I always see a lot of guys delivering street pizza on Friday nights when the bars close."

Den Of Iniquity
USED WITH ANYONE

A place where immoral activities happen, like sex, drugs, etc.

EXAMPLE 1

"Two people are having sex on the sofa, and another person is smoking marijuana by the door. This is a real den of iniquity!"

EXAMPLE 2

"I took the guy back to my little den of iniquity for sex."

Dental Dam
USED WITH FRIENDS

A piece of rubber placed over the woman's vagina during oral sex to prevent sexually transmitted diseases.

EXAMPLE 1

"I don't perform oral sex on any women without using a dental dam. It's the only way to protect myself from diseases."

IN OTHER WORDS...
"DEFECATE"

Americans are generally embarrassed by their bodies and their bodily functions. The most polite way to say that you need to defecate is to simply excuse yourself without a reason. Or, you can say "I need to visit the restroom."

When Americans are with their friends, however, they often invent funny ways to say they need to defecate.

USED WITH ANYONE

Do one's business (p. 48)

Go (p. 85)

Go check the plumbing (p. 85)

Make a pit stop (p. 123)

Poop (p. 151)

Powder one's nose (p. 153)

See a man about a horse (p. 173)

Void (p. 210)

USED WITH FRIENDS

B.M. (p. 8)

Drop one's load (p. 54)

Drop some thunder (p. 54)

Drop the kids off at the pool (p. 54)

Hang a heat stick (p. 97)

Lay a log (p. 116)

Pinch a loaf (p. 145)

Shit (p. 174)

Squat (p. 186)

Take a dump (p. 194)

Take a shit (p. 194)

EXAMPLE 2

"I never knew what a dental dam was until I performed oral sex on Linda and she insisted I use it."

Derriere
USED WITH ANYONE

Butt.

EXAMPLE 1

"Marissa has a great derriere for a woman her age."

EXAMPLE 2

"I think the derriere is the sexiest part of a man's body."

Dick
USED WITH FRIENDS

❶ Penis.

EXAMPLE 1

"Frederick wants me to put his dick in my mouth, but I won't!"

EXAMPLE 2

"Don't have sex with Hugh. His dick is really small!"

❷ A rude or nasty man.

EXAMPLE 1

"Derrick kicked my cat. What a dick!"

EXAMPLE 2

"Don't be a dick, Larry. If she said no, she means no!"

❸ To have sex with a woman.

EXAMPLE 1

"I love dicking Miki. She's really great in bed."

EXAMPLE 2

"My girlfriend's going to get a deep dicking tonight. I can't wait to have sex with her."

❍ Learn more...

- "Dick" is a common nickname for "Richard." President Richard Nixon was often called "Tricky Dick."

- You may also hear "dickhead" or "dickweed," as in "My father is a dickhead! He had sex with his secretary."

Dick With Someone
USED WITH EXTREME CAUTION

To tease or trick someone.

EXAMPLE 1

"Are you dicking with me, or did you really get a new job?"

EXAMPLE 2

"I told Hanson that I got a big raise, when I really didn't. I love dicking with him!"

Dickie And The Boys
USED WITH FRIENDS

Penis and testicles.

EXAMPLE 1

"I'm tired, but Dickie and the boys are ready for sex."

EXAMPLE 2

"Gina is having a party and told me to bring Dickie and the boys."

Dildo
USED WITH FRIENDS

A penis-shaped object used for sexual pleasure.

EXAMPLE 1

"Last week my girlfriend bought a dildo. Now she doesn't want to see me anymore!"

EXAMPLE 2

"Only a big dildo can make me have an orgasm."

Dimwit
USED WITH ANYONE

A stupid person.

EXAMPLE 1
"Sally is a dimwit. She forgets to feed her dog a lot."

EXAMPLE 2
"Don't be a dimwit. You know this answer!"

○ **Learn more...**

• A smart person is called "bright" and a stupid person is called "dim." "Wit" is another word for intelligence or humor.

Dinosaur
USED WITH ANYONE

A very old person.

EXAMPLE 1
"I'm such a dinosaur. I remember when televison was first invented!"

EXAMPLE 2
"My mother can't jog with me. She's a dinosaur!"

Dipshit
USED WITH FRIENDS

A stupid person.

EXAMPLE 1
"Les can't do anything right. He's a dipshit."

EXAMPLE 2
"You dipshit! You forgot to add eggs to the cake!"

Dipstick
USED WITH ANYONE

❶ **A stupid person.**

EXAMPLE 1
"You dipstick! You should taste your food before you salt it!"

EXAMPLE 2
"Don't invite Theo to the party. He's a dipstick."

❷ **Penis.**

EXAMPLE 1
"I gave her $50 to lick my dipstick, but she took the money and ran away."

EXAMPLE 2
"She cleaned my dipstick for 30 minutes."

○ **Learn more...**

• This is a nicer way to say "dipshit" (see previous entry).

• A "dipstick" is the part of a car used to measure oil. It became an insult because it rhymes with "dipshit."

• You may also hear the shortened version "dip."

Dirtbag
USED WITH FRIENDS

A very bad person.

EXAMPLE 1
"Hey, dirtbag! Stop trying to sell drugs to those kids!"

EXAMPLE 2
"Some dirtbag put garbage all over my car."

Dirty
USED WITH ANYONE

❶ **Sexual (bad).**

EXAMPLE 1
"That movie is too dirty for my children!"

EXAMPLE 2
"The book I'm reading is really dirty. The characters have sex too much!"

❷ **Sexual (good).**

EXAMPLE 1
"Let's go home and do something dirty!"

EXAMPLE 2
"This book is very dirty. I'm really enjoying it!"

○ **Learn more...**

• Some Americans think sex is bad and makes you "dirty."

Dirty Old Man
USED WITH ANYONE

An old man who tries to attract young men or women for sex or sexual contact.

EXAMPLE 1

"That dirty old man tried to look up my dress with a mirror on the floor."

EXAMPLE 2

"Why do all the dirty old men seem to find me on my way home from work?"

Dishonorable Discharge
USED WITH FRIENDS

Vomit.

EXAMPLE 1

"Mindy, I'm really sorry for the dishonorable discharge on your carpet last night."

EXAMPLE 2

"Matt really made the house smell with his dishonorable discharge."

Diving Suit
USED WITH FRIENDS

A condom.

EXAMPLE 1

"I make Derick put on his diving suit before we have sex."

EXAMPLE 2

"I hate wearing a diving suit during sex. You can't feel anything."

Do It
USED WITH FRIENDS

To have sex.

EXAMPLE 1

"Jill and I are going to do it tonight for the first time. I bought 36 condoms!"

EXAMPLE 2

"Hey, sexy! Let's do it on the roof of the building so everyone can see!"

Do One's Business
USED WITH ANYONE

To defecate.

EXAMPLE 1

"Please take the dog for a walk, so he can do his business."

EXAMPLE 2

"Lady, will you please stop your cat from doing his business on my driveway?"

o **Learn more...**

• Usually said when referring to pets.

Do The Deed
USED WITH FRIENDS

To have sex.

EXAMPLE 1

"Tonight I'm finally going to do the deed with Jeremy. He's really excited, but I'm nervous."

EXAMPLE 2

"Sorry I missed your phone call. I was doing the deed with Beth."

Do The Do
USED WITH FRIENDS

To have sex.

EXAMPLE 1

"I was doing the do with Yuko when the pizza delivery guy interrupted us."

EXAMPLE 2

"Gretchen likes to do the do in the car while I'm driving!"

o **Learn more...**

• The soda "Mountain Dew" is advertised with the phrase "Do the Dew!"

Do The Nasty
USED WITH FRIENDS

To have sex.

EXAMPLE 1

"Wow! My dog is trying to do the nasty with your dog! Let's watch."

EXAMPLE 2
"I never do the nasty on the first date. But I always do it on the second date!"

Do The Wild Thing
USED WITH FRIENDS

To have sex.

EXAMPLE 1
"My goal this holiday is to do the wild thing with as many women as possible."

EXAMPLE 2
"I just saw my grandmother doing the wild thing with her boyfriend. I never want to have sex again."

Dode
USED WITH ANYONE

A stupid person.

EXAMPLE 1
"You got lost driving here? What a dode!"

EXAMPLE 2
"Don't talk to Bart. He's a dode."

o **Learn more...**

- This word is used by teenagers more than adults.

"Does a bear shit in the woods?"
USED WITH FRIENDS

"Yes, of course!"

EXAMPLE 1
"Would I like a thousand dollars? Does a bear shit in the woods?"

EXAMPLE 2
SAM: "Is Tricia good at sex?"

LILLY: "Does a bear shit in the woods? She's great!"

Dog
USED WITH FRIENDS

❶ **An ugly person.**

EXAMPLE 1
DAVE: "Why don't you ask Jill for a date?"

JAY: "She's a dog. I can do better than her."

EXAMPLE 2
"Look at those dogs over there! I have never seen so many ugly girls all in one place."

❷ **A person who will say or do anything for sex.**

EXAMPLE 1
NICK: "What do you think of Billy?"

DIALOGUE
"WANTED: DOMINATRIX"

Here is a short dialogue between two Americans.

MICHAEL
"My new girlfriend doesn't know jack shit about deep throating. She bit my dick last night!"

SAM
"She needs to practice with a dildo. Of course, if you give her one, she may never want to do the nasty with you again."

MICHAEL
"Damn. Why can't I find a nice dominatrix to date?"

Don't know jack shit
(p. 51)
Deep throat (p. 45)
Dick (p. 46)

Dildo (p. 46)
Do the nasty (p. 48)

Damn (p. 44)
Dominatrix (p. 50)

KIM: "He's a dog. He's always trying to sleep with me."

EXAMPLE 2
"I thought my boyfriend was a nice guy, but more and more, I think he's just a dog."

o **Learn more...**

- You may also hear "bow-wow" to mean "ugly" as in "Jake's new girlfriend is a real bow-wow. Why is he dating her?"

- "Bow-wow" is the sound a dog makes.

Doggie-style
USED WITH FRIENDS

A sexual position where the first person penetrates the second person from behind, while the second person is on his or her hands and knees like a dog.

EXAMPLE 1
"I was having sex with Melissa doggie-style, so I wouldn't have to look at her big nose."

EXAMPLE 2
"I love when a man has sex with me doggie-style. It feels the best."

Dolt
USED WITH ANYONE

A stupid person.

EXAMPLE 1
"Bob put salt in his coffee because he thought it was sugar. What a dolt!"

EXAMPLE 2
"I feel like a dolt because I can't drive a car."

Dominant
USED WITH FRIENDS

The more active or controlling person during sexual activities.

EXAMPLE 1
"I am always the dominant one when Heather and I have sex. She does whatever I say."

EXAMPLE 2
"My wife is more dominant, and likes to tie me to the bed."

Dominatrix
USED WITH FRIENDS

A woman who enjoys controlling her sexual partner.

EXAMPLE 1
"Andrea enjoys being a dominatrix. She's great at controlling her lover."

EXAMPLE 2
"Being a dominatrix makes me enjoy sex more. I like to be in control!"

o **Learn more...**

- This phrase is sometimes used in reference to any strong woman.

"Don't get your panties in a bunch."
USED WITH FRIENDS

"Don't get upset."

EXAMPLE 1
"Don't get your panties in a bunch, Wilson. We'll clean up the mess before your parents get home."

EXAMPLE 2
GINA: "I still don't have a date for the party!"

SUE: "Don't get your panties in a bunch. I know the perfect guy for you."

Don't Give A Fuck
USED WITH EXTREME CAUTION

Not to care at all.

EXAMPLE 1

"Why are you interested in Valerie? She doesn't give a fuck about you."

EXAMPLE 2

"The executives don't give a fuck about us. They just care about themselves."

o Learn more...

- You may also hear "don't give a flying fuck."

Don't Have A Backbone
USED WITH ANYONE

To be cowardly or weak.

EXAMPLE 1

"Ron doesn't have a backbone. His wife makes all the decisions."

EXAMPLE 2

"Allison won't argue with her boss when her boss is wrong. She doesn't have a backbone!"

o Learn more...

- The backbone (or spine) helps humans stand and appear confident. If you don't have a backbone, you are considered weak.

Don't Have A Snowball's Chance In Hell
USED WITH FRIENDS

To have no chance for success.

EXAMPLE 1

"You don't have a snowball's chance in hell of passing that test tomorrow. You never even went to class!"

EXAMPLE 2

"I don't have a snowball's chance in hell with Ingrid. She's so beautiful."

o Learn more...

- "Hell" is traditionally a hot place, so a snowball would melt immediately if it were there.

Don't Know Jack Shit
USED WITH FRIENDS

To know nothing.

EXAMPLE 1

"Pam is trying to fix my car, but she doesn't know jack shit about car engines!"

EXAMPLE 2

"I don't know jack shit about marketing. You should write the report!"

o Learn more...

- You may also hear "don't know jack" or "don't know shit."

- There is a popular computer quiz game called "You Don't Know Jack."

Don't Know One's Ass From One's Elbow
USED WITH FRIENDS

To know nothing.

EXAMPLE 1

"You don't know your ass from your elbow if you think the President is doing a good job."

EXAMPLE 2

"That auto mechanic doesn't know his ass from his elbow! My car is still broken."

o Learn more...

- You may also hear "don't know one's ass from a hole in the ground."

Don't Know Shit From Shinola
USED WITH FRIENDS

To know nothing.

EXAMPLE 1

"Grandma is old, but she doesn't know shit from shinola about American history."

EXAMPLE 2

"Zak doesn't know shit from shinola about cars."

Dong
USED WITH FRIENDS

Penis.

EXAMPLE 1

"Nick has the biggest dong I've ever seen."

EXAMPLE 2

"I can't have an orgasm unless the guy has a huge dong."

Doo-doo
USED WITH ANYONE

Excrement.

EXAMPLE 1

"Mom was angry because I stepped in dog doo-doo and then walked through the house."

EXAMPLE 2

"Doo-doo smells bad, but flowers smell good."

o **Learn more...**

• Used by children or adults when talking to children.

Doofus
USED WITH ANYONE

A stupid person.

EXAMPLE 1

"Doofus! You spilled my drink!"

EXAMPLE 2

MATT: "Lisa likes me!"

KEN: "No, she doesn't, doofus!"

o **Learn more...**

• You may also hear "doof."

Dork
USED WITH ANYONE

An awkward or unpopular person.

EXAMPLE 1

"Senyo always trips and falls. He's such a dork!"

EXAMPLE 2

"I invited Sandy to the party, but she wanted to read a book instead. I didn't know she was a dork!"

o **Learn more...**

• At school, a "dork" is often a smart, unpopular person.

Double Bag It
USED WITH FRIENDS

To wear two condoms at the same time.

EXAMPLE 1

"You better double bag it if you want to have sex with Rosali. I heard she has a sexual disease."

EXAMPLE 2

"Whenever I have sex with a prostitute, I double bag it to be safe."

Douche
USED WITH FRIENDS

To clean the inside of the vagina with water or a chemical solution, usually after sex.

EXAMPLE 1

"I douche every time I have sex. I want Charles' sperm out of there!"

EXAMPLE 2

"I think I should douche. My boyfriend didn't want to perform oral sex last night."

o **Learn more...**

• Actually, "douching" isn't good for the body. It removes helpful bacteria along with the harmful ones, and can lead to infection.

Douche Bag
USED WITH FRIENDS

A stupid or irritating person.

EXAMPLE 1

"Look at that douche bag standing in the middle of the road. Get out of the way!"

EXAMPLE 2

"Hey, douche bag! Stop looking at my girlfriend's breasts!"

o **Learn more...**

• A "douche bag" is a bag used for "douching" (see previous entry).

Down There

USED WITH ANYONE

The pubic area.

EXAMPLE 1

"Carrol tried to touch me down there. I was really surprised because I just met her."

EXAMPLE 2

"I think I have a problem down there. My testicles are growing hair!"

o **Learn more...**

- Used by children or immature people.

- You may also hear "south of the border."

Drag Queen

USED WITH EXTREME CAUTION

A man who dresses like a woman.

EXAMPLE 1

"My boyfriend is a drag queen. He's always wearing dresses."

EXAMPLE 2

FRED: "She's beautiful!"

JEB: "That's a drag queen!"

o **Learn more...**

- In a "drag show," men dress as women and perform songs.

IN OTHER WORDS...
"DRUNK"

Drinking alcohol is supposed to be fun, but most of the words that mean "drunk" sound dangerous and painful! We are strange people.

USED WITH ANYONE

Blitzed (p. 18)

Bombed (p. 19)

Buzzed (p. 27)

Crocked (p. 40)

Drunk as a skunk (p. 54)

Feeling no pain (p. 64)

Hammered (p. 90)

Lit (p. 119)

Loaded (p. 120)

Looped (p. 120)

Plastered (p. 148)

Polluted (p. 150)

Ripped (p. 162)

Roaring drunk (p. 162)

Rocked (p. 163)

Sauced (p. 167)

Shattered (p. 174)

Sloshed (p. 181)

Smashed (p. 182)

Staggering drunk (p. 188)

Tanked (p. 194)

Three sheets to the wind (p. 198)

Toasted (p. 201)

Wasted (p. 211)

USED WITH FRIENDS

Shit-faced (p. 175)

Stinking drunk (p. 188)

Stupid drunk (p. 190)

Dragging Ass
USED WITH FRIENDS

To move slowly.

EXAMPLE 1

"Shannon drank too much beer last night. She's really dragging ass today."

EXAMPLE 2

"I was dragging ass all morning. Maybe I'm getting sick."

Drain The Lizard
USED WITH FRIENDS

To urinate.

EXAMPLE 1

"Phil went to drain the lizard. He'll be back soon."

EXAMPLE 2

"Which way to the bathroom? I have to drain the lizard."

○ **Learn more...**

- You may also hear "drain the vein."

Drat
USED WITH ANYONE

Indicates frustration.

EXAMPLE 1

"Drat! I failed the science test."

EXAMPLE 2

"Drat! I can't see anything in this fog!"

○ **Learn more...**

- This is a nicer way to say "damn" (p. 44).

Drive The Porcelain Bus
USED WITH FRIENDS

To vomit.

EXAMPLE 1

"I felt like I was driving the porcelain bus all the way to China last night. I vomited for hours."

EXAMPLE 2

"I love getting drunk, but I hate driving the porcelain bus home."

○ **Learn more...**

- Most toilets are made of "porcelain."

Drop One's Load
USED WITH FRIENDS

❶ **To ejaculate.**

EXAMPLE 1

"I don't like it when Bob drops his load on my sheets. I have to wash them three times a week."

EXAMPLE 2

"Laura was so drunk, I dropped my load on her face and she didn't notice."

❷ **To defecate.**

EXAMPLE 1

"Ethan dropped his load in his pants again."

EXAMPLE 2

"Sorry I'm late. I had to drop my load."

Drop Some Thunder
USED WITH FRIENDS

To defecate.

EXAMPLE 1

"I can't eat anything else until I drop some thunder."

EXAMPLE 2

"It smells terrible in here! Did you just drop some thunder?"

Drop The Kids Off At The Pool
USED WITH FRIENDS

To defecate.

EXAMPLE 1

"Sorry I'm late. I had to drop the kids off at the pool and shave before I could leave."

EXAMPLE 2

KAY: "What is that smell?"

GARY: "Oh, I just dropped the kids off at the pool."

Drunk As A Skunk
USED WITH ANYONE

Drunk.

EXAMPLE 1

"Terry is as drunk as a skunk! We can't let her drive home."

EXAMPLE 2

"My dad is always as drunk as a skunk. He needs help!"

Dry Fuck
USED WITH EXTREME CAUTION

To rub against another person as if you are having sex, but while wearing clothes.

EXAMPLE 1

"Ann didn't want to have sex, so we just kissed and dry fucked all night."

EXAMPLE 2

"Ted got a cut on his penis from dry fucking Liz last night."

o Learn more...

- You may also hear "dry hump."

Duff
USED WITH ANYONE

Butt.

EXAMPLE 1

"Get off your duff and help me clean the house!"

EXAMPLE 2

"My duff hurts from the dog bite."

Dumb As A Sack Of Rocks
USED WITH ANYONE

Very stupid.

EXAMPLE 1

"Paulo is cute, but he's as dumb as a sack of rocks!"

EXAMPLE 2

"I would ask Paige for the answer, but she's as dumb as a sack of rocks!"

o Learn more...

- You may also hear "dumb as a sack of wet mice."

Dumb As An Ox
USED WITH ANYONE

Very stupid.

EXAMPLE 1

"Dave jumped off a big rock and broke his leg. He's as dumb as an ox!"

EXAMPLE 2

"My new teacher is as dumb as an ox! He knows less than I do!"

Dumb-ass
USED WITH FRIENDS

A stupid person.

EXAMPLE 1

"Howard just yelled at his boss. What a dumb-ass!"

DIALOGUE
"RAY DELIVERS STREET PIZZA"

Here is a short dialogue between two Americans.

JACK
"I heard your dumb-ass brother Ray dicked a 17-year-old girl last night."

CARLOS
"Yeah. He met her last night when he was delivering street pizzas in front of the bar. He was drunk as a skunk, as usual."

JACK
"That dipshit loves to do it with young girls. I hope he goes to jail someday."

Dumb-ass (p. 55)
Dick (p. 46)

Deliver street pizzas
   (p. 45)
Drunk as a skunk (p. 54)

Dipshit (p. 47)
Do it (p. 48)

EXAMPLE 2

CARL: "You're stupid!"

LING: "I'm going to punch you, dumb-ass!"

Dumb-fuck
USED WITH EXTREME CAUTION

A stupid person.

EXAMPLE 1

"Dave is always getting lost. He's a real dumb-fuck."

EXAMPLE 2

"Don't be a dumb-fuck, Rita. Come with us to the party!"

Dumb-shit
USED WITH FRIENDS

A stupid person.

EXAMPLE 1

"Rick always drives when he's drunk. What a dumb-shit!"

EXAMPLE 2

"I feel like a dumb-shit. I can't remember my phone number."

Dummy
USED WITH ANYONE

A stupid person.

EXAMPLE 1

"Timmy's a dummy! He spilled juice on his shirt."

EXAMPLE 2

"You dummy! You need to start the oven before you can bake a cake!"

○ Learn more...

• You may also hear "dumdum."

• Children use this phrase more often than adults.

Dumper
USED WITH FRIENDS

Butt.

EXAMPLE 1

"Look at the cute dumper on that girl over there."

EXAMPLE 2

"I like you, but I can't date you. Your dumper is too big!"

Dunce
USED WITH ANYONE

A stupid person.

EXAMPLE 1

"If you don't study more, you'll always be a dunce!"

EXAMPLE 2

"My son is a dunce. He can't even spell his own name."

○ Learn more...

• A long time ago, school children who answered questions wrong had to wear a "dunce cap" as punishment.

Dweeb
USED WITH ANYONE

A stupid or unpopular person.

EXAMPLE 1

"The party was terrible. There were dweebs everywhere and no alcohol!"

EXAMPLE 2

"Kelly's last boyfriend was a dweeb, so I'm sure she'll like you."

Dyke
USED WITH EXTREME CAUTION

A masculine lesbian.

EXAMPLE 1

"That dyke looks like a man!"

EXAMPLE 2

"I'm only attracted to dykes. I don't like women who are too feminine."

IS FOR
EASY

Easy
USED WITH FRIENDS

A person who is usually willing to have sex with anyone.

EXAMPLE 1

"I'm having dinner with Rosali, and we all know how easy she is! I'll definitely have sex tonight."

EXAMPLE 2

"I want to have sex with Ken, but I don't want to appear easy."

○ Learn more...

- You may also hear "easy lay" as in "Nancy is an easy lay. She had sex with me on our first date!"

- Women are called "easy" more often than men.

Eat My Shorts
USED WITH FRIENDS

Phrase indicating anger or dislike.

EXAMPLE 1

"If you don't like my idea, you can eat my shorts!"

EXAMPLE 2

"All Republicans can eat my shorts! I hate those idiots."

○ Learn more...

- This phrase was made famous by Bart Simpson on Fox's animated T.V. show "The Simpsons."

- The phrase originally appeared in the 1985 movie, *The Breakfast Club*, about a group of high school kids.

"Eat shit!"
USED WITH FRIENDS

Phrase indicating anger or dislike.

EXAMPLE 1

IKE: "You look fat today."

MELANIE: "Eat shit!"

EXAMPLE 2

"Eat shit, Andrew. I never want to see you again!"

o **Learn more...**

- You may also hear "Eat shit and die!"

Eat Someone Out
USED WITH FRIENDS

To perform oral sex on a woman.

EXAMPLE 1

"Janine always wants me to eat her out. She never wants to have sex."

EXAMPLE 2

"I love it when another woman eats me out. I love to feel her tongue on my clitoris."

o **Learn more...**

- For homosexual men, to "eat someone out" refers to performing oral sex on another man's anus.

Eaten By Wolves And Shit Over A Cliff
USED WITH FRIENDS

To be ugly.

EXAMPLE 1

"Wow! She really looks like she was eaten by wolves and shit over a cliff. I've never seen anyone that ugly!"

EXAMPLE 2

"Grant is so handsome, but his brother looks like he was eaten by wolves and shit over a cliff."

Effeminate
USED WITH ANYONE

Feminine (but only said about men).

EXAMPLE 1

"I have never seen such an effeminate gay man before."

EXAMPLE 2

"My mother thinks my brother is gay because he is so effeminate."

80 (Eighty)
USED WITH FRIENDS

To have sex involving three people.

EXAMPLE 1

"My girlfriend and I love each other, but sometimes we 80 with the cute guy next door."

EXAMPLE 2

"Dave and I like to add another person and 80 whenever we can. It helps keep our sex life interesting."

88 (Eighty-eight)
USED WITH FRIENDS

Group sex.

EXAMPLE 1

"Mike is having an 88 party next weekend, and he's invited some really beautiful people. It should be fun."

EXAMPLE 2

"I was really nervous during my first 88. I wasn't sure who I should be with and when."

86'd (Eighty-six'd)
USED WITH ANYONE

To end a relationship with someone.

EXAMPLE 1

"When I realized that my girlfriend was stealing from me, I 86'd her and threw her clothes on the street."

EXAMPLE 2

"I am going to get drunk tonight because Jane just 86'd me this morning."

○ Learn more...

- "86" means "to kill" if you're a gangster in the mob.

- "To 86 something" means "to remove or discard something" as in "Let's 86 this whole idea about starting a new company. We don't have the money for that right now."

Equipment
USED WITH FRIENDS

Penis.

EXAMPLE 1

"Arthur's equipment is really big. I think it might be too big for me."

EXAMPLE 2

"Why do all the ugly guys have the best equipment?"

AT THE MOVIES
"ERIN BROCKOVICH" (2000)

The Academy Award-winning movie *Erin Brockovich*, starring Julia Roberts, is based on the true story of a single mother's fight against a California power company.

ERIN BROCKOVICH
"Did they teach you how to apologize at lawyer school? Because you suck at it."

Suck (p. 190)

—

ED MASRY
"What makes you think you can just walk in there and take whatever you want?"

ERIN BROCKOVICH
"They're called boobs, Ed."

Boob (p. 20)

—

KURT POTTER
"How did you do this?"

ERIN BROCKOVICH
"I just went out there and performed sexual favors. Six hundred and thirty-four blow jobs in five days... I'm really quite tired."

Blow job (p. 18)

—

ED MASRY
"I assumed you were off having fun."

ERIN BROCKOVICH
"Oh, and why the hell would you assume that? "

Hell (p. 97)

—

ERIN BROCKOVICH
"I don't know shit about shit, but I know right from wrong!"

Don't know jack shit (p. 51)
Shit (p. 174)

Erotica
USED WITH ANYONE

Literature or art intended to arouse sexual desire.

EXAMPLE 1
"I read a great piece of erotica yesterday. It really made me want to have sex!"

EXAMPLE 2
"That sculpture makes me think of Kim's naked body. The artist is really skilled at erotica."

Escort Service
USED WITH ANYONE

A company that provides a person with a companion, usually for sex.

EXAMPLE 1
"I need a date for the party, but I don't know any women in Chicago. I'm going to call an escort service."

EXAMPLE 2
"The best escort services are very expensive, but the women are beautiful, and you can have sex with them all night."

Eunuch
USED WITH FRIENDS

A male who has had his testicles removed.

EXAMPLE 1
"That guy must be gay or a eunuch. He's not even looking at that naked woman in front of him!"

EXAMPLE 2
"After the car accident, my father was a eunuch. He never had sex again."

Exhibitionist
USED WITH ANYONE

A person who desires attention.

EXAMPLE 1
"Jerry is an exhibitionist. He had sex at the park last week, and a dozen people saw him!"

EXAMPLE 2
"Jasmine walks through the apartment nude all the time. She's such an exhibitionist!"

F IS FOR FUCKING

F-ing
USED WITH FRIENDS

Stupid, terrible, irritating, or anything bad.

EXAMPLE 1

"My F-ing boss gave me too much work!"

EXAMPLE 2

"What's the phone number for the dentist? My F-ing tooth hurts!"

◯ Learn more...

- This is a nicer way to say "fucking" (p. 77).

Facilities
USED WITH ANYONE

Toilet or bathroom.

EXAMPLE 1

"The facilities are out of toilet paper. Can you please bring more?"

EXAMPLE 2

"This restaurant is amazing! They have the nicest facilities I've ever seen."

Facts Of Life
USED WITH ANYONE

How sex and sexual relationships work.

EXAMPLE 1

"After my father explained the facts of life to me, I hired a prostitute to practice what I learned."

EXAMPLE 2

"My sister told me about the facts of life. Now I'm scared to grow older!"

o **Learn more...**

- The popular T.V. show "The Facts of Life" (1979-1988) was about girls growing up at a boarding school.

Fag Hag
USED WITH EXTREME CAUTION

A woman who prefers homosexual men as friends.

EXAMPLE 1

"I'm becoming a fag hag! All my friends are gay guys."

EXAMPLE 2

"Brenda is a total fag hag. I think she's afraid of other women."

o **Learn more...**

- Although a "hag" is "an old, ugly woman," a "fag hag" can be any woman.

Faggot
USED WITH EXTREME CAUTION

A homosexual man.

EXAMPLE 1

"That faggot is still looking at me. He must think I'm gay."

EXAMPLE 2

"Just because I don't want to have sex with you doesn't mean that I'm a faggot."

o **Learn more...**

- You may also hear "fag."

- In British English, a "faggot" is a "bundle of wood," and a "fag" is a "cigarette."

Fairy
USED WITH EXTREME CAUTION

A homosexual man.

EXAMPLE 1

"That fairy is wearing designer sneakers. I wonder where he bought them?"

EXAMPLE 2

"Why is Tina dating Alexander? It's obvious he's a fairy."

Fake It
USED WITH ANYONE

To pretend to have an orgasm.

EXAMPLE 1

"Men never fake it. It's usually very easy for a man to have an orgasm during sex."

EXAMPLE 2

"Sex with Michael is so bad, I have to fake it so he'll stop."

Family Jewels
USED WITH ANYONE

The testicles.

EXAMPLE 1

"Just kick Matt in the family jewels, and he'll give you back your hat."

EXAMPLE 2

"I think there's something wrong with the family jewels. They've been itching since Friday."

Fanny
USED WITH ANYONE

Butt.

EXAMPLE 1

"I laughed when that girl fell on her fanny in the middle of the store."

EXAMPLE 2

"I like to touch fannies. I think I have a problem."

o **Learn more...**

- "Fanny" is also a girl's name, although it's not common.

- To the British, "fanny" is a very rude word for "vagina."

Fart

USED WITH FRIENDS

To expel gas from the anus; to flatulate.

EXAMPLE 1

"I farted at the coffee shop today and everyone laughed at me. Then they smelled it and stopped laughing."

EXAMPLE 2

"Dan farts all day, every day. I can't live with him anymore."

o Learn more...

- This is the most common way to say "flatulence."

Fat Slob

USED WITH ANYONE

A fat, messy person.

EXAMPLE 1

"Andy's a fat slob. He eats all day and never cleans!"

EXAMPLE 2

"I need to diet and exercise, or I'm going to be a fat slob!"

LEARN MORE
"FUCK" IN A SENTENCE

How are "fuck" and "fucking" used in a sentence?

These words can be used almost anywhere in a sentence to intensify the meaning.

For example, compare these sentences:

1.   **"Where is the cat?"**

2.   **"Where is the fucking cat?"**

In #1, the speaker might just be asking where the cat is. In #2, we know the speaker is serious. He or she can't find the cat, and is really upset about it.

The speaker can go even further and say:

3.   **"Where the fuck is the fucking cat?"**

Here's another set of examples. The following are all acceptable:

1.   **"Chuck forgot the tickets. We're going to miss the movie."**

2.   **"Chuck forgot the fucking tickets. We're going to miss the movie."**

3.   **"Chuck fucking forgot the fucking tickets. We're going to miss the movie."**

4.   **"Chuck fucking forgot the fucking tickets. We're going to miss the fucking movie."**

5.   **"That fuck, Chuck, forgot the fucking tickets. We're fucking going to miss the fucking movie."**

If someone is frustrated or upset, he or she may put "fuck" and "fucking" almost anywhere in a sentence and everyone will understand.

Of course, everyone will also think the person speaking is very rude.

Fat-head
USED WITH FRIENDS

A stupid person.

EXAMPLE 1

"You fat-head! You have to learn the rules before you can play the game."

EXAMPLE 2

"John called me a fat-head, but I'm a lot smarter than him!"

Fatso
USED WITH FRIENDS

A fat person.

EXAMPLE 1

"Hey, fatso! Move out of the doorway, so other people can walk into the movie theater."

EXAMPLE 2

"That fatso broke my favorite chair when he sat in it."

o **Learn more...**

• You may also hear "fatty."

Feel Like Ass
USED WITH FRIENDS

To feel tired or ill.

EXAMPLE 1

"I feel like ass today. I should have slept longer this morning."

EXAMPLE 2

"If I don't stop drinking, I'm going to feel like ass tomorrow."

Feel Someone Up
USED WITH FRIENDS

To touch another person's genitals or breasts with one's hands.

EXAMPLE 1

"Brenda has really big breasts. I was feeling her up all night."

EXAMPLE 2

"My teacher tried to feel me up yesterday. I told the police, so he can't do it to another student."

o **Learn more...**

• You may also hear "feel up someone" as in "Did you feel up Joanna last night?"

Feeling No Pain
USED WITH ANYONE

Drunk.

EXAMPLE 1

"After that last drink, I'm feeling no pain!"

EXAMPLE 2

"Gigi is feeling no pain. She drank a bottle of wine by herself!"

Fell Out Of The Ugly Tree And Hit Every Branch On The Way Down
USED WITH FRIENDS

To be very ugly.

EXAMPLE 1

"Rita's boyfriend looks like he fell out of the ugly tree and hit every branch on the way down."

EXAMPLE 2

"I would never date you! You look like you fell out of the ugly tree and hit every branch on the way down."

Fellatio
USED WITH ANYONE

Oral sex performed on a man.

EXAMPLE 1

"I bought my girlfriend a book about fellatio, and now I am the happiest man in the world."

EXAMPLE 2

"Alice is terrible at fellatio! She hurt my penis with her teeth three times."

THE SLANGMAN GUIDE TO DIRTY ENGLISH

Fetishist
USED WITH ANYONE

A person who is sexually aroused by objects or nonsexual parts of the body, and may need them for sexual satisfaction.

EXAMPLE 1

"Ted gets sexually excited by touching my feet. Why do I always date fetishists?"

EXAMPLE 2

"Emma is a fetishist. She gets sexually excited when I chain her to the bed!"

Filth
USED WITH ANYONE

Offensive material, usually sexual.

EXAMPLE 1

"I don't allow filth in this house. Take that sex movie and leave!"

EXAMPLE 2

"Jared collects filth. He has pictures of naked women all over his room."

o Learn more...

- You may also hear "filthy" as in "Tony has a filthy mouth. He's always saying bad words!"

Finger-fuck
USED WITH EXTREME CAUTION

To insert a finger in someone's rectum or vagina.

EXAMPLE 1

"Lina won't have sex with Josh, so he just finger-fucks her most of the time."

EXAMPLE 2

"I was finger-fucking Ann until dawn. My finger hurts now."

o Learn more...

- You may also hear just "finger," so be careful and listen closely to the context!

First Base
USED WITH FRIENDS

Kissing.

EXAMPLE 1

"I didn't get to first base until I was 17 years old. I was an ugly child."

EXAMPLE 2

"I let Hank get to first base last night. We kissed for three hours."

o Learn more...

- In baseball, you have to touch "first base" before you can move to "second base" (p. 172), "third base" (p. 198), and "home base" (p. 102).

Fisting
USED WITH EXTREME CAUTION

To insert the hand or fist into someone's anus or vagina.

EXAMPLE 1

"Joanie can't orgasm without ten minutes of fisting first."

EXAMPLE 2

"Dottie and I were fisting so much last night that my hand got tired!"

o Learn more...

- You may also hear "fist-fuck" as in "My wife loves fist-fucking. We're lucky I have small hands!"

Flagellation
USED WITH FRIENDS

Whipping or beating someone to orgasm.

EXAMPLE 1

"My last girlfriend liked flagellation. She had an orgasm every time I whipped her!"

EXAMPLE 2

"I was surprised that I really liked flagellation. The pain makes me very excited."

Flake
USED WITH ANYONE

A person who regularly fails to do things he or she promised to do.

EXAMPLE 1

"Marsha's a big flake! She says she'll come to my parties, but she never does."

EXAMPLE 2

"Calvin forgot to pick me up at the bus station. What a flake!"

o Learn more...

- You may also hear "flaked" as in "He was supposed to come to dinner with me, but he flaked."

- You may also hear "flaky" as in "He's flaky. He never does what he says he'll do."

Flamer
USED WITH EXTREME CAUTION

A homosexual man.

EXAMPLE 1

"Ken is a big flamer. He'd never date a woman."

EXAMPLE 2

"That flamer just kissed that other flamer on the lips."

o Learn more...

- You may also hear "flaming" as in "Everyone at Cory's party was flaming. Why weren't there any heterosexual men there?"

Flasher
USED WITH ANYONE

A person who enjoys showing people his or her genitals in public.

EXAMPLE 1

"My last boyfriend was a flasher. He loved showing old ladies his penis on the subway!"

EXAMPLE 2

"Yuck! That man over there is a flasher! He opened his coat and he was naked!"

o Learn more...

- See the illustration on the cover of this book for an example of a "flasher."

Flat
USED WITH FRIENDS

Small-breasted.

EXAMPLE 1

"Calista is flat. I have bigger breasts than she does, and I'm a guy!"

EXAMPLE 2

"I don't date flat girls. Please leave me alone."

Flatsy Patsy
USED WITH FRIENDS

A nickname for girls with no breasts.

EXAMPLE 1

"In school, the other children called my sister Flatsy Patsy because she had very small breasts."

EXAMPLE 2

"I think Flatsy Patsy will be a great swimmer without any breasts to slow her down."

Flesh Peddler
USED WITH FRIENDS

A person who finds customers for prostitutes; a prostitute's manager.

EXAMPLE 1

"That flesh peddler is always hitting his prostitutes if they don't make enough money."

EXAMPLE 2

"My goal in life is to be the best flesh peddler there is."

o Learn more...

- This is another way to say "pimp" (p. 145).

Flip One's Lid
USED WITH ANYONE

To become crazy.

EXAMPLE 1

"I think Mr. Carrington flipped his lid! He's been talking to the sky for two hours."

EXAMPLE 2

"Pauline is wearing a sweater in summer. I think she flipped her lid."

○ Learn more...

- You may also hear "flip one's wig" as in "Zach is acting crazy today. I think he's flipped his wig."

Flip Someone The Bird
USED WITH ANYONE

To show someone one's middle finger (meaning "fuck you" [p. 76]).

EXAMPLE 1

"That lady just walked in front of my car, so I flipped her the bird."

EXAMPLE 2

"I flipped Devon the bird when he started to yell at me. I don't like him."

○ Learn more...

- You may also hear "flip someone off" as in "That driver just flipped me off!"

- You may also hear "give someone the bird" as in "I just gave Aunt Celine the bird by accident! I'm in big trouble!"

AT THE MOVIES
"FIGHT CLUB" (1999)

Fight Club, starring Edward Norton, Brad Pitt, and Helena Bonham-Carter, tells the story of Jack, a man trying to find meaning in his life. He becomes involved with a mysterious stranger named Tyler, starts dating a troubled woman named Marla, and is soon part of a dangerous group called "Fight Club." The movie is violent and shocking at times, and is very popular with America's youth.

TYLER
"That crazy bitch almost fucked me in half!"

Bitch (p. 16)
Fuck (p. 72)

—

JACK
"Fuck my life. Fuck Fight Club! Fuck you and fuck Marla. I'm sick of this shit!"

Fuck (p. 72)
Shit (p. 174)

—

MARLA
"Sarcastic prick. Go fuck yourself. That's probably how you like it best."

Prick (p. 154)
Fuck (p. 72)

—

MARLA
"You want me to say I'm shit and I deserve to be treated like shit? Well, I am! And that's how you got me off, and you know it!"

Shit (p. 174)
Get off (p. 82)

—

JACK
"Did I tell you I'd call you a motherfucking asswipe dickhead?"

Motherfucking (p. 130)
Asswipe (p. 7)
Dick (p. 46)

—

JACK
"You *are* real, you son of a bitch!"

Son of a bitch (p. 184)

Flipped
USED WITH ANYONE

To become angry, excited, or crazy.

EXAMPLE 1

"My dad flipped when I told him I didn't go to school today."

EXAMPLE 2

"Bill flipped because of all the pressure at work."

o **Learn more...**

• You may also hear "flip out" as in "Jerry will flip out if I tell him I am dating his sister."

Float An Air Biscuit
USED WITH FRIENDS

To expel gas from the anus; to flatulate.

EXAMPLE 1

"I wish Frank would stop floating air biscuits. It really smells bad in here."

EXAMPLE 2

"Mandy asked if I was floating air biscuits during the movie. I lied to her and said it was Linda."

Flog The Bishop
USED WITH FRIENDS

To masturbate.

EXAMPLE 1

"I was sharing a hotel room with my sister, so I couldn't flog the bishop for two days."

EXAMPLE 2

"My hand hurts from flogging the bishop so much. I need to have sex."

Floozy
USED WITH FRIENDS

A woman who has sex often with different people.

EXAMPLE 1

"You can't bring Hanna to meet your mother. She's a floozy!"

EXAMPLE 2

"I heard that Izzy is a floozy. She's had sex with dozens of men."

o **Learn more...**

• Only women are called "floozies."

Fluffer
USED WITH FRIENDS

The person who keeps a male pornography actor's penis erect.

EXAMPLE 1

"I used to work as a fluffer, but I got tired of performing oral sex all day."

EXAMPLE 2

"Jessie used to be a fluffer. I bet she is amazing with her hands and mouth!"

Fooey
USED WITH ANYONE

Indicates frustration.

EXAMPLE 1

"Fooey! We missed the movie!"

EXAMPLE 2

"Fooey! I forgot to buy Hanna a present for her birthday!"

o **Learn more...**

• This is a nicer way to say "fuck" (p. 72).

• Almost any word starting with "f" can be used instead of fuck, like "fudge" and "fork." People understand what is meant by the context.

Fool Around
USED WITH ANYONE

To have sexual contact with someone.

EXAMPLE 1
"Susan and I just fooled around all night because she didn't want to have sex."

EXAMPLE 2
"Chilan was fooling around with every guy at the office."

For Shit
USED WITH FRIENDS

Useless.

EXAMPLE 1
"We're still lost! This map is for shit."

EXAMPLE 2
"My arm is for shit. I hurt it last night at the gym."

For The Hell Of It
USED WITH FRIENDS

For no particular reason; just for fun.

EXAMPLE 1
"I bought this dress for the hell of it. I don't even have a reason to wear it yet."

EXAMPLE 2
IAN: "Why did you kiss Janice last night?"

HANK: "Just for the hell of it."

Foreplay
USED WITH FRIENDS

Sexual activity to create sexual arousal before sex.

EXAMPLE 1
"I wish my husband knew how important foreplay is. He has sex in less than five minutes."

EXAMPLE 2
"Good foreplay should last at least 30 minutes."

Foul Language
USED WITH ANYONE

Offensive words.

EXAMPLE 1
"Mrs. Minter, your son was using foul language at school again."

LEARN MORE
FIVE NAUGHTY NUMBERS

You have to think creatively to understand how "69" came to mean "mutual oral sex."

Look at the number itself. It's actually a little picture of the sex act — just pretend the round parts are people's heads.

69

People often laugh when they hear the number "69," probably because the number itself is innocent, but it makes you think of sex when you hear it.

68 (Sixty-eight) (p. 179)

69 (Sixty-nine) (p. 179)

80 (Eighty) (p. 58)

86'd (Eighty-six'd) (p. 59)

88 (Eighty-eight) (p. 58)

Did you notice that this section is on page 69? Did you laugh when you read that?

EXAMPLE 2

"That man is always using foul language. I don't want to come to his house anymore."

Foul Mouth
USED WITH ANYONE

Said of someone who uses offensive words.

EXAMPLE 1

"You have a foul mouth for a five-year old girl."

EXAMPLE 2

"That foul-mouthed truck driver just said the most disgusting thing to me!"

Four-eyes
USED WITH ANYONE

A person who wears glasses.

EXAMPLE 1

"Watch the road while you're driving, four-eyes! You almost hit me!"

EXAMPLE 2

"Hey, four-eyes! I bet you studied for the test. Give me the answers!"

○ Learn more...

- There is a chain of stores called "FOR EYES" that sells glasses and contact lenses.

Four-letter Word
USED WITH ANYONE

An offensive word.

EXAMPLE 1

"The teacher yelled at Jim for using four-letter words in class."

EXAMPLE 2

"I won't let my daughter use any four-letter words!"

○ Learn more...

- The most popular bad words — damn, fuck, hell, and shit — have four letters.

- You may also hear something called a "four-letter word" when it has fewer or more than four letters. For example, if someone says "Vacation is a four-letter word at our company," you know that vacation is considered bad by the boss.

Fox
USED WITH ANYONE

A sexy woman.

EXAMPLE 1

"Michelle's a fox, and Mike had sex with her last night. He's really lucky!"

EXAMPLE 2

"I've never been with a fox like that. She's the most beautiful woman I've ever seen."

○ Learn more...

- You may also hear "foxy" or "foxy lady" as in "Your mother is a foxy lady! I'd love to have sex with her."

Frab
USED WITH ANYONE

To vomit.

EXAMPLE 1

"David ate too much chocolate and now he has to frab."

EXAMPLE 2

"I frabbed after drinking just one beer."

○ Learn more...

- "Frab" is "barf" (p. 11) spelled backwards.

Fraidy-cat
USED WITH ANYONE

A person who is easily scared.

EXAMPLE 1

"Don't be a fraidy cat! Come here and fight!"

EXAMPLE 2

"Katherine doesn't like to fly. What a fraidy cat!"

○ Learn more...

- Cats are surprised and scared by almost anything.

- Children use this phrase more often than adults.

Freak

USED WITH ANYONE

❶ To become angry, excited, or crazy.

EXAMPLE 1

"Dan freaked because the police caught him with drugs."

EXAMPLE 2

"I freaked when I found $500 on the street. I was screaming with joy!"

❷ An unusual or strange person.

EXAMPLE 1

"You freak! You threw my dinner on the floor!"

EXAMPLE 2

"My dad is a real freak. He wears his robe around the house every day and never leaves."

⊙ Learn more...

- You may also hear "freak out" as in "Don't freak out, we'll find your wallet. Just keep looking."

- "Freak" can also mean "obsessed" when used after another word, like "movie-freak," "car-freak," or "Jesus-freak" (p. 110). For example: "Jennifer is a chocolate-freak. She needs chocolate every five minutes!"

French Kiss

USED WITH ANYONE

To kiss and touch tongues.

EXAMPLE 1

"Tommy was French kissing me and his tongue was half-way down my throat."

EXAMPLE 2

"I practice French kissing with my dog because she has a big tongue."

⊙ Learn more...

- The 1995 movie *French Kiss*, starring Kevin Kline and Meg Ryan, was a love story between a French man and an American woman.

French Tickler

USED WITH FRIENDS

A condom with bumps or ridges to increase pleasure during sex.

EXAMPLE 1

"I bought a special French tickler to use with my girlfriend, but she couldn't feel anything different."

EXAMPLE 2

"My girlfriend loves French ticklers. Regular condoms don't excite her at all."

Friend Of Dorothy

USED WITH ANYONE

A homosexual man.

EXAMPLE 1

"Only a friend of Dorothy would have a pink car like that! This guy must be gay."

EXAMPLE 2

"I think Al is a friend of Dorothy. I saw him kissing another guy last night."

⊙ Learn more...

- This phrase refers to Dorothy from the famous 1939 movie *The Wizard of Oz*. Judy Garland, who played Dorothy, is very popular with homosexual men.

- In the 1995 movie *Clueless*, the character Murray calls another character homosexual by saying: "He's a disco dancin', Oscar Wilde readin', Streisand ticket holdin' friend of Dorothy. Know what I'm sayin'?"

Friggin'
USED WITH FRIENDS

Stupid, terrible, irritating, or anything bad.

EXAMPLE 1

"New York City has too much friggin' traffic!"

EXAMPLE 2

"My friggin' car won't start!"

○ **Learn more...**

- This is a nicer way to say "fucking" (p. 77).

Frigid
USED WITH FRIENDS

Not interested in sex.

EXAMPLE 1

"Laura hasn't had sex in so long, she has become frigid."

EXAMPLE 2

"Any woman as frigid as she is would never date a guy like me."

Frottage
USED WITH FRIENDS

Masturbation by rubbing against another person.

EXAMPLE 1

"My brother went to jail for practicing frottage on a train. The woman he rubbed against was so angry!"

EXAMPLE 2

"I like frottage. I get to have an orgasm without worrying about getting pregnant."

Fruit
USED WITH FRIENDS

A homosexual man.

EXAMPLE 1

"Gary is a fruit. He doesn't date women."

EXAMPLE 2

"I know three male flight attendants who are fruits."

○ **Learn more...**

- You may also hear "fruity" as in "Those clothes make you look fruity. If you want to attract a woman, you should change!"

- To homosexual men, a "fruit" is "a feminine homosexual man."

Fruitcake
USED WITH FRIENDS

❶ **A crazy or strange person.**

EXAMPLE 1

"Dave is a fruitcake. He added these numbers all wrong."

EXAMPLE 2

"Look at that fruitcake wearing his shoes on his hands!"

❷ **A homosexual man.**

EXAMPLE 1

"I'm no fruitcake! I'm heterosexual."

EXAMPLE 2

"I think that guy is a fruitcake. He walks and talks like a woman."

○ **Learn more...**

- Fruitcake is also a dessert often given as a gift during Christmas, although not many people like the taste.

Fuck
USED WITH EXTREME CAUTION

❶ **To have sex.**

EXAMPLE 1

"Did you fuck Brian last night? He told everyone at school that you two had sex!"

EXAMPLE 2

"I need to have sex! I would fuck my dog if I knew he wouldn't bite me."

❷ **A nasty person.**

EXAMPLE 1

"That fuck hit my car and drove away!"

EXAMPLE 2

"My father is a total fuck. He never lets me go out at night!"

❸ **Indicates surprise or displeasure.**

EXAMPLE 1

"Fuck! I can't see anything without my glasses!"

EXAMPLE 2

"I touched the pot and burned my hand. Fuck!"

❹ Used with "the" to intensify an emotion.

EXAMPLE 1
"Why the fuck did you do that?"

EXAMPLE 2
"You scared the fuck out of me!"

"Fuck a duck!"
USED WITH EXTREME CAUTION

Indicates frustration.

EXAMPLE 1
"Fuck a duck! I forgot my lunch!"

EXAMPLE 2
"I'm not getting the raise I wanted? Fuck a duck!"

Fuck Around
USED WITH EXTREME CAUTION

To spend time without doing much.

EXAMPLE 1
"Candace fucked around the house all weekend. She should have come to New York with us!"

EXAMPLE 2
"I didn't do anything fun last night. I just fucked around with Sasha."

Fuck Buddy
USED WITH EXTREME CAUTION

A friend that you have sex with but don't date.

EXAMPLE 1
"Monica is my fuck buddy. We only call each other when we want to have sex."

EXAMPLE 2
"I don't want a girlfriend because I don't have much money. I just want a fuck buddy."

❍ Learn more...

- You may also hear "fuck friend" or "sex friend."

DIALOGUE
"THE FUCKED UP FLOOZY"

Here is a short dialogue between two Americans.

LOEL
"After two hours at the bar last night, I was feeling no pain. I started talking to this floozy who tells me she's a fetishist and likes fisting guys while she performs fellatio."

Feeling no pain (p. 64)
Floozy (p. 68)
Fetishist (p. 65)
Fisting (p. 65)
Fellatio (p. 64)

BRENDAN
"That's screwed up!"

Screwed up (p. 172)

LOEL
"It gets worse. Her idea of foreplay is 20 minutes of flagellation."

Foreplay (p. 69)
Flagellation (p. 65)

BRENDAN
"It sounds like she's fucked in the head. What did you do?"

Fucked in the head (p. 77)

LOEL
"I can't remember. But we must have fucked around, because my ass really hurts today."

Fuck around (p. 73)
Ass (p. 4)

- On HBO's T.V. series "Sex and the City," Carrie makes the mistake of trying to date her "fuck buddy."

Fuck Like Bunnies
USED WITH EXTREME CAUTION

To have a lot of sex.

EXAMPLE 1
"My husband and I fucked like bunnies all morning. I'm going to be in pain later!"

EXAMPLE 2
"Tom and Tami just got married, so they'll probably fuck like bunnies for a few months."

o **Learn more...**

- Rabbits are well-known for having sex fast and frequently.

- You may also hear "bunnyfuck" as in "We only have five minutes. Let's bunnyfuck!"

"Fuck no!"
USED WITH EXTREME CAUTION

"Absolutely not!"

EXAMPLE 1
"Do I want to wait another hour? Fuck no!"

EXAMPLE 2
MICK: "Did you pass the test?"

THEA: "Fuck no! I definitely failed."

"Fuck off!"
USED WITH EXTREME CAUTION

Phrase indicating anger or dislike.

EXAMPLE 1
JAN: "You owe me money!"

MEL: "Fuck off! I don't owe you anything."

EXAMPLE 2
IAN: "You're wrong!"

BABS: "Fuck off! I don't care what you think."

Fuck Someone Over
USED WITH EXTREME CAUTION

To cheat or betray someone.

EXAMPLE 1
"Adam paid too much for his bike. The salesman really fucked him over."

EXAMPLE 2
"Don't fuck me over, Nathan. You owe me money, and I want it!"

o **Learn more...**

- You may also hear "fuck over someone" as in "Pam fucked over Gina when she stole Gina's boyfriend."

- You may also hear "fuck someone over royally" which means "to cheat or betray someone very badly."

Fuck Someone's Brains Out
USED WITH EXTREME CAUTION

To have a lot of sex.

EXAMPLE 1
"I fucked Rachel's brains out last night. She slept for sixteen hours afterwards!"

EXAMPLE 2
"I wish Michael would fuck my brains out. He's usually done in ten minutes, and I want more!"

"Fuck that noise!"
USED WITH EXTREME CAUTION

"Absolutely not!"

EXAMPLE 1
"The boss wants me to work this weekend? Fuck that noise!"

EXAMPLE 2
TINA: "I need to find a job."

ANTHONY: "Fuck that noise! We're going to Italy this summer!"

Fuck-up

USED WITH EXTREME CAUTION

A stupid or unpopular person; a failure.

EXAMPLE 1

"Betty is such a fuck-up! She forgot about the party last night."

EXAMPLE 2

"Harold never does anything right. He's a total fuck-up."

Fuck Up Someone

USED WITH EXTREME CAUTION

❶ To physically beat someone.

EXAMPLE 1

"I'm going to fuck up Jared if he touches my girlfriend."

EXAMPLE 2

"I shouldn't have fucked up Calvin last night. He's still in the hospital."

❷ To harm someone emotionally.

EXAMPLE 1

"I think I fucked up my dog. Every time I tell him to sit, he urinates on the floor."

EXAMPLE 2

"My dad really fucked up my sister. He called her fat all the time, and now she vomits after every meal so she won't gain weight."

AT THE MOVIES
"FULL METAL JACKET" (1987)

Full Metal Jacket, directed by Stanley Kubrick and nominated for an Academy Award, is considered one of the best war movies of all time. The first part of the movie takes place at a training camp for soldiers, and the second part follows those soldiers into the Vietnam War. These quotes were yelled by Gunnery Sergeant Hartman, the training camp's Drill Instructor, at the soldiers (called "privates").

GUNNERY SERGEANT
"I bet you're the kind of guy that would fuck a person in the ass and not even have the god damned common courtesy to give him a reach around!"

Fuck (p. 72)
Ass (p. 4)
God damn (p. 86)
Reach around (p. 160)

—

GUNNERY SERGEANT
"Bullshit! It looks to me like the best part of you ran down the crack of your mama's ass and ended up as a brown stain on the mattress."

Bullshit (p. 24)
Crack (p. 38)
Ass (p. 4)

—

GUNNERY SERGEANT
"Holy dog shit! Texas? Only steers and queers come from Texas, Private Cowboy."

Holy shit (p. 102)
Queer (p. 158)

—

GUNNERY SERGEANT
"Do you suck dicks?"

PRIVATE GOMER PYLE
"Sir, no, sir!"

GUNNERY SERGEANT
"Bullshit! I bet you could suck a golfball through a gardenhose!"

Dick (p. 46)

Bullshit (p. 24)
Suck a golfball through a garden hose (p. 190)

Fuck Up Something
USED WITH EXTREME CAUTION

❶ To ruin something.

EXAMPLE 1
"Amy fucked up her car because she never checked the oil."

EXAMPLE 2
"Vinnie fucked up his arm playing hockey yesterday."

❷ To make a mistake.

EXAMPLE 1
"I forgot to call Tracy yesterday. I really fucked up."

EXAMPLE 2
"If Abrams fucks up again, I'll fire him!"

○ Learn more...

• You may also hear "fuck something up" as in "I fucked my eyes up by reading in the dark."

Fuck With Someone
USED WITH EXTREME CAUTION

To tease or deceive someone.

EXAMPLE 1
"Did you really get a new job, or are you just fucking with me?"

EXAMPLE 2
"Don't fuck with me! I want an answer!"

Fuck With Something
USED WITH EXTREME CAUTION

To play with something, usually in order to fix it.

EXAMPLE 1
"Chrissy fucked with her stereo all day, but it still won't play."

EXAMPLE 2
"Stop fucking with my bike. You're going to break it!"

"Fuck yes!"
USED WITH EXTREME CAUTION

"Yes, absolutely!"

EXAMPLE 1
"Do I like chocolate? Fuck yes! I love it!"

EXAMPLE 2
HAL: "You want more beer?"

HELEN: "Fuck yes! I'm not drunk yet."

○ Learn more...

• You may also hear "Fuck yeah!"

"Fuck you!"
USED WITH EXTREME CAUTION

Phrase indicating anger or dislike.

EXAMPLE 1
THEA: "Come here."

GREG: "Fuck you! I'll do whatever I want!"

EXAMPLE 2
"Fuck you! This is my parking space!"

○ Learn more...

• You may also hear "fuck her," "fuck him," "fuck them," etc.

• You may also hear "fuck you and the horse you rode in on" for emphasis.

• You may also hear "F-U."

Fucked
USED WITH EXTREME CAUTION

In trouble.

EXAMPLE 1
"I'm fucked if I don't study for this test. I need a good grade!"

EXAMPLE 2
"If Jed wants to fight, I'm fucked! He's much stronger than me."

○ Learn more...

• You may also hear "F'd."

Fucked In The Ass
USED WITH EXTREME CAUTION

To be in trouble.

EXAMPLE 1
"Heather ruined her father's car. She's fucked in the ass!"

○ Learn more...

• You may also hear "fuck someone up" as in "My dad said he would fuck me up if I didn't clean my room."

EXAMPLE 2

"I spilled coffee on my computer, and now it won't start. I'm completely fucked in the ass."

○ Learn more...

- You may also hear "F'd in the A."

Fucked In The Head
USED WITH EXTREME CAUTION

Crazy or strange.

EXAMPLE 1

"Are you fucked in the head? Never play golf during a lightning storm!"

EXAMPLE 2

"Bill is fucked in the head. He only dates stupid women."

Fucked-up
USED WITH EXTREME CAUTION

Crazy or strange.

EXAMPLE 1

"That woman just had sex with a horse. This is one fucked-up movie."

EXAMPLE 2

"My fucked-up cat just bit the dog!"

Fucker
USED WITH EXTREME CAUTION

A nasty person.

EXAMPLE 1

"You fucker! You drank the last beer!"

EXAMPLE 2

"My boss just touched my breasts. What a fucker!"

Fuckface
USED WITH EXTREME CAUTION

A stupid or irritating person.

EXAMPLE 1

"Watch where you're going, fuckface! You almost hit me."

EXAMPLE 2

"That fuckface tried to rob me!"

○ Learn more...

- You may also hear "fuckhead."

Fucking
USED WITH EXTREME CAUTION

❶ Stupid, terrible, irritating, or anything bad.

EXAMPLE 1

"That fucking police officer gave me a ticket!"

EXAMPLE 2

"The fucking soda machine won't give me a fucking soda!"

❷ Used to intensify an emotion.

EXAMPLE 1

"Brad fucking ruined the plan! He can't follow orders at all."

EXAMPLE 2

"I'm not fucking helping Casey move! She never helps me with anything!"

○ Learn more...

- Americans often say "fucking" as "fuckin'" as in "You fuckin' bastard!"

"Fucking A!"
USED WITH EXTREME CAUTION

❶ "Yes, absolutely!"

EXAMPLE 1

"Do I think Kevin should be fired? Fucking A! He never does any work!"

EXAMPLE 2

ROY: "Did you like the movie?"

CARLA: "Fucking A! It was great!"

❷ Indicates surprise or frustration.

EXAMPLE 1

"Fucking A! Someone stole my bicycle."

EXAMPLE 2

"Fucking A! I finally sold my first book!"

Fucknut
USED WITH EXTREME CAUTION

A stupid or irritating person.

EXAMPLE 1

"Gerald is a fucknut. He asks me stupid questions all day."

EXAMPLE 2

"Hey, fucknut! Get over here and help me move this furniture."

o **Learn more...**

- You may also hear "F-nut" as in "You F-nut! Stop urinating on my carpet!"

Fuckstick
USED WITH EXTREME CAUTION

A stupid or irritating person.

EXAMPLE 1
"Hey, fuckstick! Get away from my girlfriend!"

EXAMPLE 2
"Priscilla laughed when I hurt myself. What a fuckstick!"

o **Learn more...**

- You may also hear "fuckwad."

Fudgepacker
USED WITH EXTREME CAUTION

A homosexual man.

EXAMPLE 1
"That fudgepacker can really ice skate! He won the gold medal in the Olympics."

EXAMPLE 2
"The guy who cuts my hair is a fudgepacker. He always talks about his boyfriends."

o **Learn more...**

- You may also hear "packing fudge" as in "I think that guy is packing fudge. He looks gay to me."

- "Fudgepacking" refers to the act of anal sex.

Fugly
USED WITH FRIENDS

Very ugly.

EXAMPLE 1
"That's a fugly shirt you're wearing! You should return it and get your money back."

EXAMPLE 2
"I've never seen a man as fugly as that guy."

o **Learn more...**

- This is a shortened version of "fucking ugly."

Full Of Piss And Vinegar
USED WITH FRIENDS

To be energetic and ready to fight.

EXAMPLE 1
"That old man yells at everyone. He's full of piss and vinegar."

EXAMPLE 2
"Grandma is full of piss and vinegar. Don't start a fight with her today!"

o **Learn more...**

- This is an old expression still used today, often as a joke.

Full Of Shit
USED WITH FRIENDS

Full of nonsense or lies.

EXAMPLE 1
"Gwen is full of shit. She makes promises, but she never keeps them."

EXAMPLE 2
"This report is full of shit. All of the facts are wrong!"

o **Learn more...**

- You may also hear the more polite expressions "full of it," "full of baloney," or "full of crap."

Fur Pie
USED WITH EXTREME CAUTION

Vagina.

EXAMPLE 1
"I licked Molly's fur pie until she had three orgasms."

EXAMPLE 2
"I asked Kim to shave her fur pie and she did it for my birthday last week."

Furburger
USED WITH EXTREME CAUTION

Vagina.

EXAMPLE 1
"I really want a furburger. Do you know any women who'd be willing to date me?"

EXAMPLE 2
"Brendan calls my vagina a furburger. He's so rude! I need a new boyfriend."

G IS FOR GIGOLO

G Spot
USED WITH FRIENDS

A very sensitive spot inside the woman's vagina that can bring a woman to orgasm.

EXAMPLE 1

"I've only been with one man who could find my G-spot, so I married him!"

EXAMPLE 2

"I found Marina's G-spot during sex, and she had the most incredible orgasm."

○ **Learn more...**

- The "Grafenberg spot," or "G spot," was named for the scientist who first said it existed.

- Many people, including many scientists, do not believe the "G spot" exists.

G-string
USED WITH ANYONE

A small piece of underwear worn over the genitals, usually with a thin piece of fabric that fits between the butt cheeks.

EXAMPLE 1

"Alice said she wanted some sexy underwear, so I bought her a G-string."

EXAMPLE 2

"I think women look sexy in G-strings."

Gang Bang
USED WITH EXTREME CAUTION

Group sex where one person has sex with a lot of other people.

EXAMPLE 1
"My last girlfriend wanted to be the main person in a gang bang. She really likes attention."

EXAMPLE 2
"I don't understand why any woman would like gang bangs. Who would want more than one man at the same time?"

o **Learn more...**

- If the main person is unwilling, it's called "gang rape."

Gay
USED WITH ANYONE

Homosexual.

EXAMPLE 1
"My boss is gay. He and his boyfriend are very happy together."

EXAMPLE 2
"I think I'm gay. I want to kiss my best friend Gail."

o **Learn more...**

- In old movies and T.V. shows, you'll often hear "gay" used to mean "happy." If you use it to mean "happy" these days, people will laugh.

- "Gay" is used more often than "homosexual" and is not considered offensive.

Gay Bashing
USED WITH ANYONE

Violent or verbal attacks against homosexuals.

EXAMPLE 1
"The police arrested the stupid guys who were gay bashing last night."

EXAMPLE 2
"Nick was a victim of gay bashing. He survived, but he had to kill one of his attackers."

Gay For Pay
USED WITH ANYONE

A heterosexual man who performs homosexual acts for money.

EXAMPLE 1
"That guy is gay for pay. He's got a wife, but he makes extra money performing oral sex on men."

EXAMPLE 2
"Lee's always sitting at the bar in the restaurant. He must be gay for pay and looking for customers."

Gaydar
USED WITH ANYONE

The ability to determine if someone is homosexual just by looking.

EXAMPLE 1
"My gaydar tells me that Tom Cruise is actually a homosexual."

EXAMPLE 2
"My gaydar must be broken. I don't know if Franklin is gay or not."

o **Learn more...**

- "Gaydar" is a combination of the words "gay" and "radar."

Geek
USED WITH ANYONE

A smart but strange person.

EXAMPLE 1
"Rob is a geek! He watches *Star Trek* three times a day!"

EXAMPLE 2

FRANK: "I need help with math."

PAM: "Ask Beth. She's a geek."

o **Learn more...**

- A "geek" is usually good in science, math, computers, or other technical areas.

Geez
USED WITH ANYONE

Indicates surprise or frustration.

EXAMPLE 1

"Geez! There are 200 people at this party!"

EXAMPLE 2

"Geez! The bus is always late!"

o **Learn more...**

- This is a non-religious way to say "Jesus!" (see "Jesus Christ," p. 109).

- "Gee whiz," "Gee whillikers," and "Geez Louise" are also used, but usually by older people.

Gerbiling
USED WITH FRIENDS

The insertion of a gerbil or other animal into the anus for sexual pleasure.

EXAMPLE 1

"I think Terry bought the gerbil for gerbiling, and not as a pet. He hates animals."

EXAMPLE 2

"I didn't want to tell the doctor that I had been gerbiling, but I needed to explain how the gerbil got into my butt."

o **Learn more...**

- "Gerbiling" is more of a legend than a common practice.

Get A Little Action
USED WITH FRIENDS

To have sexual contact with someone.

EXAMPLE 1

"Larry's wearing his best suit because he is hoping to get a little action tonight."

EXAMPLE 2

"I like to wash the sheets on my bed if I think I might get a little action that night."

o **Learn more...**

- You may also hear "get some action" as in "I went to the bar to get some action, but didn't meet anyone."

Get A Piece Of Ass
USED WITH EXTREME CAUTION

To have sexual contact or sex.

EXAMPLE 1

"Look at that beautiful woman! I would love to get a piece of that ass."

IN OTHER WORDS...
"GAY MEN"

Homosexual men are politely called "gays." Most other words are considered offensive.

USED WITH ANYONE

Gay (p. 80)

USED WITH FRIENDS

Canned fruit (p. 29)

Friend of Dorothy (p. 71)

Fruit (p. 72)

Fruitcake (p. 72)

Mary (p. 124)

Nellie (p. 133)

USED WITH EXTREME CAUTION

Butt pirate (p. 27)

Faggot (p. 62)

Fairy (p. 62)

Flamer (p. 66)

Fudgepacker (p. 78)

Homo (p. 102)

Limp-wrist (p. 118)

Manhole inspector (p. 124)

Pillow-biter (p. 145)

Queen (p. 157)

Queer (p. 158)

Rump Ranger (p. 164)

Screaming Fairy (p. 168)

Sissy (p. 178)

EXAMPLE 2

"I'm going out tonight and I'm not coming home until I get a piece of ass."

Get Into Someone's Pants
USED WITH FRIENDS

To have sexual contact with someone.

EXAMPLE 1

"I've been trying to get into Mrs. Bush's pants for two years."

EXAMPLE 2

"I don't let a guy get into my pants until I'm sure he has an expensive car."

❶ Learn more...

- You may also hear "get into someone's underwear" or "get into someone's panties."

Get It On
USED WITH FRIENDS

To have sexual contact or sex.

EXAMPLE 1

"I would pay $100 to get it on with her for ten minutes."

EXAMPLE 2

"I think Jay wants to get it on. He just took off his pants."

Get It Up
USED WITH FRIENDS

To achieve an erect penis.

EXAMPLE 1

"Keith is taking special medicine to help him get it up. He can't get an erection without his pills."

EXAMPLE 2

"I'm 74 years old and I have no problem getting it up."

Get Laid
USED WITH FRIENDS

To have sex.

EXAMPLE 1

"If I could get laid by a different, beautiful woman every day for the rest of my life, I would be the luckiest man on Earth."

EXAMPLE 2

"I'm sleepy today because I got laid last night."

Get Off
USED WITH EXTREME CAUTION

To orgasm.

EXAMPLE 1

"I can't get off unless the woman I'm having sex with calls me Mr. President. Is that strange?"

EXAMPLE 2

"I need a man with a big penis to get me off! Or a big vibrator!"

Get One's Ass in Gear
USED WITH FRIENDS

❶ To hurry.

EXAMPLE 1

"You need to get your ass in gear if you want to get to the movie before it starts!"

EXAMPLE 2

"The game is about to start, so get your ass in gear. I don't want to be late!"

❷ To start working harder.

EXAMPLE 1

"If Alyssa wants to leave work early today, she needs to get her ass in gear!"

EXAMPLE 2

"Kale failed history because he never got his ass in gear."

Get One's Rocks Off
USED WITH EXTREME CAUTION

To orgasm.

EXAMPLE 1

"If my girlfriend doesn't get my rocks off soon, I will find someone who can."

EXAMPLE 2

LINDA: "Will you spank my butt while you have sex with me?"

JAKE: "Whatever gets your rocks off. Let's try it."

Get One's Shit Together
USED WITH FRIENDS

To become organized or focused.

EXAMPLE 1

"If Garret doesn't get his shit together, he won't get the project done by Monday."

EXAMPLE 2

"I have to get my shit together or the coach will not let me play on the team."

Get Some
USED WITH FRIENDS

To have sexual contact or sex.

EXAMPLE 1

"Johnny said he got some last night. That's why he's still sleeping today."

EXAMPLE 2

"If I knew where to get some, I would be there getting some."

Get Some Ass
USED WITH EXTREME CAUTION

To have sex.

EXAMPLE 1

"I need to get some ass before I forget how to have sex."

EXAMPLE 2

KIP: "Where is Lou?"

JIM: "He's out getting some ass. He'll be back tonight."

Get The Lead Out Of One's Ass
USED WITH FRIENDS

"Hurry!"

EXAMPLE 1

"Donald, we have to leave. Get the lead out of your ass!"

EXAMPLE 2

"Get the lead out of your ass or we'll miss the first part of the movie."

○ Learn more...

• You may also hear the more polite expression "Get the lead out" as in "We're late for work. Get the lead out!"

• Lead is a very heavy metal.

DIALOGUE
"GET YOUR GAYDAR FIXED!"

Here is a short dialogue between two Americans.

ANTHONY
"Hey, is that guy gay? My gaydar isn't working on him."

PHILLIP
"He's as queer as a three-dollar bill. And he looks like a good lay, too."

ANTHONY
"I don't give a shit about sex. I'm just looking for someone to go down on me. I've been so tense lately. But I'm not greedy—I'll give head in return."

PHILLIP
"Then get your ass in gear and go ask him for a date!"

Gay (p. 80)
Gaydar (p. 80)

Queer as a three-dollar bill (p. 158)
Good lay (p. 87)

Give a shit (p. 84)
Go down on someone (p. 85)
Give head (p. 84)

Get one's ass in gear (p. 82)

Gigolo
USED WITH ANYONE

A male prostitute.

EXAMPLE 1

"Margaret hired a gigolo when her husband was in New York last week!"

EXAMPLE 2

"I became a gigolo to earn extra money for college, and I really enjoyed all the sex!"

o **Learn more...**

- There is a 1999 movie called *Deuce Bigalow: Male Gigolo,* starring comedian Rob Schneider, about a man who charges women money for sex.

Give A Shit
USED WITH FRIENDS

To care.

EXAMPLE 1

"You don't give a shit about this project, or you would work harder."

EXAMPLE 2

"Yes, I do give a shit about you. I love you!"

Give Head
USED WITH EXTREME CAUTION

To perform oral sex.

EXAMPLE 1

"Rob's mother gives the best head. I wonder if Rob knows?"

EXAMPLE 2

"Give me head or I won't clean the apartment!"

"Give me some sugar."
USED WITH ANYONE

"Kiss me."

EXAMPLE 1

"I love you. Give me some sugar!"

EXAMPLE 2

"Give me some sugar, Jill. I want you!"

o **Learn more...**

- The character Ash (played by Bruce Campbell) in the 1993 movie *Army Of Darkness* is famous for saying, "Give me some sugar, baby!" when he wants a kiss.

- You may see this written as "Gimme some sugar," which is closer to how the phrase is pronounced.

Give Someone Shit
USED WITH FRIENDS

To argue with someone.

EXAMPLE 1

"Jamie is so annoying! He's always giving me shit."

EXAMPLE 2

"I don't want to give you shit, but why did you have sex with Bill last night?"

Give Someone The Eye
USED WITH ANYONE

To flirt with someone.

EXAMPLE 1

"That beautiful guy over there has been giving you the eye since he sat down."

EXAMPLE 2

"I tried giving her the eye from across the room, but she wasn't interested."

o **Learn more...**

- You may also hear "make eyes at someone" as in "That man by the bar is making eyes at me. I'm going to go talk to him!"

Glory Hole
USED WITH FRIENDS

A small hole in the wall between two toilets in a men's bathroom through which people can have oral sex.

EXAMPLE 1

"Whenever I want oral sex, I just find a glory hole and someone makes me ejaculate."

EXAMPLE 2

"That gay bar has three glory holes in the bathroom."

Go
USED WITH ANYONE

To urinate or defecate.

EXAMPLE 1

"Mommy, I have to go. I have to go now!"

EXAMPLE 2

"Dan, please stop the car when you see an exit. I have to go."

Go All The Way
USED WITH ANYONE

To have sex.

EXAMPLE 1

"Dixie and I are going to go all the way tonight."

EXAMPLE 2

"Ron wants to go all the way, but I'm not ready yet."

Go Bananas
USED WITH ANYONE

❶ **To become excited or crazy.**

EXAMPLE 1

"Be careful when you give sugar to children. It makes them go bananas."

EXAMPLE 2

"If Sue wins the contest, she'll go bananas!"

❷ **To become angry.**

EXAMPLE 1

"My father will go bananas when he sees that I broke his favorite coffee mug."

EXAMPLE 2

"I'll go bananas if the restaurant is closed. I'm so hungry!"

Go Check The Plumbing
USED WITH ANYONE

To urinate or defecate.

EXAMPLE 1

"Please excuse me while I go check the plumbing."

EXAMPLE 2

"Terry went to check the plumbing. He should be back in a minute."

Go Down On Someone
USED WITH EXTREME CAUTION

To perform oral sex.

EXAMPLE 1

"After two years of dating, I finally went down on my boyfriend for the first time. I hated it."

EXAMPLE 2

"I can make any woman have an orgasm when I go down on her."

❍ **Learn more...**

- You may also hear "go down" or "go downtown."

- In 1995, Alanis Morisette released her *Jagged Little Pill* CD with the song "You Oughta Know" containing the words "Would she go down on you in a theater?"

Go Down The Dirt Road
USED WITH EXTREME CAUTION

To have anal sex.

EXAMPLE 1

"Derrick wants to go down the dirt road again, but my butt still hurts from the last time."

EXAMPLE 2

"Henry's anus is too small to go down the dirt road. He starts screaming in pain immediately."

Go On And On
USED WITH ANYONE

To talk too much.

EXAMPLE 1
"I love my cat! I can go on and on about her."

EXAMPLE 2
"I was so bored last night! Ernie went on and on about his new car."

"Go to hell!"
USED WITH FRIENDS

Indicates anger or dislike.

EXAMPLE 1
WILL: "You look terrible today."

MINDY: "Go to hell!"

EXAMPLE 2
"If you're having sex with my sister, you can go to hell!"

○ **Learn more...**

• Although "Hell" is part of the Judeo-Christian religion, today people of all religions use it.

Go Wee
USED WITH ANYONE

To urinate.

EXAMPLE 1
"Mom said I can go wee by myself now."

EXAMPLE 2
"Sometimes I go wee in my bed when I am sleeping."

○ **Learn more...**

• Children use this phrase more often than adults.

"God!"
USED WITH FRIENDS

Indicates frustration or surprise.

EXAMPLE 1
"God! Why did I eat all the cake? I feel sick."

EXAMPLE 2
"Why can't they find the person who killed my father? God! I'm so angry!"

God Damn
USED WITH FRIENDS

❶ **Indicates frustration.**

EXAMPLE 1
"God damn! I think I just broke my finger."

EXAMPLE 2
"I failed another test yesterday. God damn!"

❷ **Stupid, terrible, irritating, or anything bad.**

EXAMPLE 1
"Those God damn politicians are always lying to us!"

EXAMPLE 2
"Where's the money for the God damn rent? Did you spend it?"

○ **Learn more...**

• You may also hear "God damned" used the same way as definition 2.

• You may also hear "God dammit!" which is a combination of the words "God, damn it."

Golden Shower
USED WITH FRIENDS

The act of urinating on another person for sexual pleasure.

EXAMPLE 1
"I love getting a golden shower from my boyfriend. It makes me very excited."

EXAMPLE 2
"Missy really likes golden showers, but I don't think I can urinate on her. I'd be too nervous!"

Gonads
USED WITH FRIENDS

Testicles.

EXAMPLE 1
"When Fran kicked me in the gonads, I knew I didn't want to marry her anymore."

EXAMPLE 2
"My gonads are so big that I have to buy special underwear."

○ **Learn more...**

• You may also hear "nads."

Gonorrhea

USED WITH ANYONE

A sexually transmitted disease.

EXAMPLE 1

"The doctor just told me that I have gonorrhea. I never thought it would happen to me."

EXAMPLE 2

"Gonorrhea is really painful, but they have good medicine to cure it now."

"Good grief!"

USED WITH ANYONE

Indicates surprise.

EXAMPLE 1

"Good grief! You're sick again?"

EXAMPLE 2

"Good grief! The dog ruined the carpet!"

○ **Learn more...**

- This is a non-religious way to say "Good God!"

- Another less popular version of this phrase is "Good gravy!"

- Charlie Brown, one of the "Peanuts" characters created by Charles Schultz, always says "Good grief!" when something goes wrong.

Good Lay

USED WITH FRIENDS

❶ **A fun session of sex.**

EXAMPLE 1

"She won't feel so angry after a good lay from her boyfriend."

EXAMPLE 2

"I really need a good lay to forget about my ex-girlfriend."

❷ **A person who is good at sex.**

EXAMPLE 1

"Cheryl is a good lay. I had sex with her yesterday, and I can't stop thinking about it!"

EXAMPLE 2

"I heard Tom was a good lay, but I think he's terrible at sex!"

DIALOGUE
"DON'T BARF IN THE CAR"

Here is a short dialogue between two Americans.

ALICE
"I had a shitty day at work. I need to get hammered."

Shitty (p. 177)
Hammered (p. 90)

VINCE
"I'll drive, but you have to promise not to yak in my car."

Yak (p. 218)

ALICE
"I've been blitzed a million times and I've never barfed."

Blitzed (p. 18)
Barf (p. 11)

VINCE
"Ok, but if you do, your ass is grass."

Someone's ass is grass
(p. 184)

Goof Ball
USED WITH ANYONE

A silly person.

EXAMPLE 1

"Thea loves to sing and dance while she's naked. What a goof ball!"

EXAMPLE 2

JOHN: "I wish I could fly!"

ARIEL: "You goof ball! You're afraid of heights!"

Goon
USED WITH ANYONE

❶ A stupid person.

EXAMPLE 1

"Sometimes Andy sleeps during class. What a goon!"

EXAMPLE 2

"Louis lifted a huge rock and hurt his back. What a goon!

❷ A person hired for his or her strength, usually in order to threaten someone else.

EXAMPLE 1

"I owe Mike money, so he sent his goons to get it!"

EXAMPLE 2

"Greg's goons broke my leg because I insulted him."

o Learn more...

• Men are called "goons" more often than women.

Goose
USED WITH ANYONE

To touch someone's butt.

EXAMPLE 1

"There's a man goosing the women on the train each morning. I'm going to tell the police!"

EXAMPLE 2

"The suit salesman goosed me while he was measuring me!"

Grease the Bayonet
USED WITH FRIENDS

To masturbate.

EXAMPLE 1

"Maybe I'm masturbating too much. Yesterday I greased the bayonet 16 times."

EXAMPLE 2

"Is it strange if I think about kittens while I'm greasing the bayonet?"

Grind
USED WITH FRIENDS

To have sex.

EXAMPLE 1

"Want to go back to my place to grind?"

EXAMPLE 2

"My penis hurts from grinding all night long with those three girls."

Gross
USED WITH ANYONE

❶ Ugly.

EXAMPLE 1

"He's gross! I would never kiss him."

EXAMPLE 2

"Mom, everyone at school thinks I'm gross. I will never find a date."

❷ Disgusting.

EXAMPLE 1

"Look at the trash floating in the ocean. That's gross."

EXAMPLE 2

"I think I ate a spider by accident. How gross!"

Group Grope
USED WITH FRIENDS

A group of people touching one person's genitals.

EXAMPLE 1

"Everyone got so drunk that the party turned into a group grope with me at the center."

EXAMPLE 2

"I hope Mary is coming to the party tonight. I have a group grope waiting for her."

o **Learn more...**

- Some people mean "group sex" when they use this phrase.

Grow Some Sack
USED WITH FRIENDS

To stop being a coward.

EXAMPLE 1

"Laura always yells at Ralph. He needs to grow some sack and yell back at her!"

EXAMPLE 2

"I used to hit Wally a lot, but he grew some sack. Now I'm afraid to fight with him."

o **Learn more...**

- "Sack" is another way to say "testicles."

- You may also hear "get some sack."

Guns
USED WITH FRIENDS

Breasts.

EXAMPLE 1

"That woman has some nice guns. I'd love to hold them in my hands."

EXAMPLE 2

"I think that girl's guns are pointing at me."

o **Learn more...**

- A man's "guns" are his "biceps" (upper-arm muscles).

Guppie
USED WITH FRIENDS

A "Gay Urban Professional."

EXAMPLE 1

"Stephen got a new job as a lawyer. He and his boyfriend are real guppies now!"

EXAMPLE 2

"This party is full of guppies! Let's go somewhere else."

o **Learn more...**

- A "yuppie" is a "Young Urban Professional," a person who has a good job and is on the path to success. A lot of people don't like yuppies.

Gutless
USED WITH ANYONE

A coward.

EXAMPLE 1

"Will you race me, or are you gutless?"

EXAMPLE 2

"Henry is gutless! He won't eat raw fish because he's afraid."

o **Learn more...**

- We say that a brave person has "guts," so a "gutless" person is a coward.

- You may also hear "gutless wonder" (a person who is such a coward that it's amazing).

Gym Queen
USED WITH EXTREME CAUTION

A muscular homosexual man who is usually at the gym.

EXAMPLE 1

"Joel is a gym queen. He'll only date muscular men from his gym."

EXAMPLE 2

"I go to the gay gym across the street three times a day. I guess you can say I'm a gym queen."

o **Learn more...**

- This phrase is used by homosexuals more often than heterosexuals.

H IS FOR HOOTERS

Half-assed
USED WITH FRIENDS

Bad; inadequate.

EXAMPLE 1
"The painter did a half-assed job. He forgot to paint the kitchen!"

EXAMPLE 2
"I wrote the report half-assed. I just don't care what the boss thinks!"

Hammered
USED WITH ANYONE

Drunk.

EXAMPLE 1
"Larry got hammered and vomited on my sofa!"

EXAMPLE 2
"I can't walk when I get hammered. The room spins!"

Hand Job
USED WITH FRIENDS

Masturbation of a man using the hands for stimulation.

EXAMPLE 1
"Stacy has very strong hands, so she gives great hand jobs."

EXAMPLE 2

"I got a hand job from my babysitter when I was 13 years old. I'll never forget her!"

Handballing
USED WITH FRIENDS

Using the hand or fist as a penis in one's anus or vagina.

EXAMPLE 1

"Phil was handballing me for 30 minutes this morning, and now my vagina hurts."

EXAMPLE 2

"Both guys were handballing me at the same time. It hurt a little, but felt great!"

Hanky-panky
USED WITH ANYONE

Sexual contact or play.

EXAMPLE 1

"Don't try any of your hanky-panky with me!"

EXAMPLE 2

"I'm not interested in hanky-panky. Let's just talk."

○ **Learn more...**

- This is usually said as a joke.

Happy As A Pig In Shit
USED WITH FRIENDS

To be very happy.

EXAMPLE 1

"Lennie has been as happy as a pig in shit since he got his new job."

EXAMPLE 2

"If you bring me ice cream, I'll be as happy as a pig in shit!"

Hard-ass
USED WITH FRIENDS

A tough or strict person.

EXAMPLE 1

"If you're late for work, you'll get fired. Our boss is a hard-ass!"

EXAMPLE 2

"Don't be such a hard-ass, Lilly. Let your daughter go to the party!"

Had Hard Miles
USED WITH FRIENDS

To look tired and worn, like a person who has had a difficult life.

EXAMPLE 1

"Those guys look like they've had some hard miles. I hope I never look like that."

EXAMPLE 2

"My father was handsome when he was young. He has had many hard miles since then."

○ **Learn more...**

- This is usually said about older people.

Hard On The Eyes
USED WITH FRIENDS

Ugly.

EXAMPLE 1

"If Frank wasn't so hard on the eyes, I would marry him. He's really funny and nice."

EXAMPLE 2

KENT: "What do you think of Beth?"

JAMES: "She's pretty hard on the eyes. I don't like her face."

○ **Learn more...**

- Someone is attractive if he or she is "easy on the eyes."

Hard-on
USED WITH FRIENDS

An erect penis.

EXAMPLE 1

"Whenever I see a picture of Brad Pitt, I get a hard-on."

EXAMPLE 2

"When I hugged my English teacher, I could feel his hard-on."

Hardbody
USED WITH ANYONE

A person who is in perfect physical shape.

EXAMPLE 1

"I love watching the hardbodies at the beach on Saturday mornings."

EXAMPLE 2

"There is a beautiful hardbody that works at the coffee shop near my apartment."

Hardcore
USED WITH FRIENDS

❶ **Sexual material that shows every detail.**

EXAMPLE 1

"This movie is hardcore! I can see everything!"

EXAMPLE 2

"Hardcore pornography is boring. I like to use my imagination!"

❷ **Extreme.**

EXAMPLE 1

"Jerry is hardcore about swimming. He goes to the pool three times a day."

EXAMPLE 2

"I'm studying hardcore for this test. I have to get a good grade!"

Haul Ass
USED WITH FRIENDS

Hurry.

EXAMPLE 1

"We need to haul ass, so we're not late to work!"

EXAMPLE 2

"If you don't haul ass, you're going to miss the movie!"

o Learn more...

- You may also hear "move ass."

Have a Bug Up One's Ass
USED WITH FRIENDS

To be in a bad mood.

EXAMPLE 1

"Kev's been rude all morning. Why does he have a bug up his ass?"

EXAMPLE 2

"Samantha has a bug up her ass because I borrowed her favorite T-shirt and spilled coffee on it."

o Learn more...

- You may also hear "have a stick up one's ass" as in "Monica must have a stick up her ass today. She keeps yelling at me for no reason!"

- You may also hear "What flew up someone's ass?" as in "Fran is yelling at everyone today. What flew up her ass?"

Have A Bun In The Oven
USED WITH ANYONE

To be pregnant.

EXAMPLE 1

"Danielle can't go on the rollercoaster because she has a bun in the oven."

EXAMPLE 2

"Franco is marrying Alice because she has a bun in the oven."

Have A Dirty Mind
USED WITH ANYONE

To think or say sexual things a lot.

EXAMPLE 1

"Rick has a dirty mind. He's always talking about sex."

EXAMPLE 2

"Carl put all my dolls in sexual positions. He has such a dirty mind!"

Have A Headache

USED WITH ANYONE

To be uninterested or unwilling to have sex.

EXAMPLE 1

"Every night I tell my husband I have a headache, so I don't have to have sex with him."

EXAMPLE 2

"My wife always says she has a headache when I want to have sex."

o Learn more...

- Women use the excuse "I have a headache" more often than men.

Have A Nooner

USED WITH FRIENDS

To have sex during the time one would normally be eating lunch at work.

EXAMPLE 1

"I must hurry because I'm meeting Sharon for a nooner during my lunch break."

EXAMPLE 2

"Every Tuesday and Friday, I take an extra ten minutes for lunch so I can have a nooner with my girlfriend at her apartment."

Have A One-Night Stand

USED WITH ANYONE

To have a single sexual encounter with someone (usually a stranger).

EXAMPLE 1

"I've never had a one-night stand, but I really want to!"

EXAMPLE 2

"Janis seems to have one-night stands a few times each week. She can't even remember their names."

Have A Screw Loose

USED WITH ANYONE

To be crazy or strange.

EXAMPLE 1

"People who drive drunk have a screw loose!"

EXAMPLE 2

"You must have a screw loose if you think eating ice cream with a knife is a good idea."

o Learn more...

- You may also hear "have a few screws loose" as in "You must have a few screws loose if you think Brad Pitt is ugly."

IN OTHER WORDS... "SURPRISE"

Here are some of the most popular ways to express surprise or frustration at a situation.

USED WITH ANYONE

"D'oh!" (p. 43)

"Darn!" (p. 44)

"Geez!" (p. 81)

"Good grief!" (p. 87)

"Heck!" (p. 97)

"Holy cow!" (p. 101)

"Shoot!" (p. 177)

USED WITH FRIENDS

"Crap!" (p. 38)

"Damn!" (p. 44)

"God!" (p. 86)

"God damn!" (p. 86)

"Hell!" (p. 97)

"Hell's bells!" (p. 98)

"Holy shit!" (p. 102)

"Jesus Christ!" (p. 109)

"No shit!" (p. 134)

"What the hell!" (p. 213)

USED WITH EXTREME CAUTION

"Fuck!" (p. 72)

"Fucking A!" (p. 77)

"What the fuck!" (p. 213)

Have A Shit Fit
USED WITH FRIENDS

To display extreme anger or frustration.

EXAMPLE 1
"Don't have a shit fit! I'll pay you for the damage I caused."

EXAMPLE 2
"Jeremy had a shit fit when he saw his wife kissing another man."

Have Bats In The Belfry
USED WITH ANYONE

To be crazy or strange.

EXAMPLE 1
"That woman is always talking to her feet. She must have bats in the belfry."

EXAMPLE 2
"Kevin has bats in the belfry. He wants me to pay for his new car!"

Have Carnal Knowledge Of Someone
USED WITH ANYONE

To have had sex with someone.

EXAMPLE 1
"I have carnal knowledge of Juliette ever since we dated last summer."

EXAMPLE 2
"Yes, I know Linus. I even have carnal knowledge of him!"

○ **Learn more...**

- This is an old phrase still used as a joke or by very educated people.

Have Diarrhea Of The Mouth
USED WITH FRIENDS

To talk too much.

EXAMPLE 1
"Billy asked me about my job, and I had diarrhea of the mouth. I talked for almost an hour!"

EXAMPLE 2
"Ron had diarrhea of the mouth last night. He talked about his last wife the whole time!"

Have No Lead In One's Pencil
USED WITH FRIENDS

To be impotent or sterile.

EXAMPLE 1
"Reggie doesn't have any children because he has no lead in his pencil."

EXAMPLE 2
"Katie can't get pregnant because I don't have any lead in my pencil."

Have Nothing Upstairs
USED WITH ANYONE

To be stupid or strange.

EXAMPLE 1
"Many people think fashion models have nothing upstairs, but many of them are very smart."

EXAMPLE 2
"Martin has nothing upstairs. I know him from school, and he isn't smart."

○ **Learn more...**

- "Upstairs" refers to a person's head.

- You may also hear "don't have much upstairs" as in "That guy doesn't have much upstairs if he thinks he can run faster than a car."

Have One's Back Teeth Floating

USED WITH FRIENDS

To need to urinate.

EXAMPLE 1

"I drank so much water watching the movie that my back teeth are floating."

EXAMPLE 2

"It's been ten hours since I urinated. My back teeth are floating!"

○ **Learn more...**

- The (disgusting) idea behind this phrase is that your body is so full of urine that your teeth are floating in it.

Have One's Head Up One's Ass

USED WITH FRIENDS

To be very stupid.

EXAMPLE 1

"Jonah has his head up his ass if he thinks we can finish this project today."

EXAMPLE 2

"I had my head up my ass all morning. I just couldn't think!"

Have One's Mind In The Gutter

USED WITH ANYONE

To be thinking about sexual or offensive things.

EXAMPLE 1

"I'm not talking about sex! Your mind is always in the gutter!"

EXAMPLE 2

"Get your mind out of the gutter and think about work!"

○ **Learn more...**

- A person's mind can be "in" or "out" of "the gutter."

DIALOGUE
"HOOKING UP WITH A HOT CHICK"

Here is a short dialogue between two Americans.

MORGAN
"Geez, you look fucking horrible!"

Geez (p. 81)
Fucking (p. 77)

JAMES
"I got hammered at the party last night and I've been yorking all morning. "

Hammered (p. 90)
York (p. 219)

MORGAN
"I heard there were a lot of pretty women at the party. Did you hook up with anyone?"

Hook up (p. 102)

JAMES
"I fooled around with a really hot chick, but I was too blitzed to actually have sex."

Fool around (p. 69)
Hot (p. 104)
Chick (p. 31)
Blitzed (p. 18)

MORGAN
"Tough shit. I couldn't even go to the party."

Tough shit (p. 202)

Have One's Thumb Up One's Ass
USED WITH FRIENDS

To act slowly or not at all.

EXAMPLE 1
"Jamie did nothing to stop Charles. She just sat there with her thumb up her ass."

EXAMPLE 2
"I need to find a job, but I just sit on the couch with my thumb up my ass all day."

Have Relations
USED WITH ANYONE

To have a sexual relationship.

EXAMPLE 1
"Mr. Cox and Ms. Littles have been having relations for more than a year."

EXAMPLE 2
"Martin was married, but he was having relations with three other women at the same time."

o **Learn more...**

- This is often said in courts of law to mean "have sex or oral sex with."

Have Shit For Brains
USED WITH FRIENDS

To be very stupid.

EXAMPLE 1
"Mandy gave dog food to the cats! She must have shit for brains."

EXAMPLE 2
"I gave Clem money and he lost it. He has shit for brains!"

Have Someone By The Balls
USED WITH FRIENDS

To have power over someone.

EXAMPLE 1
"I have Nate by the balls because I know he's been having sex with the boss' wife."

EXAMPLE 2
"The manager has me by the balls because I signed that contract."

Have Someone By The Short Hairs
USED WITH FRIENDS

To have power over someone.

EXAMPLE 1
"The company won't give us any more money, and we need our jobs. They really have us by the short hairs."

EXAMPLE 2
"I have him by the short hairs. He'll be calling soon to negotiate again."

o **Learn more...**

- "Short hairs" are pubic hairs — very painful if pulled!

Have Someone's Ass
USED WITH FRIENDS

To intend to punish someone.

EXAMPLE 1
"I'll have your ass if you ever lie to me again!"

EXAMPLE 2
"The professor will have Brian's ass! He cheated on the test, and she knows it!"

Have The Hots For Someone
USED WITH ANYONE

To be attracted to someone.

EXAMPLE 1
"I have the hots for any guy wearing a uniform. I think police officers are so cute!"

EXAMPLE 2
"Several of my students have the hots for me, but I'm only dating three of them."

Head
USED WITH ANYONE

Toilet or bathroom.

EXAMPLE 1
"We just got on the boat, and already you have to visit the head?"

EXAMPLE 2
"The captain is in the head. He should be out soon."

o **Learn more...**

- This is the term used for the toilet on a boat or ship.

Headcase
USED WITH ANYONE

A crazy or strange person.

EXAMPLE 1

"Fred is a headcase. I don't trust him to drive my car."

EXAMPLE 2

"I think anyone who only eats mushrooms is a headcase. Mushrooms are disgusting!"

○ **Learn more...**

- This is a rude way to say "crazy."

Headlights
USED WITH FRIENDS

Breasts.

EXAMPLE 1

"I've never seen headlights that big on such a short woman."

EXAMPLE 2

"Garret wants to see my headlights, but I don't want to show him."

Hang A Heat Stick
USED WITH FRIENDS

To defecate.

EXAMPLE 1

"Let's go, Joe! How long does it take you to hang a heat stick?"

EXAMPLE 2

"How can I hang a heat stick when I can't lock the door to the bathroom?"

Heave
USED WITH FRIENDS

To vomit.

EXAMPLE 1

"My stomach hurts from heaving all night."

EXAMPLE 2

"Never eat the shrimp at a casino or you'll heave later."

Heck
USED WITH ANYONE

❶ **Indicates surprise or frustration.**

EXAMPLE 1

"Heck! I forgot my doctor's appointment!"

EXAMPLE 2

"Heck! When did you arrive in town?"

❷ **Used with "the" to intensify an emotion.**

EXAMPLE 1

"You're early. When the heck did your flight arrive?"

EXAMPLE 2

"Why the heck does Kyle keep watching us?"

○ **Learn more...**

- This is a nicer way to say "hell" (p. 97).

Heinie
USED WITH ANYONE

Butt.

EXAMPLE 1

"Daddy's heinie is much bigger than Mommy's heinie."

EXAMPLE 2

"Karen's heinie was all I could see from my seat under the stairs."

○ **Learn more...**

- Some people call a Heineken beer a "Heinie."

Hell
USED WITH FRIENDS

❶ **Indicates surprise or frustration.**

EXAMPLE 1

"Hell! I just won a million dollars in the lottery!"

EXAMPLE 2

"Hell! I just got a parking ticket."

❷ **Used with "the" to intensify an emotion.**

EXAMPLE 1

"How the hell did you get a golf ball stuck in your mouth?"

EXAMPLE 2

"What the hell are you doing with my favorite dress? I didn't say you could borrow that!"

❸ **In many religions, the terrible place where bad people are sent to suffer after they die.**

EXAMPLE 1

"If you steal, you're going to hell!"

EXAMPLE 2

"I'm so tired! I feel like I've been to hell and back."

❹ **Pain and suffering.**

EXAMPLE 1

"I went through hell at my last job. I worked all the time and my boss still yelled at me."

EXAMPLE 2

"Harold puts me through hell. If I don't cook his dinner every night, he beats me."

○ **Learn more...**

- Although "Hell" is part of the Judeo-Christian religion, today people of all religions use it.

Hell On Something
USED WITH FRIENDS

Damaging to something.

EXAMPLE 1

"I love to ski, but it's hell on my knees. I'm usually in a lot of pain afterwards."

EXAMPLE 2

"This job is hell on my nerves. I'm so stressed from working nights and weekends."

Hell-raiser
USED WITH FRIENDS

A rowdy person or someone who makes trouble.

EXAMPLE 1

"I was a real hell-raiser when I was young. I drank too much and got in fights all the time."

EXAMPLE 2

"I'm a hell-raiser when I'm having a good time. I like to take my shirt off and show everyone my breasts."

Hell To Pay
USED WITH FRIENDS

Big trouble.

EXAMPLE 1

"If I don't get home before midnight, there will be hell to pay. My dad gets really angry when I'm late."

EXAMPLE 2

"There will be hell to pay if Lisa's pregnant. My wife will never understand!"

"Hell's bells!"
USED WITH FRIENDS

Indicates surprise or frustration.

EXAMPLE 1

"Hell's bells! We're two hours late!"

EXAMPLE 2

"Hell's bells! If I don't have sex soon, I'm going to explode!"

Hella
USED WITH ANYONE

Very.

EXAMPLE 1

"This ice cream is hella good."

EXAMPLE 2

"Sarah is hella sexy."

○ **Learn more...**

- Cartman, one of the animated characters from the T.V. show "South Park," says "hella" often.

- A popular band called *No Doubt* released the song "Hella Good" in 2001 containing the line "You've got me feeling hella good."

Helluva
USED WITH FRIENDS

Special, big, or important.

EXAMPLE 1

"That's a helluva big scar on your face. How did you get it?"

EXAMPLE 2

"I had a helluva good time at Tracey's house last night."

o **Learn more...**

* This is a shortening of the phrase "hell of a" as in "That's a hell of a nice car, Ted."

Helmet
USED WITH FRIENDS

The tip of the penis.

EXAMPLE 1

"Kathy likes to put my helmet in her mouth and rub her tongue all over it."

EXAMPLE 2

"My favorite thing is when my girlfriend plays with my helmet."

o **Learn more...**

* You may also hear "purple helmet."

Hermaphrodite
USED WITH ANYONE

A person with both male and female genitalia.

EXAMPLE 1

"Some people think hermaphrodites are lucky because they have a penis and a vagina."

EXAMPLE 2

"If I were a hermaphrodite, I would have sex with myself all the time!"

AT THE MOVIES
"HOME ALONE" (1990)

Home Alone, starring Macaulay Culkin, tells the story of a young boy accidentally left at home when his parents fly to France for Christmas. When the house is attacked by thieves, the boy (Kev) uses his brain to defeat them. Most Americans consider this movie appropriate for older children, despite the dangerous words it uses.

KEV "I'm over here, you big horse's ass! "	**Ass** (p. 4)
—	
GANGSTER "I'm gonna give you to the count of ten to get your ugly, yellow, no-good keester off my property."	**Yellow** (p. 219) **Keester** (p. 112)
—	
KATE McCALLISTER "I have been awake for almost 60 hours. I have been from Chicago to Paris to Dallas to...where the hell am I?"	**Hell** (p. 97)
—	
KEV "I don't want to sleep with Fuller. He'll pee all over me, I know it."	**Pee** (p. 143)
—	
KEV "Did anyone order me a plain cheese [pizza]? " **BUZZ McCALLISTER** "Yeah we did. But if you want any, someone's gonna have to barf it all up because it's gone."	**Barf** (p. 11)

Herpes
USED WITH ANYONE

An incurable sexually transmitted disease that affects the genitals and the mouth.

EXAMPLE 1

"I only had sex without a condom once, but that was enough to get herpes."

EXAMPLE 2

"I would never have sex with someone unless they knew I had herpes, and they were okay with that."

Hershey Highway
USED WITH FRIENDS

Anus.

EXAMPLE 1

"Always wear a condom if you plan on visiting someone's Hershey highway."

EXAMPLE 2

"I love to put my penis in Kelly's Hershey highway, and she loves it, too."

o **Learn more...**

• Hershey Food Corporation is famous for its chocolate.

Hershey Squirts
USED WITH FRIENDS

Diarrhea.

EXAMPLE 1

"Willy ate some bad fish and now he has the Hershey squirts. He's been in the bathroom for hours!"

EXAMPLE 2

"Kent can't go swimming because he has the Hershey squirts."

Hickey
USED WITH ANYONE

A red area on the skin caused by sucking.

EXAMPLE 1

"I was really embarrassed when I noticed that Laura gave me a hickey yesterday."

EXAMPLE 2

"My mother was angry when I came home from studying with three hickeys on my neck."

Highbeams
USED WITH FRIENDS

Breasts with erect nipples.

EXAMPLE 1

"It's so cold in our house that Nancy always has her highbeams on."

EXAMPLE 2

"I love the winter months because most women use their highbeams more."

o **Learn more...**

• "Highbeams" is another name for "a car's headlights set to their brightest level."

Hippo
USED WITH FRIENDS

A fat person.

EXAMPLE 1

"I haven't seen a hippo like that woman since I was at the zoo last week."

EXAMPLE 2

"Hey, hippo! Stop eating those potato chips and maybe you'll be able to walk more than 20 feet a day."

Hit In The Face With A Hot Bag Of Nickles
USED WITH FRIENDS

Very ugly.

EXAMPLE 1

"How did that man find a wife? He looks like he was hit in the face with a hot bag of nickels."

EXAMPLE 2

"I want to have sex with her even though she looks like she was hit in the face with a hot bag of nickels. I'll just keep the lights off."

Hit On
USED WITH ANYONE

To flirt or try to attract another person.

EXAMPLE 1

"I hit on 14 different girls tonight, and none of them were interested in me."

EXAMPLE 2

"Officer, are you hitting on me?"

H-I-V
USED WITH ANYONE

A condition that slowly destroys a person's immune system.

EXAMPLE 1

"If you have H-I-V, you have to be very careful. Almost any illness can kill you."

EXAMPLE 2

"You can hug me even though I have H-I-V. You can't get it that way."

o **Learn more...**

• People with "H-I-V" are called "H-I-V positive." People who have been tested but don't have it are called "H-I-V negative."

Ho
USED WITH FRIENDS

A prostitute.

EXAMPLE 1

"You're such a ho! You'll have sex with anyone!"

EXAMPLE 2

"I saw your mother kissing Mr. Sanders. She's such a ho!"

o **Learn more...**

• This is another way to say "whore" (p. 214).

Hog
USED WITH FRIENDS

A fat or greedy person.

EXAMPLE 1

"That hog ate all the food at the buffet!"

EXAMPLE 2

"Wow! That hog is eating a piece of turkey during the funeral. How rude!"

Hole
USED WITH EXTREME CAUTION

❶ **Vagina.**

EXAMPLE 1

"I want to fill her hole with my penis."

EXAMPLE 2

"Her hole is so big, I barely feel anything when we have sex."

❷ **Anus.**

EXAMPLE 1

"Wendel enjoys having his hole licked during sex."

EXAMPLE 2

"Pull your finger out of your hole and come help me do the laundry!"

Holler At The Toilet
USED WITH FRIENDS

To vomit.

EXAMPLE 1

"I couldn't sleep last night because you were hollering at the toilet for so long."

EXAMPLE 2

"Stay away from the oysters, or you'll be hollering at the toilet all night."

Holy Cow
USED WITH ANYONE

Indicates surprise.

EXAMPLE 1

"Holy cow! This painting is cheap!"

EXAMPLE 2

"Holy cow! It's December already?"

o **Learn more...**

• This is a non-religious way to say "Holy Christ!"

• You may also hear "Holy moley," a non-religious way to say "Holy Moses."

- You can make your own version by adding almost any word after "holy," like "Holy hard test!" or "Holy hotcakes!" It sounds better if the other words also start with "h."

"Holy shit!"
USED WITH FRIENDS

Indicates surprise.

EXAMPLE 1

"Holy shit! That lady just broke her leg!"

EXAMPLE 2

"You got married in Las Vegas? Holy Shit!"

o **Learn more...**

- You may also hear "Holy cripes."

Home Base
USED WITH FRIENDS

Sex.

EXAMPLE 1

"Carrie let Fred get to home base yesterday."

EXAMPLE 2

"I went to home base with Mathew when we were both 15 years old. I wish I had waited!"

o **Learn more...**

- In baseball, you have to touch "home base" in order to score a point (a "run") for your team.

Homo
USED WITH EXTREME CAUTION

A homosexual.

EXAMPLE 1

"He's not my boyfriend, he's a homo! He likes other men."

EXAMPLE 2

"My sister is a homo, so we go looking for women together."

Honey Pot
USED WITH FRIENDS

Vagina.

EXAMPLE 1

"Her honey pot was so sweet, I was licking it for an hour."

EXAMPLE 2

"She let me stick my penis in the honey pot and now it's sticky."

Hook Shop
USED WITH FRIENDS

A place of prostitution.

EXAMPLE 1

"Johnson is still at the hook shop. He must really like that prostitute."

EXAMPLE 2

"I once had an apartment next to a hook shop. I saw men coming and going all through the night."

Hook Up
USED WITH ANYONE

To get together, sometimes in a sexual way.

EXAMPLE 1

"Sarah and I hooked up for dinner last night. She's my best friend."

EXAMPLE 2

"I finally hooked up with Jake! The sex was wonderful!"

o **Learn more...**

- People use "hook up" in a lot of ways. It can mean "get together" with friends, "kiss," or even "have sex." Only context will help you decide which definition is right!

Hooker
USED WITH FRIENDS

A prostitute.

EXAMPLE 1

"Your mother dresses like a hooker! You must be so embarrassed."

EXAMPLE 2

"I'm dating a hooker. It's expensive, but all my friends are jealous."

Hooters

USED WITH FRIENDS

Breasts.

EXAMPLE 1

"Melissa has the smallest hooters of any woman I know."

EXAMPLE 2

"This bar is full of great hooters."

o Learn more...

- There is a famous restaurant chain called "Hooters" where all the waitresses have large breasts and wear tight shirts.

Hop In The Sack

USED WITH ANYONE

To have sex.

EXAMPLE 1

"I know we're friends, but I think we should hop in the sack just once to see how it feels."

EXAMPLE 2

"Alice and I were going to hop in the sack, but the phone rang."

Horn Dog

USED WITH FRIENDS

A man who is always looking for sex.

EXAMPLE 1

"Do you see that horn dog asking every woman in the club to have sex with him?"

LEARN MORE
TRICKY TECHNICAL TERMS

These are the technical (official) names for various legal and illegal sexual acts. These words are considered polite when used to discuss another person.

Here are some examples of polite usage:

1. "The police are chasing a pedophile in my neighborhood."

2. "Sue was a victim of incest. That's why she doesn't talk to her father."

3. "The prostitute was performing fellatio on the actor Hugh Grant when the police found them."

However, these words are very dangerous when the speaker is talking about himself or herself.

Here are some examples of dangerous usage:

1. "Bestiality really arouses me. I see a sheep and I want to have sex with it."

2. "I'm a sadist. I love to beat my lovers until they bleed."

3. "I've always been interested in necrophilia. Do you know where I can find a dead body?"

Some of these technical terms are:

Bestiality (p. 14)

Cunnilingus (p. 42)

Fellatio (p. 64)

Incest (p. 107)

Masochist (p. 124)

Necrophiliac (p. 133)

Orgy (p. 139)

Pederast (p. 142)

Pedophile (p. 143)

Sadist (p. 167)

Sadomasochist (p. 167)

EXAMPLE 2

"Gina won't go on a date with me because she thinks I'm a horn dog."

Horny

USED WITH FRIENDS

To desire sex or sexual contact.

EXAMPLE 1

"I've never been this horny before. I really need to have sex!"

EXAMPLE 2

"My girlfriend gets really horny when I hit her butt with a wooden spoon."

o **Learn more...**

- The movie character Austin Powers (played by Mike Myers) is famous for saying "Do I make you horny, baby?"

Horse Around

USED WITH ANYONE

To be with someone in a non-sexual way.

EXAMPLE 1

"Cheryl and I were just horsing around all night. We watched a movie and talked."

EXAMPLE 2

"We just horsed around until the band started to play."

Hose

USED WITH FRIENDS

Penis.

EXAMPLE 1

"Dina wants my hose in her mouth. She loves to perform oral sex on me."

EXAMPLE 2

"Kara is depressed, so I'm going to her house to give her the hose."

Hot

USED WITH ANYONE

Sexy, attractive.

EXAMPLE 1

"Harrison Ford is hot! I would love to have sex with him."

EXAMPLE 2

"Asian women are much hotter than European women, in my opinion."

Hot And Bothered

USED WITH FRIENDS

Ready for sex.

EXAMPLE 1

"After watching that sex movie, I'm really hot and bothered."

EXAMPLE 2

"We were both hot and bothered when the doorbell rang. It was his parents!"

Hot Shit

USED WITH FRIENDS

Amazing or impressive.

EXAMPLE 1

"Andrew thinks he's hot shit since he got a new car."

EXAMPLE 2

"My new boyfriend is hot shit! He has a great job and great hair."

o **Learn more...**

- You may also hear "king shit" as in "Ever since he went to Harvard, Nick acts like he's king shit."

Hot To Trot

USED WITH ANYONE

Ready for sex.

EXAMPLE 1

"I am hot to trot for my big date tonight! I'm wearing my sexiest underwear."

EXAMPLE 2

"Roy is always hot to trot, but no one will have sex with him."

o **Learn more...**

- This is an older phrase used as a joke today.

"Hot Damn!"

USED WITH FRIENDS

"Great!"

EXAMPLE 1

"Hot damn! Wanda agreed to go on a date with me!"

EXAMPLE 2

"My parents are buying me a new car. Hot damn!"

House Of Ill Repute
USED WITH ANYONE

A place of prostitution.

EXAMPLE 1

"Senator McNeel was discovered at a house of ill repute last night."

EXAMPLE 2

"Jennifer's first job was washing the sheets at a house of ill repute."

o Learn more...

- You may also hear "house of delight," "house of ill fame," "house of joy," or "joy house."

Hummer
USED WITH EXTREME CAUTION

Oral sex performed on a man.

EXAMPLE 1

"The best night of my life is when Susan learned how to give me a hummer."

EXAMPLE 2

"Giving hummers should be a course in college that all women are required to attend."

o Learn more...

- It is rumored that if the person performing oral sex on someone hums, it feels great.

- A "Hummer" is also a brand of car, so listen closely to the context!

Hump
USED WITH ANYONE

To have sex.

EXAMPLE 1

"I've never seen a horse humping another horse before."

EXAMPLE 2

"I humped Ashley until she almost fainted."

Hung
USED WITH FRIENDS

To have a big penis.

EXAMPLE 1

"I know Dave is a small guy, but he's really hung."

EXAMPLE 2

"Everyone knows Chris is hung. He can have sex with any woman he wants."

o Learn more...

- Someone who is "hung like a horse" has a very big penis.

Hurl
USED WITH FRIENDS

To vomit.

EXAMPLE 1

"If I eat another piece of cake, I'll have to hurl."

EXAMPLE 2

"I almost hurled when I saw my grandmother naked."

Hustle
USED WITH ANYONE

❶ To sell or get something in an illegal or unethical way.

EXAMPLE 1

"We hustled stolen jewelry and made a lot of money!"

EXAMPLE 2

"Ed hustled $100 from me when we played pool. He never told me he was a professional pool player!"

❷ To find customers for a prostitute or "pimp" (p. 145).

EXAMPLE 1

"We have to find another place to look for customers. Another woman hustles on this street."

EXAMPLE 2

"I need a man to hustle clients for me. I hate looking for them myself."

o Learn more...

- "Hustler" is a famous magazine featuring naked women.

I IS FOR IMPOTENT

Impotent
USED WITH ANYONE

Unable to achieve an erect penis.

EXAMPLE 1
"Ben is impotent from using so many drugs when he was young."

EXAMPLE 2
"I love my husband, but we never have sex because he's impotent."

In Deep Shit
USED WITH FRIENDS

To be in big trouble.

EXAMPLE 1
"If I can't find a new job, I'll be in deep shit."

EXAMPLE 2
"Hanson is in deep shit with his girlfriend. She found him with another woman!"

In One's Birthday Suit
USED WITH ANYONE

Totally naked.

EXAMPLE 1
"Martha went to the party in her birthday suit. She's crazy, but she looked great!"

EXAMPLE 2
"That man just ran across the soccer field in his birthday suit! The police will probably arrest him."

o Learn more...

• Because a "suit" is a piece of clothing, you can use the verb "wear" with "birthday suit."

- Everyone is naked when they are born, so your "birthday suit" is nothing!

In The Buff
USED WITH ANYONE

Totally naked.

EXAMPLE 1

"Let's go swimming in the buff! If we turn the lights off, no one will see."

EXAMPLE 2

"Margot took a picture of me in the buff, then sent it to my girlfriend!"

In The Mood
USED WITH ANYONE

Interested in having sex.

EXAMPLE 1

"My husband is never in the mood. I haven't had sex in three years."

EXAMPLE 2

"Whenever I'm in the mood, my wife says that she has a headache."

In The Raw
USED WITH ANYONE

Totally naked.

EXAMPLE 1

"I always sleep in the raw. The sheets feel so good on my skin!"

EXAMPLE 2

"Mario was in the raw when I went into his house. I should have knocked on the door before entering!"

Incest
USED WITH ANYONE

Sex between two people who are part of the same family.

EXAMPLE 1

"Incest is a crime in most states. It's illegal to have sex with your direct family."

EXAMPLE 2

"I hear that incest is a big problem in some states."

Indecent Exposure
USED WITH ANYONE

Showing one's body, usually genitals, in a public place.

EXAMPLE 1

"Joel was arrested for indecent exposure. He took his pants off in a busy store!"

EXAMPLE 2

"If you urinate outside, you could get arrested for indecent exposure!"

J IS FOR JERK OFF

Jack Off
USED WITH FRIENDS

To masturbate.

EXAMPLE 1
"I wanted to masturbate so much on the flight home that I went into the airplane bathroom to jack off."

EXAMPLE 2
"When I was 10 years old, I saw my neighbor jacking off using a watermelon. I don't eat watermelon anymore."

Jack-off
USED WITH FRIENDS

A stupid person.

EXAMPLE 1
"Hey, jack-off! You're driving too slow! Get off the road!"

EXAMPLE 2
"Some jack-off stole my car. Now I have to call the police and file a report."

Jackass
USED WITH FRIENDS

A very rude person.

EXAMPLE 1
"You jackass! You bought pizza with my money!"

EXAMPLE 2
"Michael is such a jackass. I asked him for help, but he wanted to watch T.V. instead!"

O Learn more...

- There is an MTV television show (and a movie) called "Jackass" where young men do very stupid or disgusting things to get laughs.

Jail Bait
USED WITH FRIENDS

A person too young to have sex legally.

EXAMPLE 1
"Sarah is jail bait. She looks 20, but she's only 15!"

EXAMPLE 2
"Alan wants to have sex with the jail bait at the high school. He's crazy!"

O Learn more...

- If you have sex with someone who is too young, you could go to jail.

- "15 will get you 20" is a common phrase meaning "If you have sex with a 15 year old, you'll go to jail for 20 years."

Jerk
USED WITH ANYONE

A rude person.

EXAMPLE 1
"Josh broke my pencil. What a jerk!"

EXAMPLE 2
"Sheamus is such a jerk! He promised to help me last night, but he didn't."

Jerk Off
USED WITH FRIENDS

To masturbate.

EXAMPLE 1
"What a terrible day! I need to go home and jerk off."

EXAMPLE 2
"You don't want to have sex because you just jerked off in the bathroom!"

Jerk-off
USED WITH FRIENDS

A rude or irritating person.

EXAMPLE 1
"That guy knocked over my shopping cart. What a jerk-off!"

EXAMPLE 2
"You jerk-off! Don't leave your trash on my doorstep!"

Jerkin' The Gherkin
USED WITH FRIENDS

To masturbate.

EXAMPLE 1
"Masturbation is great! I would be jerkin' the gherkin all day if I didn't have to go to work."

EXAMPLE 2
RAY: "What is that sound?"

JIM: "Nick is jerkin' the gherkin is his room again. Sounds like he just finished."

O Learn more...

- "Jerking" is pronounced "jerkin'" in this phrase so it rhymes with "gherkin." To "jerk" something is to "move something with a lot of force."

- A "gherkin" is a kind of pickle.

"Jesus Christ!"
USED WITH FRIENDS

Indicates frustration or surprise.

EXAMPLE 1
"Jesus Christ! How many pairs of shoes do you own?"

EXAMPLE 2
"Jesus Christ! They impeached President Bush! That's great!"

O Learn more...

- You may also hear just "Jesus!" or "Christ!"

Jesus-freak
USED WITH FRIENDS

A very religious Christian.

EXAMPLE 1

"That Jesus-freak just tried to sell me a Bible in the coffee shop."

EXAMPLE 2

"I used to be a Jesus-freak, but then I realized there's no God."

Jism
USED WITH FRIENDS

Sperm or fluid from an ejaculation.

EXAMPLE 1

"My boyfriend and I had sex in the living room and he got jism all over the couch. If my mother sees it, I'm in big trouble!"

EXAMPLE 2

"I like to suck the jism out of his penis during oral sex. It makes me feel powerful."

o Learn more...

• You may also hear "jiz."

Jock Strap
USED WITH ANYONE

A piece of clothing used to keep a man's genitals in place while he does a sports activity.

EXAMPLE 1

"If you're going to practice football, you need to wear a jock strap!"

EXAMPLE 2

"I forgot my jock strap, so my testicles were bouncing everywhere during the soccer game."

John
USED WITH ANYONE

❶ A prostitute's customer.

EXAMPLE 1

"My last john was fast. We had sex for five minutes, and he was done!"

EXAMPLE 2

"Let's go to the other alley. There are more johns over there."

❷ Bathroom.

EXAMPLE 1

"Excuse me, please. Which way to the john?"

EXAMPLE 2

"The line for the john is too long. Let's go somewhere else."

Johnson
USED WITH FRIENDS

Penis.

EXAMPLE 1

"Nate likes to touch his johnson in the office."

EXAMPLE 2

"Phil Johnson has a really small johnson. I feel bad for him."

Joystick
USED WITH FRIENDS

Penis.

EXAMPLE 1

"I wish I could find a woman who wanted to play with my joystick."

EXAMPLE 2

"Trish would be great at video games. She's a master with my joystick."

o Learn more...

• A "joystick" is the controller used for many video games.

Jugs
USED WITH FRIENDS

Breasts.

EXAMPLE 1

"Do you want to see a picture of my girlfriend's jugs?"

EXAMPLE 2

"My history teacher has the biggest jugs. I never hear a thing she says in class!"

Jump Someone's Bones
USED WITH FRIENDS

To have sex.

EXAMPLE 1

"Cassandra already knows that I want to jump her bones. She doesn't want to have sex with me though."

EXAMPLE 2

"Everything was going well. I was just about to jump her bones when she asked me to take her home."

○ **Learn more...**

• You may also hear "jump someone."

Junior
USED WITH FRIENDS

Penis.

EXAMPLE 1

"Junior makes most of my decisions. I just do the talking."

EXAMPLE 2

"I know I need to wear a condom when I have sex, but junior doesn't like it."

Junk
USED WITH FRIENDS

Genitals.

EXAMPLE 1

"Man, put your junk back in your pants. I don't want to see that when I'm trying to eat."

EXAMPLE 2

"Yeah, Jane wants my junk. She's always asking me to have sex with her."

○ **Learn more...**

• A person with "junk in the trunk" has a nice butt.

AT THE MOVIES
"JAWS" (1975)

The Academy Award-winning movie *Jaws* is one of the most famous movies ever made. It tells the story of three men trying to destroy a huge, man-eating shark that's been terrorizing the vacation town of Amity.

QUINT
"What are you, some kind of half-assed astronaut?"

—

Half-assed (p. 90)

QUINT
"You've got city boy hands, Hooper."

HOOPER
"I don't need this working-class-hero crap. "

—

Crap (p. 38)

PRATT
"I'll stuff your friggin' head in there, man, and find out whether or not it's a man-eater!"

—

Friggin' (p. 72)

HOOPER
"You are going to ignore this particular problem until it swims up and bites you on the ass!"

—

Ass (p. 4)

BRODY
"Smile, you son of a bitch!"

—

Son of a bitch (p. 184)

ELLEN BRODY
"Wanna get drunk and fool around?"

BRODY
"Oh, yeah!"

Fool around (p. 69)

K IS FOR KINKY

"Keep your panties on."
USED WITH FRIENDS

"Don't get upset."

EXAMPLE 1
ISABELLE: "We're lost! We're both going to die!"

LYNN: "Keep your panties on. I can use my cell phone to call for help."

EXAMPLE 2
TOM: "I forgot to study for today's test!"

WILL: "Keep your panties on. You can cheat from me."

Keester
USED WITH ANYONE

Butt.

EXAMPLE 1
"My grandmother fell on her keester when she got drunk last Christmas."

EXAMPLE 2
"The doctor says I need to stay off my keester for one week so it can heal."

Kick Ass
USED WITH FRIENDS

To do really well.

EXAMPLE 1
"I'm going to kick ass on this test. I studied all night!"

EXAMPLE 2

"The company hired me because I kicked ass in the interview!"

Kick-ass
USED WITH FRIENDS

Great or wonderful.

EXAMPLE 1

"I love my new car. It's so kick-ass!"

EXAMPLE 2

"I'm saving money to buy a kick-ass stereo system."

Kick Someone's Ass
USED WITH FRIENDS

❶ **To hurt someone physically.**

EXAMPLE 1

"If you touch my girlfriend again, I'm going to kick your ass!"

EXAMPLE 2

"Mike tried to grab my breast last night, so I kicked his ass."

❷ **To do better than someone in a contest.**

EXAMPLE 1

"I kicked Mary's ass on the history test, and I didn't even study!"

EXAMPLE 2

"Sheila can kick your ass at tennis. She's been playing her whole life."

○ **Learn more...**

• In the popular action movie *Charlie's Angels*, Drew Barrymore's character beats up several men and says "And that's kicking your ass!"

Kinky
USED WITH ANYONE

Strange or unusual.

EXAMPLE 1

"Vince likes kinky sex. The stranger, the better!"

EXAMPLE 2

"I like wearing leather. It makes me feel kinky."

Kiss Ass
USED WITH FRIENDS

To try to gain someone's support any way one can.

EXAMPLE 1

"If you want the promotion, you should start kissing ass right now!"

EXAMPLE 2

"I'm going over to Gina's house to kiss ass again. I hope she forgives me!"

DIALOGUE
"HARRIS NEEDS TO KISS ASS"

Here is a short dialogue between two Americans.

HARRIS
"The boss just saw me looking at her knockers. She's probably going to fire me now!"

Knockers (p. 114)

DAMIEN
"Keep your panties on. Maybe she's kinky and liked it."

"Keep your panties on." (p. 112)
Kinky (p. 113)

HARRIS
"You jackass! Of course she didn't like it. She's married!"

Jackass (p. 108)

DAMIEN
"Well, then you'd better start kissing ass. Just don't look at her keester when you're doing it!"

Kiss ass (p. 113)
Keester (p. 112)

Kiss-ass
USED WITH FRIENDS

A person who tries to gain someone's support any way he or she can.

EXAMPLE 1

"Dave is such a kiss-ass. He bought lunch for the boss because he wants a raise."

EXAMPLE 2

"I want to give the teacher an apple, but I don't want to look like a kiss-ass."

Knocked Up
USED WITH FRIENDS

Pregnant.

EXAMPLE 1

"Melinda got knocked up, and she doesn't know who the father is."

EXAMPLE 2

"My father told me to always wear a condom so my girlfriend doesn't get knocked up."

o **Learn more...**

• You may also hear "knock up someone" as in "I tried to knock up Melissa so she'd stay with me, but she didn't get pregnant."

Knockers
USED WITH FRIENDS

Breasts.

EXAMPLE 1

"That prostitute has great knockers, and she'll let you touch them for $1."

EXAMPLE 2

"My wife wants to have surgery to make her knockers bigger."

Know-it-all
USED WITH ANYONE

A person who thinks he or she knows everything.

EXAMPLE 1

"Lisa answered every question the teacher asked. I hate know-it-alls!"

EXAMPLE 2

"Hank went fishing once, and now he talks like he's an expert. What a know-it-all!"

Kook
USED WITH ANYONE

A crazy or strange person.

EXAMPLE 1

"That old guy is a kook. He always asks what my favorite color is."

EXAMPLE 2

"People who believe in aliens are kooks!"

o **Learn more...**

• You may also hear "kooky" as in "That was a kooky movie. I didn't understand it."

L IS FOR LECHER

La Petite Mort

USED WITH FRIENDS

A female orgasm.

EXAMPLE 1

"Finally Akira gave me la petite mort. It took him over an hour, but he did it."

EXAMPLE 2

"La petite mort, chocolate ice cream, and traveling are the three most important things in my life."

o Learn more...

- A French phrase which translates as "the little death."

Ladies' Man

USED WITH ANYONE

A man who is successful with women.

EXAMPLE 1

"Cal is a real ladies' man! He can get any woman he wants!"

EXAMPLE 2

"When I was young, I was a ladies' man. Now I can't even get a date!"

o Learn more...

- Actor Tim Meadows plays a character called "the Ladies' Man" on the popular T.V. show "Saturday Night Live."

Lady Of The Evening
USED WITH ANYONE

A nice way of saying "prostitute."

EXAMPLE 1

"You look like a lady of the evening in that cheap dress!"

EXAMPLE 2

"I think Will's new girlfriend is actually a lady of the evening. She's too beautiful for him!"

o **Learn more...**

- You may also hear "lady of the night."

Lam-o
USED WITH ANYONE

A stupid or boring person.

EXAMPLE 1

"Ian is a lam-o. He never wants to have fun."

EXAMPLE 2

ADAM: "I need to study tonight."

SARAH: "You lam-o! Come with us to the concert!"

o **Learn more...**

- "Lam-o" is pronounced "Lame-Oh."

- You may also hear "lamebrain."

Lame
USED WITH ANYONE

Stupid, boring.

EXAMPLE 1

"This party is lame! Let's go somewhere else."

EXAMPLE 2

"That movie was so lame! I'm sorry we paid to see it."

Lard-ass
USED WITH FRIENDS

A fat person.

EXAMPLE 1

"My brother is a lard-ass. He eats pizza all day and never exercises."

EXAMPLE 2

"Which one of you lard-asses ate all the cereal this morning?"

Laugh At The Lawn
USED WITH FRIENDS

To vomit.

EXAMPLE 1

"We had to come home from the party early so Jim could go laugh at the lawn."

EXAMPLE 2

"I saw six different people laughing at the lawn on the way home from the bar tonight."

Laugh One's Ass Off
USED WITH FRIENDS

To laugh a lot.

EXAMPLE 1

"I laughed my ass off when Rob fell off his bike!"

EXAMPLE 2

"That comedian makes me laugh my ass off!"

o **Learn more...**

- You may also hear "laugh one's butt off" and "laugh one's socks off."

- When you see "LMAO" in an Internet chat room, it means "laugh my ass off."

Lay A Log
USED WITH FRIENDS

To defecate.

EXAMPLE 1

"I hope Ken gets out of the bathroom soon because I have to lay a log."

EXAMPLE 2

"Someone layed a log on the toilet seat. I'm not going to clean it up."

Lay Pipe
USED WITH FRIENDS

To have sex.

EXAMPLE 1

"I have to get home early. My wife wants me to lay pipe tonight."

EXAMPLE 2

"I think my husband Morty has been laying pipe all over town. Strange women call him in the middle of the night."

Leather Queen
USED WITH EXTREME CAUTION

A homosexual man who likes to wear leather clothes.

EXAMPLE 1

"Oliver is a leather queen. He always wears leather pants, even in the summer!"

EXAMPLE 2

"I like my men dressed in leather. I'm such a leather queen!"

Lecher
USED WITH ANYONE

A man with strong, usually inappropriate, sexual desires.

EXAMPLE 1

"My last boyfriend was a lecher. He talked about having sex with my mother all the time!"

EXAMPLE 2

"My father is always dating women half his age. He's such a lecher."

o **Learn more...**

- You may also hear "lech" as in "Robert is a total lech! I saw him drooling over some schoolgirls after work yesterday."

Les-be-friends
USED WITH FRIENDS

Lesbians or lesbian friends.

EXAMPLE 1

"I'm going to a meeting with my les-be-friends tonight."

EXAMPLE 2

"I think those two woman are les-be-friends. Do you see the way they're touching each other?"

o **Learn more...**

- "Les-be-friends" sounds like "lesbians" and has a positive meaning.

Lesbian
USED WITH ANYONE

A homosexual woman.

EXAMPLE 1

"Those two women must be lesbians. They're always kissing each other."

EXAMPLE 2

"I thought I was heterosexual until I saw Tierza. Now I know I'm a lesbian!"

Lesbo
USED WITH FRIENDS

Lesbian.

EXAMPLE 1

"Is Donna a lesbo? She won't go on a date with me, and I'm the cutest guy in school!"

IN OTHER WORDS... "LESBIANS"

Homosexual women are politely called "lesbians" or "gays." Most other words are considered offensive.

USED WITH ANYONE

Gay (p. 80)

Lesbian (p. 117)

USED WITH FRIENDS

Lesbo (p. 117)

Lipstick lesbian (p. 119)

USED WITH EXTREME CAUTION

Beaver-eater (p. 14)

Bulldyke (p. 23)

Dyke (p. 56)

Homo (p. 102)

Queer (p. 158)

EXAMPLE 2
"It's my goal in life to have sex with three beautiful lesbos at the same time."

o Learn more...

- You may also hear "lezzie" as in "My best friend is a lezzie."

Let One Fly
USED WITH FRIENDS

To expel gas from the anus; to flatulate.

EXAMPLE 1
"My girlfriend doesn't care if I let one fly in bed. She's great!"

EXAMPLE 2
"Paul let one fly yesterday. It smelled so bad that I told him to go to the doctor to make sure he wasn't dying."

o Learn more...

- You may also hear "let one go" as in "Cover your nose. I just let one go."

Lewd
USED WITH ANYONE

Crude or sexual.

EXAMPLE 1
"Ben said many lewd things at the party. It was very inappropriate."

EXAMPLE 2
"My boss has a lewd sense of humor. He's always making sexual jokes."

Light In The Loafers
USED WITH ANYONE

Feminine (but only said about men).

EXAMPLE 1
"Alan seems a little light in the loafers. Are you sure he's married to a woman?"

EXAMPLE 2
"Gary said I'm light in the loafers, but no one else thinks I'm feminine."

"The lights are on, but nobody's home."
USED WITH ANYONE

"That person is very stupid."

EXAMPLE 1
"Chuck's really handsome, but he's not very smart. The lights are on, but nobody's home."

EXAMPLE 2
"Yeah, Trish is dumb. The lights are on but nobody's home."

o Learn more...

- This phrase compares a person to a house. The person is present and alive, but he or she isn't thinking clearly.

Like Hell
USED WITH FRIENDS

Used to intensify an emotion.

EXAMPLE 1
"Joe ran like hell when the police started chasing him."

EXAMPLE 2
"If you touch me, I'm going to scream like hell!"

Limp-wrist
USED WITH EXTREME CAUTION

A homosexual man.

EXAMPLE 1
"Brad is such a limp-wrist! He could never win a fight against Larry."

EXAMPLE 2
"It's difficult to believe that those limp-wrists were married before."

o Learn more...

- You may also hear "limp-wristed."

Lip-lock
USED WITH FRIENDS

To kiss.

EXAMPLE 1
"Tom and Joan were lip-locked during the whole party. How rude!"

EXAMPLE 2
"Lip-locking with Corey is terrible. He uses his tongue too much!"

Lipstick Lesbian
USED WITH FRIENDS

A very attractive lesbian.

EXAMPLE 1
"Tucia is the most beautiful lipstick lesbian I've ever seen."

EXAMPLE 2
HANK: "She's beautiful!"

SUE: "She's a lipstick lesbian."

Lit
USED WITH ANYONE

Drunk.

EXAMPLE 1
"I'm totally lit! I need a ride home."

EXAMPLE 2
"I got lit before I met my girlfriend's parents. She's really angry at me!"

Little Black Book
USED WITH ANYONE

A book, created and maintained by a man, that contains the names and phone numbers of women.

EXAMPLE 1
"Franklin's little black book has more than 150 womens' names in it."

EXAMPLE 2
"Whenever I need a date, I just call one of the girls in my little black book."

Little Shit
USED WITH FRIENDS

An annoying person.

EXAMPLE 1
"That little shit just took the last piece of cake."

EXAMPLE 2
"Some little shit over there threw a snowball in my face."

DIALOGUE
"MARRIED TO A LOW-LIFE"

Here is a short dialogue between two Americans.

WENDY
"Cheryl's husband is so lewd! She never should have married such a lecher."

KEVIN
"Yeah, he's a real loser. Now I understand why she's completely lit all the time. I'd drink too if I were living with that low-life."

WENDY
"I'm going to laugh my ass off when she finally leaves that little shit."

Lewd (p. 118)
Lecher (p. 117)

Loser (p. 121)
Lit (p. 119)
Low-life (p. 121)

Laugh one's ass off
(p. 116)
Little shit (p. 119)

Live In Sin
USED WITH ANYONE

To live (and have sex) with someone without being married.

EXAMPLE 1
"Jane and I aren't married. If we live together, her parents think we'll be living in sin."

EXAMPLE 2
"My mother won't let me live in sin with my boyfriend."

Loaded
USED WITH ANYONE

Drunk.

EXAMPLE 1
"I've never been this loaded while having sex. I shouldn't have had that whiskey."

EXAMPLE 2
"Juan is so loaded that he can't drive home."

o **Learn more...**

• "Loaded" also means "rich" as in "My dad is loaded. He won the lottery last year!"

Look Like Death Warmed Over
USED WITH FRIENDS

To look tired or sick, like a person who has had a difficult life.

EXAMPLE 1
"John has been working for 63 hours without sleep. That's why he looks like death warmed over now."

EXAMPLE 2
"I think most taxi drivers in New York City look like death warmed over."

Loon
USED WITH ANYONE

A crazy or strange person.

EXAMPLE 1
"I am such a loon. I forgot my keys in my apartment again."

EXAMPLE 2
"Only a loon would burn money."

o **Learn more...**

• You may also hear "loony" or "loony-tune" as in "This loony-tune house has no doors."

• "Loon" is taken from "lunatic" which means someone who is crazy. (And "luna" in "lunatic" means "moon"!)

Looped
USED WITH ANYONE

Drunk.

EXAMPLE 1
"I get really looped after drinking just one glass of beer."

EXAMPLE 2
"Rick got looped from mixing different types of alcohol and drinking them fast."

Loose
USED WITH FRIENDS

Willing to have sex often with different people.

EXAMPLE 1
"Did you have sex with Tom? You shouldn't be so loose!"

EXAMPLE 2
"Bonnie used to be loose, but now she's married to Jonathan."

o **Learn more...**

• Women are called "loose" more often than men.

Lose One's Lunch
USED WITH ANYONE

To vomit.

EXAMPLE 1
"I almost lost my lunch when I heard that I won the lottery."

EXAMPLE 2
"My husband lost his lunch when I told him I was pregnant."

Lose One's Marbles
USED WITH ANYONE

To become crazy.

EXAMPLE 1
"I can't remember my own name. I think I am losing my marbles."

EXAMPLE 2
"My grandmother lost her marbles years ago. She doesn't know anything now."

Loser
USED WITH ANYONE

A stupid or unpopular person; a failure.

EXAMPLE 1
"Why did you give Brian money? He's a loser!"

EXAMPLE 2
"Peggy is a loser. No one wants to be her friend."

o **Learn more...**

- You can also call someone a "loser" by making the shape of an "L" with your fingers and holding them up to your forehead.

Loudmouth
USED WITH ANYONE

A person who talks too much, usually revealing private information.

EXAMPLE 1
"Heather is a loudmouth. She told everyone that I failed the test."

EXAMPLE 2
GEORGE: "Where's my coat? I know I put it here somewhere."

HANK: "Be quiet, you loudmouth! I'm trying to sleep!"

Love Dungeon
USED WITH EXTREME CAUTION

Vagina.

EXAMPLE 1
"The only thing Hank wants is a trip to my love dungeon."

EXAMPLE 2
"You can play in the love dungeon after you apologize for being rude to me."

Love Handles
USED WITH ANYONE

Fat around a person's waist.

EXAMPLE 1
"I know I have love handles, but that just means you have more of me to love."

EXAMPLE 2
"I like girls with love handles so I have something to hold on to during sex."

o **Learn more...**

- Men have "love handles" more often than women.

Love Muscle
USED WITH EXTREME CAUTION

Penis.

EXAMPLE 1
"Did you see Pete's love muscle? He got an erection while he was talking to Gina!"

EXAMPLE 2
"Why don't you lick my love muscle, and I'll think about taking off your handcuffs."

Low-down, No-good
USED WITH ANYONE

Phrase used to intensify an insult.

EXAMPLE 1
"Hale is always trying to steal from people. He's a low-down, no-good thief!"

EXAMPLE 2
"You low-down, no-good jerk! Why did you kill my dog?"

Low-life
USED WITH ANYONE

A very bad person.

EXAMPLE 1
"That low-life just tried to touch my breasts when I walked near him."

EXAMPLE 2
"I don't go to that bar because there are so many low-lifes."

M IS FOR MASTURBATE

Mack
USED WITH ANYONE

❶ To flirt with someone.

EXAMPLE 1
"Jerry was macking on all the women in the bar, but no one was interested."

EXAMPLE 2
"I was doing some serious macking last night, and got three phone numbers!"

❷ A person who is good at flirting and does it a lot.

EXAMPLE 1
"I won't go to the bar with Sam. He's a total mack! It's so embarrassing."

EXAMPLE 2
"Oliver is a real mack. He would have sex with a different woman every night if he could."

○ Learn more...

• You may also hear "mack daddy" as in "I'm a mack daddy. Women can't resist my charms!"

Maggot
USED WITH FRIENDS

A very bad person.

EXAMPLE 1
"Hey, maggot! Stop trying to sell drugs to children!"

EXAMPLE 2
"That maggot always says mean things to the new students."

Make A Pit Stop
USED WITH ANYONE

To urinate or defecate.

EXAMPLE 1
"Do you mind if I make a pit stop before we continue shopping?"

EXAMPLE 2
"I'll be ready to leave in two minutes. I just have to make a pit stop."

Make An Anal Announcement
USED WITH FRIENDS

To expel gas from the anus; to flatulate.

EXAMPLE 1
"Larry was standing in front of the class to give a speech, but he gave an anal announcement instead. The smell was terrible."

EXAMPLE 2
"Tom gave the smelliest anal announcement ever. I almost vomited."

Make Love
USED WITH ANYONE

To have sex.

EXAMPLE 1
"Men call it having sex, but women call it making love."

EXAMPLE 2
"I am excited to make love outside, under the stars tonight."

○ **Learn more...**

- A famous phrase from the 1960s is "Make love, not war."

- "Make love" is one of the most romantic ways to say "have sex."

Make Out
USED WITH ANYONE

To kiss.

EXAMPLE 1
"We like to sit in the back of the movie theater so we can make out without anyone seeing us."

EXAMPLE 2
"Anna and Chris were making out for 30 minutes last night at the party."

Make The Beast With Two Backs
USED WITH FRIENDS

To have sex.

EXAMPLE 1
"Dan and I were making the beast with two backs when you called earlier."

EXAMPLE 2
"Dirk and Donna were making the beast with two backs all day. They'll be too tired to go out tonight."

○ **Learn more...**

- During sex, two people make one creature with two backs.

Make Whoopee
USED WITH ANYONE

To have sex.

EXAMPLE 1
"Son, sex is a natural part of life. Your mother and I were making whoopee just last night."

EXAMPLE 2
"It smells strange in this room, like someone was making whoopee in here."

○ **Learn more...**

- This is an old phrase still used today, usually as a joke.

- ABC's T.V. game show "The Newlywed Game" (1966-1974) asked four recently married couples questions about their relationships. The host, Bob Eubanks, always said "make whoopee" instead of "have sex."

Man Juice
USED WITH EXTREME CAUTION

Sperm or fluid from an ejaculation.

EXAMPLE 1
"Wait! You're going to get your man juice all over my new bed!"

EXAMPLE 2
"I'm sorry, but I won't swallow your man juice. I don't care how much you pay me!"

Man Pussy
USED WITH EXTREME CAUTION

A man's anus.

EXAMPLE 1

"Don loves it when I lick his man pussy. It really excites him!"

EXAMPLE 2

"I want to touch your man pussy before we have anal sex."

o **Learn more...**

- This word is used by homosexuals more than heterosexuals.

Man-hater
USED WITH FRIENDS

A woman who hates men.

EXAMPLE 1

"Joan wants equal rights for women, but that doesn't mean she's a man-hater!"

EXAMPLE 2

"I'm a lesbian, so you think I'm a man-hater? My best friend is a guy!"

Manhole Inspector
USED WITH EXTREME CAUTION

A homosexual man.

EXAMPLE 1

"Drew's a manhole inspector. He dates guys, not women."

EXAMPLE 2

"When did you become a manhole inspector? I thought you were heterosexual!"

o **Learn more...**

- Normally, a "manhole" is a hole on a road which goes to the sewer. Here, a "man hole" is the anus.

Maracas
USED WITH FRIENDS

Breasts.

EXAMPLE 1

"That woman asked me if I wanted to touch her maracas. What should I do?"

EXAMPLE 2

"I want to lick Anita's maracas all night long."

o **Learn more...**

- A "maraca" is a musical instrument (shaped like a ball on a stick) that makes a rattling noise when you shake it.

Mary
USED WITH FRIENDS

A homosexual man or a man with feminine qualities.

EXAMPLE 1

"Look at that Mary over there! He's not strong enough to lift his own suitcase!"

EXAMPLE 2

"I'm no Mary! I like to have sex with women."

o **Learn more...**

- This word is used by homosexuals more than heterosexuals.

- On an episode of the popular television show "Seinfeld," George gets very upset when some kids call him a "Mary."

Masochist
USED WITH ANYONE

A person who gets sexual pleasure from pain.

EXAMPLE 1

"I think my husband is a masochist. He asked me to bite him last night!"

EXAMPLE 2

"I'm not a masochist, but I do like rough sex."

Massage Parlor
USED WITH FRIENDS

A place of prostitution.

EXAMPLE 1

"The only girls I have sex with are the girls at the massage parlor."

EXAMPLE 2

"The massages are terrible, but the sex is great at the massage parlor."

o Learn more...

- Because prostitution is illegal in most states, many places of prostitution advertise themselves as "massage parlors."

- There are many "massage parlors" that just give massages!

Master
USED WITH FRIENDS

The dominant or controlling person in a sexual situation.

EXAMPLE 1

"Vanessa's always the master in the bedroom. I just do whatever she says."

EXAMPLE 2

"My master hits me with a whip if I don't do what he wants in bed."

o Learn more...

- The rock group *Depeche Mode* released a song in 1990 entitled "Master and Servant" about sexual and emotional domination.

IN OTHER WORDS...
"MASTURBATE"

Masturbation is an embarrassing topic for most Americans. When men discuss it, they generally joke about it, using creative phrases. They imply the meaning more in how they say the phrase than in what the phrase means.

USE WITH FRIENDS

Beat off (p. 13)

Beat one's meat (p. 13)

Bleed the weasel (p. 17)

Choke the chicken (p. 32)

Collar the cock (p. 35)

Date Rosy Palm and her five sisters (p. 44)

Flog the bishop (p. 68)

Grease the bayonet (p. 88)

Jack off (p. 108)

Jerk off (p. 109)

Jerkin' the gherkin (p. 109)

Milk the chicken (p. 127)

Play with oneself (p. 149)

Polish the knob (p. 150)

Punch the clown (p. 155)

Roll the fuzzy dice (p. 164)

Rub the rod (p. 164)

Shake hands with the governor (p. 174)

Slap the snake (p. 180)

Tickle the tiger (p. 200)

Tune one's organ (p. 204)

Whack off (p. 212)

Whip the weenie (p. 213)

Yank the yak (p. 218)

Matinee
USED WITH FRIENDS

Sex in the afternoon.

EXAMPLE 1

"Keiko invited me to her house this afternoon for a matinee."

EXAMPLE 2

"Sunday afternoon is a great time for a matinee with your boyfriend."

Meat
USED WITH FRIENDS

Penis.

EXAMPLE 1

"Naomi loves my meat. She's always touching it when we're together."

EXAMPLE 2

"Kate is so sexy! I'd love to give her some of my meat."

Meat And Two Vegetables
USED WITH FRIENDS

Penis and testicles.

EXAMPLE 1

"If you're hungry, I've got some meat and two vegetables you can have!"

EXAMPLE 2

"Something is wrong with my meat and two vegetables. I need to see a doctor!"

o **Learn more...**

• This phrase is not used often.

Meat Market
USED WITH FRIENDS

A place where people look for sex.

EXAMPLE 1

"I don't want to go to that bar. It's such a meat market! I just want a beer."

EXAMPLE 2

"My gym is a total meat market! All the women wear makeup and try not to sweat."

o **Learn more...**

• A "meat market" is literally a "place where meat is sold."

Meathead
USED WITH ANYONE

A stupid person.

EXAMPLE 1

"You meathead! You missed the movie!"

EXAMPLE 2

"Oscar is a meathead. He doesn't know the president's name!"

o **Learn more...**

• The character Archie Bunker from the 1970s sitcom "All in the Family" called his son-in-law "Meathead" instead of "Mike."

Melons
USED WITH FRIENDS

Breasts.

EXAMPLE 1

"I would love to see Donna in a bathing suit because she has a great pair of melons."

EXAMPLE 2

"Helen has some ripe melons, and I'm hungry. Oh, yeah!"

o **Learn more...**

• You may also hear "watermelons," "grapefruit," "coconuts," "gourds," or any other large, round object.

Menage A Trois
USED WITH FRIENDS

Sex between three people at the same time.

EXAMPLE 1

"Now I'm dating two women. I wish I could have a menage a trois with both of them!"

EXAMPLE 2

"Barry is my hero because he just had a menage a trois with beautiful, 21-year-old twin sisters."

o Learn more...

- "Menage a trois" is a French phrase meaning "house of three."

Mercy Fuck
USED WITH FRIENDS

To have sex with someone because you feel sorry for him or her.

EXAMPLE 1

"I know it was just a mercy fuck, but I finally had sex with Katrina yesterday."

EXAMPLE 2

"Greg won't stop asking me to have sex with him. I really don't like him, but I may decide to give him a mercy fuck to make him stop."

o Learn more...

- You may also hear "pity fuck."

Milf
USED WITH FRIENDS

A "mom I'd like to fuck" — an attractive mother teenage boys want to have sex with.

EXAMPLE 1

"Sarah's mom is a milf! I really want to have sex with her."

EXAMPLE 2

"My boyfriend wants to have sex with my mother. I wish she wasn't such a milf!"

o Learn more...

- In the popular 1999 movie *American Pie*, a group of high school boys call Stifler's Mom a "milf." Later in the film, the character Finch has sex with her!

Milk Bottles
USED WITH FRIENDS

Breasts.

EXAMPLE 1

"Baby loves Mommy's milk bottles, and so does Daddy."

EXAMPLE 2

"I'm thirsty. Can I take a drink from your milk bottles?"

Milk The Chicken
USED WITH FRIENDS

To masturbate.

EXAMPLE 1

"I like milking the chicken too, but sex is much better if you can get it."

EXAMPLE 2

"Every guy milks the chicken sometime in his life. Masturbation is the best part about being a guy."

Mindfuck
USED WITH EXTREME CAUTION

❶ To mislead or trick someone.

EXAMPLE 1

"Bev is always mindfucking her employees. She promises to give them raises, but never does."

EXAMPLE 2

"Do you want to have sex or not? Stop mindfucking me!"

❷ Something confusing.

EXAMPLE 1

"That movie was a mindfuck! I have no idea what happened."

EXAMPLE 2

"I'm angry at Danny, but I still love him. This is such a mindfuck!"

Missionary Position
USED WITH FRIENDS

A sexual position in which the man is on top, laying down and facing his partner.

EXAMPLE 1

"Mary likes to have sex in the missionary position so she can see Jed's eyes."

EXAMPLE 2

"Eric thinks the missionary position is boring. He likes to have sex while hanging from the ceiling."

Mistress

USED WITH ANYONE

A female sexual partner who is not one's wife.

EXAMPLE 1

"I love Emma, but I enjoy sex with my mistress Sally better."

EXAMPLE 2

"I heard that Charles has a mistress! I hope his wife and children don't know."

Molest

USED WITH ANYONE

To make unwanted sexual contact with someone.

EXAMPLE 1

"I wonder if the priest in my neighborhood is molesting children?"

EXAMPLE 2

"Nadine thinks that anyone who molests children should be killed!"

Money Shot

USED WITH FRIENDS

The scene in pornographic movies where the man ejaculates.

EXAMPLE 1

"We can turn off the video after I see the money shot."

EXAMPLE 2

"That was the longest money shot I have ever seen in a pornographic movie."

o **Learn more...**

• A "money shot" is literally the most important scene, the scene that people will pay to see.

Montezuma's Revenge

USED WITH ANYONE

Diarrhea.

EXAMPLE 1

"As soon as I arrived in Mexico, I got Montezuma's revenge. I spent the next three days in the bathroom."

EXAMPLE 2

"I've heard so many bad stories about people getting Montezuma's revenge that I don't want to go to Mexico anymore."

o **Learn more...**

• Montezuma was the ruler of the Aztec people of Mexico from 1502-1520. Because his people were conquered, his "revenge" is to cause visitors to get sick.

Monthly Visitor

USED WITH FRIENDS

Menstruation.

EXAMPLE 1

"Dorris can't go to the beach because her monthly visitor came early."

EXAMPLE 2

"I've been crying all day. My monthly visitor must be coming."

Moon

USED WITH ANYONE

To show one's naked butt to others.

EXAMPLE 1

"Tom likes to moon people when he gets drunk. I've seen his butt 43 times."

EXAMPLE 2

"I like to moon my sister's friends. She gets so embarrassed!"

Morning-after Pill

USED WITH ANYONE

A drug taken within 72 hours after unprotected sex to prevent pregnancy.

EXAMPLE 1

"My mother doesn't want me to take the morning-after pill. She wants me to have the baby if I'm pregnant."

EXAMPLE 2

"I asked Monique to take the morning-after pill because I forgot to wear a condom."

Mosquito Bites

USED WITH FRIENDS

Small breasts.

EXAMPLE 1

"My last two girlfriends didn't have breasts, they had mosquito bites."

EXAMPLE 2

"Emily can't be in *Playboy* magazine with mosquito bites like those."

Mother

USED WITH FRIENDS

❶ Something very difficult.

EXAMPLE 1

"This test is a mother! I should have studied more."

EXAMPLE 2

"That's a mother of a problem. I don't think you can solve it."

❷ A very bad person.

EXAMPLE 1

"My boss makes me work a lot. He's a real mother!"

EXAMPLE 2

"Chuck's a mother for breaking my computer!"

❸ Learn more...

- This is a nicer way to say "motherfucker" (p. 130).

- The "mother" of something is "the creator or inspiration of something," as seen in the common proverb "Necessity is the mother of invention."

AT THE MOVIES
"MY COUSIN VINNY" (1992)

In the Academy Award-winning comedy *My Cousin Vinny*, starring Joe Pesci, Marisa Tomei and Ralph Macchio, two boys are falsely accused of murder. Because they can't afford an expensive lawyer, their cousin Vinny and his girlfriend attempt to prove the boys' innocence. Much of the movie's humor involves Vinny's New York accent and attitude.

VINNY
"Hey Stan, you're in Ala-Fucking-Bama."

Fucking (p. 77)

—

VINNY
"Everything that guy just said is bullshit."

Bullshit (p. 24)

—

VINNY
"I got thirty fucking minutes to take a shower, get a new suit, get dressed, and get to the fucking courthouse."

Fucking (p. 77)

LISA
"You fucking shower, I'll get your fucking suit."

—

VINNY
"Look, it's either me or them. You're getting fucked one way or the other."

Fucked (p. 76)

—

STAN
"Beans make you fart."

Fart (p. 63)

—

VINNY
"How the fuck did I get into this shit?"

Fuck (p. 72)
Shit (p. 174)

Motherfucker
USED WITH EXTREME CAUTION

A bad person.

EXAMPLE 1

"That motherfucker stole my favorite CD!"

EXAMPLE 2

"You motherfucker! If I see you again, I'll kill you."

o **Learn more...**

- You may also hear "mofo" as in "That mofo tried to kiss my wife!"

- Samuel L. Jackson's character in the 1994 movie *Pulp Fiction* carries a wallet with the words "bad motherfucker" on it.

Motherfucking
USED WITH EXTREME CAUTION

Stupid, terrible, irritating, or anything bad.

EXAMPLE 1

"This motherfucking hotel always loses my reservation!"

EXAMPLE 2

"I took the motherfucking test and failed!"

Motormouth
USED WITH ANYONE

A person who talks too much.

EXAMPLE 1

"If you ask Helen a question, she'll talk forever! She's a motormouth."

EXAMPLE 2

"I'm late for dinner because Trevor is a motormouth. He talked about his car for an hour!"

o **Learn more...**

- If a person's mouth was "motorized," it would go faster and run longer than a regular mouth.

Mr. Happy
USED WITH FRIENDS

Penis.

EXAMPLE 1

"Mr. Happy is always ready for sex with Danielle. She has a great body."

EXAMPLE 2

"Mr. Happy likes to see beautiful women wearing bathing suits!"

o **Learn more...**

- For some reason, men often refer to their penises as if they were people.

Muff
USED WITH EXTREME CAUTION

A woman's pubic area or vagina.

EXAMPLE 1

"Tanya's muff is so sweet! It smells like strawberries."

EXAMPLE 2

"Caitlin's muff gets so wet that we don't need lubrication when we have sex."

o **Learn more...**

- A "muff" is also "a piece of fur or cloth used to keep one's hands warm."

Muff-diver
USED WITH EXTREME CAUTION

A person who likes to perform oral sex on women.

EXAMPLE 1

"My husband is a real muff-diver. He loves to perform oral sex on me, and I'm not complaining!"

EXAMPLE 2

"Jill is a muff-diver? I thought she was heterosexual."

Muffin
USED WITH EXTREME CAUTION

Vagina.

EXAMPLE 1

"Dave says his girlfriend's muffin tastes great."

EXAMPLE 2

"My wife never let's me lick her muffin. Sex is fine, but she doesn't like oral sex."

Munch Box
USED WITH EXTREME CAUTION

To perform oral sex on a woman.

EXAMPLE 1

"My girlfriend is glad I love to munch box. Sometimes she asks me to do it three times a day."

EXAMPLE 2

"The best way to munch box is to spell the alphabet with your tongue. All the women I know love it when I do that."

o **Learn more...**

- You may also hear "munch someone's box" as in "Look at that sexy woman! I would love to munch her box."

- "Munch" is another way to say "eat."

- "Box" (p. 22) is another word for "vagina."

Munch Carpet
USED WITH EXTREME CAUTION

To perform oral sex on a woman.

EXAMPLE 1

"The video I rented last night shows lesbians munching carpet."

EXAMPLE 2

"I would love to munch her carpet. She has a great body."

o **Learn more...**

- You may also hear "munch someone's carpet" as in "If you let me, I'll munch your carpet forever!"

- You may also hear "munch rug," "carpet-muncher," or "rug-muncher."

- "Munch" is another way to say "eat."

- Rugs and carpets are made with short, sometimes tough, threads that resemble pubic hair.

Muscle Mary
USED WITH FRIENDS

A muscular homosexual man who lifts weights in a gym.

EXAMPLE 1

"That muscle Mary is always looking at me. I want to tell him that I'm only here to get exercise, not find dates."

EXAMPLE 2

"David loves going to the gym. He met all of his boyfriends there. He's a big muscle Mary.

o **Learn more...**

- This phrase is used by homosexuals more often than heterosexuals.

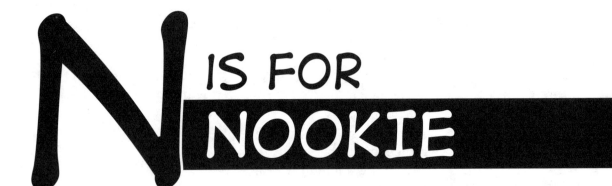

N IS FOR NOOKIE

Nail
USED WITH EXTREME CAUTION

To have sex with someone.

EXAMPLE 1
"I nailed Heather in a coffee shop bathroom yesterday. She loves having sex in public places."

EXAMPLE 2
"When I was 14 years old, I nailed my brother's girlfriend. She was 18 years old and really sexy."

Naked As A Jaybird
USED WITH ANYONE

Totally naked.

EXAMPLE 1
"My mom walked into my bedroom and saw me naked as a jaybird! It was terrible!"

EXAMPLE 2
"Jay and I got naked as jaybirds together. What fun!"

"Nature is calling"
USED WITH ANYONE

"I need to use the bathroom."

EXAMPLE 1
"Mom, can I talk to you later? Nature is calling."

EXAMPLE 2
"Can you take the dog for a walk? I think nature is calling him."

Neck

USED WITH ANYONE

To kiss a lot, usually around the neck and head.

EXAMPLE 1

"Ralph and I necked for over an hour! My lips hurt."

EXAMPLE 2

"I wanted to have sex, but we just necked instead."

Necrophiliac

USED WITH ANYONE

A person who enjoys having sex with dead people.

EXAMPLE 1

"My grandfather was a necrophiliac, so he wasn't upset when my grandmother died."

EXAMPLE 2

"Addison is a necrophiliac! The police caught him in the graveyard digging up bodies."

Nellie

USED WITH FRIENDS

A feminine homosexual man.

EXAMPLE 1

"What a nellie! Did you see the way Malcolm laughed at that joke? He sounds like my sister!"

EXAMPLE 2

"I thought that person was a woman, but it's just a nellie with long hair."

Nerd

USED WITH ANYONE

A smart person, usually with bad social skills.

EXAMPLE 1

"Those nerds wear ugly clothes!"

EXAMPLE 2

"Matt is a nerd. He studies too much and never dates!"

○ **Learn more...**

- You may also hear that someone is "nerdy," as in "Don't wear those glasses. They make you look nerdy."

- In the popular 1984 movie *Revenge of the Nerds*, the college's athletes tease and insult the nerds. Finally, the nerds fight back using their intelligence and defeat the athletes.

Nincompoop

USED WITH ANYONE

A stupid person.

EXAMPLE 1

"You nincompoop! Don't jump in the lake with your clothes on!"

EXAMPLE 2

"David kicked his computer and broke it. What a nincompoop!"

○ **Learn more...**

- This word is often used in cartoons.

Nipple Clips

USED WITH FRIENDS

Clips placed on one's nipples for sexual pleasure.

EXAMPLE 1

"My girlfriend loves the nipple clips I bought her."

EXAMPLE 2

"I would never try nipple clips. They'd hurt too much."

Nitwit

USED WITH ANYONE

A stupid person.

EXAMPLE 1

"Wendy, you nitwit! Give me a hammer, not a flashlight!"

EXAMPLE 2

JASON: "What's the capital of California?"

JILL: "It's Sacramento, you nitwit!"

"No shit!"
USED WITH FRIENDS

❶ "Everyone knows that!"

EXAMPLE 1
"You think Michael Jordan is a good basketball player? No shit!"

EXAMPLE 2
WENDY: "I don't have any money."

GILLIAN: "No shit! You just bought six new dresses!"

❷ Indicates surprise.

EXAMPLE 1
EVE: "I'm getting married!"

STAN: "No shit! That's great!"

EXAMPLE 2
MANNY: "I won two million dollars!"

VIV: "No shit! Can I have some?"

○ Learn more...

• You may also hear "No shit, Sherlock!" to mean "Everyone knows that." This is even more sarcastic because Sherlock Holmes is a famous detective.

No Spring Chicken
USED WITH ANYONE

An old person.

EXAMPLE 1
"I'm no spring chicken, but I can still run five miles a day."

EXAMPLE 2
"Oliver's no spring chicken. He shouldn't be out dancing all night!"

Nocturnal Emission
USED WITH FRIENDS

Ejaculation that happens during sleep.

EXAMPLE 1
"If I don't have sex with Sunish before we go to bed, he'll have a noctural emission in the middle of the night."

EXAMPLE 2
"Kel washes his sheets every day because he has nocturnal emissions."

Nookie
USED WITH FRIENDS

To have sexual contact or sex.

EXAMPLE 1
"I am going to a party tonight with 45 beautiful girls, and I'm going to get some nookie!"

EXAMPLE 2
"Hello, ladies. I'm looking for some nookie. Are any of you interested in spending the night with me?"

○ Learn more...

• The popular musical group *Limp Bizkit* released a song called "Nookie" in 1999 with the chorus "I did it all for the nookie."

Not All There
USED WITH ANYONE

A stupid or strange person.

EXAMPLE 1
DAVE: "Look at that guy fishing in a swimming pool!"

GARY: "He's not all there."

EXAMPLE 2
"Kelly's not all there. I wouldn't ask her to do anything important for you."

Not Cooking On All Four Burners
USED WITH ANYONE

To be crazy or strange.

EXAMPLE 1
"People who pray to Elvis aren't cooking on all four burners."

EXAMPLE 2
"Greg isn't cooking on all four burners. He eats his socks."

○ Learn more...

- Most stoves have four burners, so a person who isn't "cooking on all four burners" isn't using all of their brain.

Not Playing With A Full Deck
USED WITH ANYONE

A crazy or strange person.

EXAMPLE 1
"Anyone who keeps a loaded gun in their car is not playing with a full deck."

EXAMPLE 2
"If you like to eat rocks, you aren't playing with a full deck."

○ Learn more...

- This expression refers to a deck of playing cards which would be useless if the deck was not complete.

Not To Have A Pot To Piss In
USED WITH FRIENDS

To be poor.

EXAMPLE 1
"Six months from now, I won't have a pot to piss in. I'm spending more money than I'm earning!"

EXAMPLE 2
"Rodney hasn't worked for months. He doesn't have a pot to piss in."

Numb-nuts
USED WITH FRIENDS

A stupid person.

EXAMPLE 1
"You numb-nuts! The milk goes in the refrigerator, not in the oven!"

EXAMPLE 2
"Hey, numb-nuts! Bring me another beer."

○ Learn more...

- Only men are called "numb-nuts."

- "Nuts" (p. 136) is a slang word for "testicles."

Number One
USED WITH ANYONE

Urinate.

EXAMPLE 1
"I drank a lot of coffee today. Now I have to go number one."

EXAMPLE 2
FRED: "I just went to the bathroom."

BILL: "Number one?"

○ Learn more...

- This is a nicer way to say "urinate."

- This phrase is often used with children.

DIALOGUE
"NADINE'S NO NYMPHOMANIAC"

Here is a short dialogue between two Americans.

NADINE
"I thought Josh was a nerd, so I asked him to help me with my science project. But when I got to his house last night, he was naked as a jaybird!"

Nerd (p. 133)
Naked as a jaybird (p. 132)

JILL
"No shit! What did you do?"

"No shit!" (p. 134)

NADINE
"We necked for a while, and then I left. I don't want him to think I'm a nymphomaniac."

Neck (p. 133)
Nymphomaniac (p. 136)

Number Two
USED WITH ANYONE

Defecate.

EXAMPLE 1

"The baby went number two in his diapers."

EXAMPLE 2

"I haven't gone number two since Friday!"

o **Learn more...**

- This is a nicer way to say "defecate."

- This phrase is often used with children.

Numbskull
USED WITH ANYONE

A stupid person.

EXAMPLE 1

"You numbskull! Japan is an island, not part of China!"

EXAMPLE 2

"Kim bought a new dress instead of paying rent. What a numbskull!"

Nut Case
USED WITH ANYONE

A crazy or strange person.

EXAMPLE 1

"I can't believe you don't know how to cook eggs. Any nut case knows how to do that!"

EXAMPLE 2

"I'm sorry, but I think your friend Henry is a nut case. He keeps licking my hand."

o **Learn more...**

- You may also hear "nut job" as in "That nut job was driving so fast he almost hit me!"

Nuts
USED WITH ANYONE

❶ **A crazy person.**

EXAMPLE 1

"Helen is nuts! She always takes her clothes off in the movie theater."

EXAMPLE 2

"If you think I'm going to jump out of an airplane, you're nuts!"

❷ **Testicles.**

EXAMPLE 1

"I just paid a prostitute $20 to lick my nuts."

EXAMPLE 2

"I was dating that guy for a while, but his nuts were so big that they scared me. I had to leave him."

o **Learn more...**

- You may also hear "nutty" to mean "crazy" as in "That is a nutty idea, it will never work."

- The 1996 movie *The Nutty Professor*, starring Eddie Murphy, is about a crazy scientist.

Nymphomaniac
USED WITH ANYONE

A woman who wants to have sex all the time.

EXAMPLE 1

"Sally is a nyphomaniac! I can't keep her satisfied."

EXAMPLE 2

"Some day I want to date a nymphomaniac. If a women wanted to have sex as much as I do, we'd never leave the bedroom!"

o **Learn more...**

- You may also hear the shortened version "nympho."

- In the 1800s, many women were told they had "nymphomania" because it was considered abnormal for women to want or enjoy sex as much as men did. Back then, people thought it was a medical problem.

- The medical word for men who want sex all the time is "satyriasis," but it's almost never used. It's considered normal for men to want sex all the time.

O IS FOR ORGY

Off One's Rocker

USED WITH ANYONE

Crazy or strange.

EXAMPLE 1
"You're off your rocker if you think the president is doing a good job."

EXAMPLE 2
"Bill's off his rocker if he thinks I'm afraid of him. I'll fight him anytime."

Off The Deep End

USED WITH ANYONE

To become crazy.

EXAMPLE 1
"Terry went off the deep end. She's screaming at the boss!"

EXAMPLE 2
"My mother has finally gone off the deep end. She wants me to clean the entire house by tomorrow!"

Off The Wagon

USED WITH ANYONE

To drink alcohol after trying to stop.

EXAMPLE 1
"Dan was definitely off the wagon when I saw him. He was carrying three bottles of wine!"

EXAMPLE 2
"I fell off the wagon last night and had some beer."

Off-color
USED WITH ANYONE

Offensive.

EXAMPLE 1

"You shouldn't tell off-color jokes. Someone may get angry."

EXAMPLE 2

"This magazine has many off-color articles. I don't like it!"

"Oh, hell!"
USED WITH FRIENDS

Indicates frustration or loss.

EXAMPLE 1

"Oh, hell! I think I lost my wedding ring."

EXAMPLE 2

"Oh, hell. Alice's mother just died."

o **Learn more...**

• You may also hear "Aw, hell!"

Old Maid
USED WITH ANYONE

An older woman who never married.

EXAMPLE 1

"Why would Henry date that old maid? She must be 20 years older than him."

EXAMPLE 2

"Cassie would rather die an old maid than marry a man she doesn't love."

On Someone's Ass
USED WITH FRIENDS

To pressure someone constantly.

EXAMPLE 1

"My dad is on my ass to get a job, but I just want to party!"

EXAMPLE 2

"Jessie won't finish the report unless you stay on her ass."

On The Make
USED WITH ANYONE

To look for sex.

EXAMPLE 1

"Mary is on the make again after sleeping in the street all afternoon."

EXAMPLE 2

"I love to watch all the men on the make in the nightclub. They'll do anything to have sex!"

On The Sauce
USED WITH ANYONE

To drink alcohol on a regular basis.

EXAMPLE 1

"I think Dave is on the sauce again. When he called this morning, he sounded drunk."

EXAMPLE 2

"Hey, you're not on the sauce again, are you? You're going to get fired!"

On The Wagon
USED WITH ANYONE

To stop drinking alcohol.

EXAMPLE 1

"Ben is back on the wagon after the police arrested him for driving his car while he was drunk."

EXAMPLE 2

"Kendra is on the wagon again. She hasn't had a beer in three weeks."

One-eyed Monster
USED WITH FRIENDS

Penis.

EXAMPLE 1

"I took my one-eyed monster out of my pants, and Julia started laughing."

EXAMPLE 2

"Karl's one-eyed monster is seven inches long."

o **Learn more...**

• You may also hear "one-eyed wonder."

Open A Can Of Whoop-ass
USED WITH FRIENDS

To become aggressive.

EXAMPLE 1

"We were losing the game until we opened a can of whoop-ass and scored fifteen points!"

EXAMPLE 2

"Don't make me open a can of whoop-ass. I'll beat you until you cry!"

Opposite Sex
USED WITH ANYONE

One's opposite gender.

EXAMPLE 1

"I'm heterosexual. I'm only interested in the opposite sex."

EXAMPLE 2

"Lisa's only eight years old. We have a few more years before she starts noticing the opposite sex."

Orgy
USED WITH ANYONE

Group sex.

EXAMPLE 1

"I got invited to an orgy. How many condoms should I bring?"

EXAMPLE 2

"Orgies are fun. You can't tell who you're touching or who is touching you!"

Out Of It
USED WITH ANYONE

❶ Crazy or strange.

EXAMPLE 1

"That woman is talking to a sock! She's really out of it."

EXAMPLE 2

"That guy is out of it. He's wearing a hat on his foot."

❷ To be unable to focus on the current situation.

EXAMPLE 1

"I'm sorry. Can you please say that again? I'm out of it today."

EXAMPLE 2

"The medicine my mother takes makes her out of it. She just watches T.V. for hours."

Out Of One's Mind
USED WITH ANYONE

Crazy or strange.

EXAMPLE 1

"My father is out of his mind! Whenever we go to a restaurant for dinner, he steals something."

EXAMPLE 2

"If Reggie thinks I want to marry him, he's out of his mind. I would never marry him."

❍ Learn more...

- You may also hear "out of one's head," "out of one's gourd," and "out of one's skull."

Out There
USED WITH ANYONE

Crazy or strange.

EXAMPLE 1

"My uncle thinks he's a doctor and a nurse. He's really out there."

IN OTHER WORDS...
"ORGASM"

The technical word is "orgasm," and many people use that word even in romantic or sexual situations. Here are some other options.

USED WITH ANYONE

Climax (p. 33)

USED WITH FRIENDS

La petite mort (p. 115)

The big "O" (p. 195)

USED WITH EXTREME CAUTION

Bust a nut (p. 26)

Cream (p. 40)

Cream one's jeans (p. 40)

Cum (p. 41)

Get off (p. 82)

Get one's rocks off (p. 82)

EXAMPLE 2

"Van Gogh was a great artist, but he was out there. I can't imagine cutting off my own ear!"

Out To Lunch
USED WITH ANYONE

Crazy or strange.

EXAMPLE 1

"Don't ask Mindy for help. She's been out to lunch since her husband left her."

EXAMPLE 2

"I asked Kavi a question during the meeting, but he was out to lunch. I think he was sleeping with his eyes open!"

Over The Hill
USED WITH ANYONE

Very old.

EXAMPLE 1

"I was a football player when I was young, but now I'm over the hill."

EXAMPLE 2

SALLY: "Dad will be 70 years old tomorrow."

BOB: "He's over the hill!"

Overcoat
USED WITH FRIENDS

A condom.

EXAMPLE 1

"Rachel doesn't want to get pregnant. She won't let my penis outside of my pants without an overcoat."

EXAMPLE 2

"I wore my overcoat while we had sex so I wouldn't get any diseases."

P IS FOR PISSED OFF

P.O.'d
USED WITH ANYONE

Angry.

EXAMPLE 1
"I'm P.O.'d that Stacy ruined my sweater!"

EXAMPLE 2
"Dan got P.O.'d because I forgot to return his bicycle."

o Learn more...

- This is a nicer way to say "pissed off" (p. 146).

- Pronounced "P-O'd."

Package
USED WITH FRIENDS

The testicles and penis.

EXAMPLE 1
"I'll bet that my package is bigger than anyone else's in this room."

EXAMPLE 2
"I need to find a man with a package big enough to satisfy me."

Pain In The Ass
USED WITH FRIENDS

o An annoying person.

EXAMPLE 1
"Kevin is a pain in the ass. He asks too many questions!"

EXAMPLE 2

"My mom is a pain in the ass. She won't let me go to the party because I didn't clean my room."

❷ **Annoying.**

EXAMPLE 1

"My pain-in-the-ass brother hid my cell phone."

EXAMPLE 2

"Did your pain-in-the-ass boss make you work late again?"

Party Hat
USED WITH FRIENDS

A condom.

EXAMPLE 1

"Stacy and I are going to have sex tonight, so I'm bringing a party hat."

EXAMPLE 2

"Linda said we aren't going to party if I don't wear my party hat."

Pass Gas
USED WITH ANYONE

To expel gas from the anus; to flatulate.

EXAMPLE 1

"If you must pass gas, please go outside so it won't smell in here."

EXAMPLE 2

"Joan passes gas so much that she had to buy six air fresheners for her apartment."

○ **Learn more...**

• This is a polite way to say "fart" (p. 63).

Pat
USED WITH FRIENDS

A person who looks both male and female.

EXAMPLE 1

"My history teacher is a Pat. He looks like a man and a woman."

EXAMPLE 2

"I don't know if that is a woman or a man! It's Pat."

○ **Learn more...**

• "Pat" can be a woman's name or a man's name.

• The T.V. show "Saturday Night Live" featured a skit called "It's Pat" where people tried to determine the gender of the character "Pat."

Pearl Necklace
USED WITH EXTREME CAUTION

Sperm ejaculated onto a person's neck (that looks like a necklace of pearls).

EXAMPLE 1

"I know I don't have a lot of money, but I can give you a lot of pearl necklaces!"

EXAMPLE 2

"That's a nice ring, Jill. The only thing my boyfriend will give me on our anniversary is a pearl necklace."

Pecker
USED WITH FRIENDS

Penis.

EXAMPLE 1

"When I hugged Nathan after the movie, I could feel his pecker against my leg. I guess he really liked the movie!"

EXAMPLE 2

"Jake likes it when I play with his pecker using my feet."

Peckerhead
USED WITH FRIENDS

A nasty or irritating person.

EXAMPLE 1

"My dad is a real peckerhead. He divorced my mom and married his secretary!"

EXAMPLE 2

"You're such a peckerhead! You never buy me flowers."

○ **Learn more...**

• Only men are called "peckerheads."

Pederast
USED WITH ANYONE

A man who has sex or anal sex with a boy.

EXAMPLE 1

"I heard Michael is a pederast! Don't let him babysit your children."

EXAMPLE 2

"Billy is only six, and you want to have sex with him? You pederast! "

Pedophile
USED WITH ANYONE

An adult who is sexually attracted to children.

EXAMPLE 1

"Most pedophiles get jobs where they can be close to children."

EXAMPLE 2

"Pedophiles like to touch little boys and girls in a sexual way."

Pee
USED WITH ANYONE

❶ Urine.

EXAMPLE 1

"I smell pee. Did you let your cat use my carpet as a toilet?"

EXAMPLE 2

"There's pee in the kitchen. Trevor was too drunk to find the bathroom last night."

❷ To urinate.

EXAMPLE 1

"My new dog pees everywhere. Yesterday, he peed on my dinner!"

EXAMPLE 2

"The doctor asked me to pee in a cup and give it to the nurse."

Pee-pee
USED WITH ANYONE

❶ Penis.

EXAMPLE 1

"Little Michael has the smallest pee-pee I've ever seen."

EXAMPLE 2

"I took a picture of my boyfriend's pee-pee when he was sleeping."

❷ To urinate.

EXAMPLE 1

"We're about to get on the airplane. Does anyone have to go pee-pee first?"

EXAMPLE 2

"Angela went pee-pee in her diapers. Can you change them for me?"

❸ Urine.

EXAMPLE 1

"Johnny's clothes smell like pee-pee."

EXAMPLE 2

"Is that pee-pee or juice on your clothes?"

❍ Learn more...

- This phrase is usually used by children or adults talking to children.

DIALOGUE
"WHAT A PAIN IN THE ASS"

Here is a short dialogue between two Americans.

SHELLEY
"My boss is a psycho. He pissed off the president of the company, so now I have to work all weekend. What a pain in the ass!"

Psycho (p. 154)
Pissed off (p. 146)
Pain in the ass (p. 141)

KEN
"My boss is worse. He's such a pervert that all the women in our department quit. No one wants to work for such a piece of shit."

Pervert (p. 144)
Piece of shit (p. 144)

SHELLEY
"Come on, let's go piss away our salaries at the bar."

Piss away (p. 146)

Peeping Tom
USED WITH ANYONE

A person who likes to secretly watch other people.

EXAMPLE 1

"Barbara saw a peeping Tom looking at her when she stepped out of the shower naked."

EXAMPLE 2

"The police found the peeping Tom in a tree outside the women's college."

Period
USED WITH ANYONE

Menstruation.

EXAMPLE 1

"I thought I was pregnant, but I just got my period."

EXAMPLE 2

"I don't want to get married at the end of the month because that's when I get my period."

Pervert
USED WITH ANYONE

A person whose sexual behavior is considered socially unacceptable.

EXAMPLE 1

"That pervert was under the stairs looking up my dress."

EXAMPLE 2

"Only a pervert would sell pictures of naked children."

○ **Learn more...**

- You may also hear the shortened version "perv" as in "That guy on the subway touched my butt. What a perv!"

Peter
USED WITH FRIENDS

Penis.

EXAMPLE 1

"My peter is cold. I stood out in the rain too long!"

EXAMPLE 2

"I told Gregor I never want his peter in my mouth again."

Peter-eater
USED WITH FRIENDS

A person who enjoys performing oral sex on a man.

EXAMPLE 1

"My boyfriend thinks I'm a peter-eater machine. He always wants me to suck his penis."

EXAMPLE 2

"The best peter-eater is a gay man. He knows best how to perform oral sex on a man."

Pick Up
USED WITH ANYONE

To flirt or try to attract another person.

EXAMPLE 1

"I picked up a girl yesterday at the supermarket. We were both buying beer, so we started talking."

EXAMPLE 2

"Keaver was so drunk, I wasn't sure if he was trying to pick me up or get me to drive him home."

Piddle
USED WITH ANYONE

To urinate.

EXAMPLE 1

"That little dog piddles everywhere in the house."

EXAMPLE 2

"Little Danny piddled again. Get a towel to clean it."

Piece Of Shit
USED WITH FRIENDS

❶ **A nasty person.**

EXAMPLE 1

"Geof is a piece of shit. He'll do anything to get what he wants."

EXAMPLE 2

"Tallia is mean to everyone. She's a real piece of shit!"

❷ **Worthless.**

EXAMPLE 1
"This T.V. is a piece of shit. I can't get it to work!"

EXAMPLE 2
"Felicia's car won't start. What a piece of shit!"

Pig
USED WITH ANYONE

A fat or nasty person.

EXAMPLE 1
"That pig asked for my phone number! I told him I don't have a phone."

EXAMPLE 2
"Why would a woman like that be interested in a pig like him?"

○ **Learn more...**

• You may also hear "fat pig" or "porker."

Pigfuck
USED WITH EXTREME CAUTION

A disaster.

EXAMPLE 1
"There's no more beer or food. This party is a pigfuck!"

EXAMPLE 2
"The meeting was a pigfuck. Everyone started yelling at the same time."

Pillow-biter
USED WITH EXTREME CAUTION

A homosexual man.

EXAMPLE 1
"That pillow-biter wants to have sex with Bill and Grant at the same time."

EXAMPLE 2
"I tried being a pillow-biter once in college, but I didn't like it."

Pimp
USED WITH ANYONE

A person who finds customers for prostitutes; a prostitute's manager.

EXAMPLE 1
"If you want to hire a prostitute, you need to talk to a pimp first!"

EXAMPLE 2
"A pink fur coat? You look like a pimp in that outfit!"

○ **Learn more...**

• "Pimps" are usually men.

• "Pimps" are famous for their outrageous clothes.

Pimp Slap
USED WITH FRIENDS

To slap someone as if he or she is less important.

EXAMPLE 1
"I'm going to pimp slap you until you cry."

EXAMPLE 2
"Come over here so I can pimp slap you."

○ **Learn more...**

• Traditionally, a "bitch slap" described the way a "pimp" (see previous entry) hit his prostitutes.

Pinch A Loaf
USED WITH FRIENDS

To defecate.

EXAMPLE 1
"Mark was so drunk last night that he pinched a loaf in his bed."

EXAMPLE 2
"I just pinched the biggest loaf ever! It won't go down the toilet."

Pinhead
USED WITH ANYONE

A stupid person.

EXAMPLE 1
"Sam sat on his guitar and broke it. What a pinhead!"

EXAMPLE 2
"You pinhead! I wanted coffee, not soda!"

o **Learn more...**
- A "pinhead" has a head and brains the size of a pin.

Pipsqueak
USED WITH ANYONE

A very small, weak person.

EXAMPLE 1
"You must be a pipsqueak if you can't lift this box."

EXAMPLE 2
"My younger brother is a pipsqueak. He's only six years old."

Piss
USED WITH FRIENDS

To urinate.

EXAMPLE 1
"I have to piss. Where's the bathroom?"

EXAMPLE 2
"Don't piss on the flowers. You'll kill them!"

o **Learn more...**
- You may also hear "go to the pisser."

Piss Away
USED WITH FRIENDS

To lose or ruin something.

EXAMPLE 1
"Dad says I'll piss away my future if I don't go to college."

EXAMPLE 2
"Adam had $200,000 but he pissed it away in Las Vegas while gambling."

Piss Hard-on
USED WITH FRIENDS

An erect penis caused by the need to urinate.

EXAMPLE 1
"I always get a piss hard-on in the morning. It makes it hard to urinate without hitting the wall!"

EXAMPLE 2
"Fred woke me up when his piss hard-on poked me in the back while we were sleeping."

"Piss on that!"
USED WITH FRIENDS

"Absolutely not!"

EXAMPLE 1
"The boss wants us to work on the weekend. Piss on that! I won't do it."

EXAMPLE 2
"Piss on that! I'm not going to buy you dinner if you won't have sex with me."

Piss-poor
USED WITH FRIENDS

Terrible.

EXAMPLE 1
"I had a few ideas for the new project, but they were really piss-poor."

EXAMPLE 2
"The bridge broke because the guy who built it did a piss-poor job."

Pissant
USED WITH FRIENDS

A worthless person.

EXAMPLE 1
"Tommy's a pissant. He'll never get a raise."

EXAMPLE 2
"You pissant. You'll never find a woman."

o **Learn more...**
- Pronounced "piss-ant."

Pissed Off
USED WITH FRIENDS

Angry.

EXAMPLE 1
"Barbara broke my camera. I'm so pissed off at her!"

EXAMPLE 2
"Gary got really pissed off when I ended our relationship."

o Learn more...

- You may also hear the shortened version "pissed" as in "You lied to me? Yes, I'm pissed!"

Pisser
USED WITH FRIENDS

o A frustrating event.

EXAMPLE 1
"The bus came two hours late. What a pisser!"

EXAMPLE 2
"What a pisser! I have to work late tonight."

❷ The bathroom.

EXAMPLE 1
"Hold my coat, please. I'm going to the pisser."

EXAMPLE 2
"I have to go to the pisser before we leave."

Pistol
USED WITH FRIENDS

Penis.

EXAMPLE 1
"I want to have sex tonight, so make sure your pistol is ready!"

EXAMPLE 2
"Jerry's pistol is much smaller than I thought it would be."

IN OTHER WORDS...
"PENIS"

Most of the words for penis are based on its shape — long and thick. In fact, almost anything can look like a penis, including a train, the Eiffel Tower, or a rocket. If the object is moving back and forth or up and down, even better!

USED WITH ANYONE

Pee-pee (p. 143)

Tool (p. 201)

USED WITH FRIENDS

Battering ram (p. 12)

Bazooka (p. 12)

Blue-veined throbber (p. 19)

Bone (p. 19)

Cucumber (p. 41)

Cyclops (p. 42)

Dick (p. 46)

Dipstick (p. 47)

Dong (p. 52)

Equipment (p. 59)

Hose (p. 104)

Johnson (p. 110)

Joystick (p. 110)

Junior (p. 111)

Meat (p. 126)

Mr. Happy (p. 130)

One-eyed monster (p. 138)

Pecker (p. 142)

Peter (p. 144)

Pistol (p. 147)

Pole (p. 150)

Ramrod (p. 160)

Rod (p. 163)

Salami (p. 167)

Shlong (p. 177)

Staff (p. 187)

Thing (p. 198)

Third leg (p. 198)

Trouser snake (p. 203)

Unit (p. 206)

Wiener (p. 214)

Willie (p. 215)

USED WITH EXTREME CAUTION

Cock (p. 34)

Love muscle (p. 121)

Prick (p. 154)

Pitch A Tent
USED WITH FRIENDS

To have an erect penis.

EXAMPLE 1
"I saw Sharon naked so I was pitching a tent for the rest of the day."

EXAMPLE 2
"I don't like to go to the department store with Hank because the cute women cause him to pitch a tent in his pants."

o **Learn more...**

- An erect penis in a man's pants looks like a small tent.

Pitcher
USED WITH FRIENDS

For homosexual men, the man who penetrates the other man with his penis.

EXAMPLE 1
"I heard Perry is a pitcher. He'll never let you penetrate him."

EXAMPLE 2
BEN: "I like to pitch."

CURTIS: "Great, I like pitchers!"

o **Learn more...**

- In baseball, the "pitcher" throws balls towards the "catcher" (p. 30).

Pizza-face
USED WITH FRIENDS

A person with a lot of acne or acne scars on his or her face.

EXAMPLE 1
"Hey, pizza-face! Buy some soap!"

EXAMPLE 2
"I have so much acne! I'm going to be a pizza-face soon."

Plant One On Someone
USED WITH ANYONE

To kiss someone.

EXAMPLE 1
"I haven't seen you in months! Come over here and plant one on me."

EXAMPLE 2
"When I saw Paul last night, he planted one on me without asking!"

Plastered
USED WITH ANYONE

Drunk.

EXAMPLE 1
"I just got fired. I want to get plastered tonight!"

EXAMPLE 2
"Should we go see a movie or get plastered at Edith's party?"

Platonic
USED WITH ANYONE

Non-sexual.

EXAMPLE 1
"My relationship with Dave's sister is just platonic."

EXAMPLE 2
"Nate and I are no longer dating. Our relationship is just platonic now."

Play Bouncy-Bouncy
USED WITH FRIENDS

To have sex.

EXAMPLE 1
"Amanda's breasts are so big, it's fun to play bouncy-bouncy with her."

EXAMPLE 2
"I walked into my mom's bedroom and saw her playing bouncy-bouncy with our neighbor. I'm going to tell dad!"

Play Doctor
USED WITH FRIENDS

To pretend to be a doctor and a patient while engaging in sexual activities.

EXAMPLE 1
"Lucy and I were playing doctor last night. She has a great body!"

EXAMPLE 2

"When I was eight years old, my best friend wanted to play doctor. I showed her my penis and she screamed!"

Play "Hide The Sausage"
USED WITH FRIENDS

To have sex.

EXAMPLE 1

"Lisa comes to my house every Monday night to play 'hide the sausage' with me."

EXAMPLE 2

"Jeff is crazy if he thinks I am going to play 'hide the sausage' with him on the first date."

○ **Learn more...**

• "Sausage" is a slang word for "penis."

Play The Skin Flute
USED WITH FRIENDS

To perform oral sex on a man.

EXAMPLE 1

"Melinda promised to play the skin flute for me tonight. It's been so long since I've had oral sex!"

EXAMPLE 2

"Homosexual men are the best at playing the skin flute, since they know what feels good."

Play Tonsil Hockey
USED WITH FRIENDS

To kiss deeply using tongues.

EXAMPLE 1

"We played tonsil hockey for a while, then had sex."

EXAMPLE 2

"I hate it when Carl tries to play tonsil hockey. His tongue is huge!"

○ **Learn more...**

• "Tonsils" are located at the back of the mouth, near the throat. When you "play tonsil hockey," you are joking that your tongue is so far in your partner's mouth that you could play with his or her tonsils like a hockey player plays with a hockey puck.

Play With Oneself
USED WITH FRIENDS

To masturbate.

EXAMPLE 1

"I enjoy playing with myself, but I hate cleaning the mess after."

EXAMPLE 2

"I wonder if anyone knows I am playing with myself in the bathroom?"

○ **Learn more...**

• You may also hear "stroke oneself" as in "I cannot stop stroking myself. I do it all day long because it feels so good."

Plays For The Other Team
USED WITH ANYONE

To be homosexual.

EXAMPLE 1

"I heard Gary won't date Ellie because he plays for the other team."

EXAMPLE 2

"I can't possibly be the man that raped that woman, officer. I play for the other team!"

○ **Learn more...**

• You may also hear "pitches for the other team."

P-M-S
USED WITH ANYONE

Pre-Menstrual Syndrome, the time just before a woman begins menstruating.

EXAMPLE 1

"I've been feeling depressed lately. I hope it's just P-M-S."

EXAMPLE 2

"Every time I get angry at work, my boss asks if it's P-M-S. It's not fair!"

○ **Learn more...**

• You may also hear "P-M-S-ing" as in "I hate being around my mother when she's P-M-S-ing. She yells at me for everything."

Pocket Pool
USED WITH FRIENDS

To masturbate using a pocket in one's pants.

EXAMPLE 1

"The teacher found Gary playing pocket pool in class."

EXAMPLE 2

"Rick always has his hands in his pockets. I think he's playing pocket pool."

Poke
USED WITH FRIENDS

❶ To have sex.

EXAMPLE 1

"I poked Nina in every sexual position we knew."

EXAMPLE 2

"I hate Bill. He poked my wife while I was on a business trip last year."

❷ A session of sex.

EXAMPLE 1

"Anne had a terrible day at work. She wants a good poke tonight to make her happy."

EXAMPLE 2

"Mandy is coming over early for a quick poke before we go to dinner."

⊙ Learn more...

- You may also hear "poke in the hay."

Pole
USED WITH FRIENDS

Penis.

EXAMPLE 1

"Your girlfriend told me you have a small pole. Is it true?"

EXAMPLE 2

"Maggie was touching my pole during the whole movie."

Polish The Knob
USED WITH FRIENDS

To masturbate.

EXAMPLE 1

"All Jose ever does is talk about women. He should just go home and polish the knob."

EXAMPLE 2

"If I have to spend another Friday night polishing the knob, I'm going to scream."

⊙ Learn more...

- You may also hear "polish the lance" as in "My date cancelled tonight, so I guess I will stay home and polish the lance."

Polluted
USED WITH ANYONE

Drunk.

EXAMPLE 1

"I got so polluted that I was vomiting all night."

EXAMPLE 2

"Frank was completely polluted after drinking those three bottles of wine."

Poo-Poo
USED WITH ANYONE

Excrement.

EXAMPLE 1

"Little Lisa has dog poo-poo all over her face."

EXAMPLE 2

"The poo-poo smell is still in the car. We should buy an air freshener."

⊙ Learn more...

- Children use this phrase more often than adults.

Poonani
USED WITH EXTREME CAUTION

Vagina; sex with a woman.

EXAMPLE 1

"Richard only calls me when he wants some poonani."

EXAMPLE 2

"I'm going out for poonani, and I'm not coming home until I get some."

Poontang
USED WITH EXTREME CAUTION

Vagina; sex with a woman.

EXAMPLE 1

"Vera won't return my calls because she thinks I only want her poontang."

EXAMPLE 2

"The only thing most men care about is poontang."

○ **Learn more...**

• You may also hear the shortened expressions "poon" or "tang."

Poop

USED WITH ANYONE

❶ **To defecate.**

EXAMPLE 1

"Did you poop today, Sally?"

EXAMPLE 2

"Jonathan pooped in his pants!"

❷ **Indicates frustration.**

EXAMPLE 1

"Oh, poop! I missed Tracy's phone call."

EXAMPLE 2

"Poop! I should have studied more for the test."

❸ **Details.**

EXAMPLE 1

"Tell me the poop on what happened last night."

EXAMPLE 2

"What's the poop on the new person in the sales department?"

❹ **Excrement.**

EXAMPLE 1

"Hank's dog left a pile of poop on my lawn! Hank should come over and pick it up."

AT THE MOVIES
"PULP FICTION" (1994)

The Academy Award-winning movie *Pulp Fiction* tells the violent but funny stories of two mobsters, a boxer, and two thieves. The movie jumps from story to story, and only at the end do we see how all the characters fit together. Directed by Quentin Tarantino, the movie stars Samuel L. Jackson, Bruce Willis, John Travolta, and Uma Thurman.

JULES
"Eating a bitch out and giving a bitch a foot massage ain't even the same fucking thing."

Eat someone out (p. 58)
Bitch (p. 16)
Fucking (p. 77)

—

YOLANDA
"Any of you fucking pricks move, and I'll execute every motherfucking last one of you."

Fucking (p. 77)
Prick (p. 154)
Motherfucking (p. 130)

—

JIMMIE
"Dorks. They look like a couple of dorks."

Dork (p. 52)

—

VINCENT
"Hey, look man, I didn't mean to shoot the son of a bitch!"

Son of a bitch (p. 184)

—

JULES
"Well believe it now, motherfucker! We gotta get this car off the road. You know cops tend to notice shit like you're driving a car drenched in fucking blood."

Motherfucker (p. 130)
Shit (p. 174)
Fucking (p. 77)

—

JULES
"Oh man, I will never forgive your ass for this. This is some fucked-up, repugnant shit!"

Ass (p. 4)
Fucked-up (p. 77)
Shit (p. 174)

EXAMPLE 2

"Stop playing with the cat's poop, Willy!"

o Learn more...

- This is a nicer way to say "shit" (p. 174).

- This word is often used with children to describe defecation.

Poop Chute
USED WITH FRIENDS

Anus.

EXAMPLE 1

"Martha won't let me put anything in her poop chute during sex."

EXAMPLE 2

"Jamison stuck a cucumber in his poop chute and couldn't get it out. What an idiot!"

Pop Someone's Cherry
USED WITH FRIENDS

To have sex with a woman who is a virgin.

EXAMPLE 1

"Maya won't let me pop her cherry, and we've been dating for three years!"

EXAMPLE 2

"When I was in high school, I popped more cherries than any of my friends."

o Learn more...

- The blood that comes out of a woman's vagina when she has sex for the first time is red like a cherry.

Porn
USED WITH ANYONE

Sexual material (books, movies, pictures, etc.).

EXAMPLE 1

"Did you bring me any porn? I want to look at nude women!"

EXAMPLE 2

"I don't like porn. I like having sex, but I don't want to watch other people doing it!"

o Learn more...

- This is another way to say "pornography" (p. 152).

- You may also hear "porno," which usually refers to pornographic movies.

Pornographic
USED WITH ANYONE

Sexually explicit.

EXAMPLE 1

"That painting is pornographic. You can see the woman's breasts!"

EXAMPLE 2

"I want to pose naked for a pornographic magazine, but my husband will be angry if he sees it."

Pornography
USED WITH ANYONE

Sexual material (books, movies, pictures, etc.).

EXAMPLE 1

"Your photographs aren't pornography. The people are nude, but they're not very sexual."

EXAMPLE 2

"You can't survive being a teenage boy without a lot of pornography!"

Pot
USED WITH FRIENDS

Toilet or bathroom.

EXAMPLE 1

"Why can't I find the pot? I have to urinate so bad it hurts."

EXAMPLE 2

"The pot is really dirty. You should go somewhere else."

o Learn more...

- "Pot" is also slang for "marijuana."

Potty
USED WITH ANYONE

Toilet or bathroom.

EXAMPLE 1
"We should go home soon. Sally needs to use the potty."

EXAMPLE 2
"Mommy, the potty is too high for me to sit on! Can you help me?"

○ **Learn more...**
- This is usually said when speaking to children, or a term that children use to say "toilet."

Powder One's Nose
USED WITH ANYONE

To go to the bathroom in order to urinate or defecate.

EXAMPLE 1
"Excuse me while I powder my nose."

EXAMPLE 2
"Martha is in the bathroom powdering her nose. She'll be out in a minute."

○ **Learn more...**
- Women sometimes say this when they want to check their makeup ("powder their noses").

Powder Room
USED WITH ANYONE

The bathroom.

EXAMPLE 1
"Why do women spend so much time in the powder room?"

EXAMPLE 2
"Sheena has been gone a long time. How much can she do in the powder room?"

Pray To The Porcelain God
USED WITH ANYONE

To vomit.

EXAMPLE 1
"You can't go into the bathroom yet. Ben is still praying to the porcelain god."

IN OTHER WORDS...
"PROSTITUTION"

Ah, prostitution. One of the oldest professions in the world. Americans go to these places if they're willing to pay for sex!

Prostitutes (male and female) have a lot of names, too.

USED WITH ANYONE

Bordello (p. 21)
Brothel (p. 23)
House of ill repute (p. 105)
Red-light district (p. 161)

USED WITH FRIENDS

Cathouse (p. 30)
Chicken ranch (p. 31)
Hook shop (p. 102)
Massage parlor (p. 125)
Service station (p. 173)
Whorehouse (p. 214)

USED WITH ANYONE

Gigolo (p. 84)
Lady of the evening (p. 116)
Streetwalker (p. 189)
Working girl (p. 216)

USED WITH FRIENDS

Ass-peddler (p. 6)
Call boy (p. 29)
Call girl (p. 29)
Ho (p. 101)
Hooker (p. 102)
Whore (p. 214)

EXAMPLE 2

"The last time I drank vodka, I was praying to the porcelain god all night. I'll never drink it again!"

o Learn more...

- You may also hear "pray to the porcelain goddess."

- Most toilets are made of porcelain, and when one vomits in a toilet, one kneels in front of it as if the toilet were a god.

Precum
USED WITH FRIENDS

A small amount of fluid that comes out of the penis before orgasm.

EXAMPLE 1

"I removed my penis from her vagina before orgasm, so it must have been some precum that got her pregnant."

EXAMPLE 2

"My girlfriend stopped performing oral sex on me when some precum got into her mouth."

Premature Ejaculation
USED WITH ANYONE

Ejaculation that happens before sex or sexual contact begins.

EXAMPLE 1

"T.J. suffers from premature ejaculation, but he won't see a doctor. His wife hasn't had an orgasm in almost two years!"

EXAMPLE 2

"Premature ejaculation is embarrassing to men who have it, and frustrating for their sexual partners."

Prick
USED WITH EXTREME CAUTION

o Penis.

EXAMPLE 1

"Amelia only dates men with big pricks. She doesn't care what the guys look like."

EXAMPLE 2

"Put your prick back in your pants! We're not having sex tonight."

o A rude or nasty man.

EXAMPLE 1

"You prick! You ate the last piece of pizza!"

EXAMPLE 2

"Johnson is a prick. He stole my promotion!"

Private Parts
USED WITH ANYONE

Genitals.

EXAMPLE 1

"When I was a young boy, my neighbor would always try to touch my private parts."

EXAMPLE 2

"You need a bathing suit to cover all of your private parts."

o Learn more...

- You may also hear "privates" as in "Donna touched my privates during the movie. She likes me!"

- Radio personality Howard Stern called his autobiography and movie "Private Parts."

Psycho
USED WITH ANYONE

o A crazy person.

EXAMPLE 1

"My old boyfriend is a psycho. He follows me everywhere I go and takes pictures of me."

EXAMPLE 2

JAY: "You psycho! Stop touching me!"

BILL: "Relax. I'm just trying to get you upset."

JAY: "It worked."

❷ Crazy.

EXAMPLE 1

"I'm going to go psycho if my mother tells me to get a job one more time!"

EXAMPLE 2

"My psycho boss wants me to work 18 hours a day!"

○ Learn more...

- Alfred Hitchcock's famous 1960 movie *Psycho* (starring Anthony Perkins) involves an insane killer who thinks his dead mother is still alive.

Puke
USED WITH FRIENDS

To vomit.

EXAMPLE 1

"There's a strange smell in this place that makes me want to puke."

EXAMPLE 2

"Whatever happens, please don't puke on the stereo. It's new and very expensive."

○ Learn more...

- In his 1998 movie *The Wedding Singer*, Adam Sandler's character Robbie says "Oh, I don't think anybody could puke more than that kid. I think I saw a boot come out of him."

Pull Shit
USED WITH FRIENDS

To do something nasty or annoying.

EXAMPLE 1

"Heather won't take us to the airport after she promised she would. She's always pulling shit like this!"

EXAMPLE 2

"Don't pull that shit! You promised to pay the bills, and now you have to!"

○ Learn more...

- You may also hear "shit someone pulls" as in "The shit Amy pulls is amazing! She should be in jail."

Punch The Clown
USED WITH FRIENDS

To masturbate.

EXAMPLE 1

"I just heard Bob punching the clown in his office. I wish he'd go to the bathroom to do that!"

EXAMPLE 2

"Keith never gets tired of punching the clown. Masturbation is his life."

Punk-ass
USED WITH FRIENDS

A stupid or irritating person.

EXAMPLE 1

"That punk-ass Jerry made me wait two hours at the mall!"

EXAMPLE 2

"You punk-ass! You shouldn't read while you're driving!"

○ Learn more...

- You may also hear "punk-ass bitch" for emphasis, as in "That punk-ass bitch stole my wallet!"

Pussy
USED WITH EXTREME CAUTION

❶ Vagina; sex with a woman.

EXAMPLE 1

"Kaylee has a nice tight pussy. I love having sex with her."

EXAMPLE 2

"I need to get some pussy tonight. Do you have any female friends who might be interested?"

❷ A coward.

EXAMPLE 1

"Alex is always worried about something. He's such a pussy."

EXAMPLE 2

"Don't be a pussy! Meet me in the cemetary at midnight!"

o Learn more...

- Some people use "pussy" or "pussycat" to mean "cat."

- Only women can *have* "pussies" (vaginas), but only men can *be* "pussies" (cowards).

Pussy-whipped
USED WITH EXTREME CAUTION

Dominated or controlled by a woman.

EXAMPLE 1
"Malcolm is so pussy-whipped! He won't do anything without asking his wife if it's okay."

EXAMPLE 2
"Are you coming to the bar with us, or are you too pussy-whipped by your girlfriend?"

"Put a sock in it."
USED WITH ANYONE

"Stop talking."

EXAMPLE 1
"I was talking during the movie and someone told me to put a sock in it."

EXAMPLE 2
"Put a sock in it, Reggie. I don't want to hear about your political views."

o Learn more...

- In this phrase, "it" is "one's mouth."

Put Out
USED WITH FRIENDS

To have sex.

EXAMPLE 1
"I heard that Donna puts out. I'm going to ask her for a date."

EXAMPLE 2
"I bought Amy dinner, a movie, dessert, a massage, and a puppy, but she still won't put out."

Put The Moves On Someone
USED WITH ANYONE

To flirt or try to attract another person.

EXAMPLE 1
"I put my best moves on Monique, but she wasn't interested."

EXAMPLE 2
"My girlfriend's mother puts the moves on me every time I see her."

Putz
USED WITH ANYONE

A stupid or irritating person.

EXAMPLE 1
"Leo forgot to wash his car again. What a putz!"

EXAMPLE 2
"Marty is a total putz. He sneezed on my food!"

o Learn more...

- This word is Yiddish for "penis."

- Men are called "putzes" more often than women.

Q IS FOR QUICKIE

Queef
USED WITH EXTREME CAUTION

The quick release of air from the vagina, which usually makes a noise.

EXAMPLE 1
"I heard Melissa queef while we were having sex last night."

EXAMPLE 2
"I queefed during yoga class this morning! I was so embarrassed."

o Learn more...

- "Queef" is sometimes spelled "kweef."

Queen
USED WITH EXTREME CAUTION

A feminine homosexual man.

EXAMPLE 1
"I didn't realize that Enriquez was such a queen. It took him two hours to get dressed for our date!"

EXAMPLE 2
"Not every gay man is a queen. The queens just attract more attention."

Queer
USED WITH EXTREME CAUTION

❶ Homosexual.

EXAMPLE 1

"I'm queer, and proud of it!"

EXAMPLE 2

"That guy seems queer. Is he gay?"

❷ A homosexual.

EXAMPLE 1

"That queer tried to kiss Ed in the parking lot behind the store."

EXAMPLE 2

"I thought only a queer would know so much about musicals and opera music, but Jonathan isn't gay."

○ Learn more...

- Although many people use "queer" as an insult, many homosexuals now use the word with pride.

- Showtime's T.V. show "Queer As Folk" follows the lives of three different homosexual men.

- "Queer" used to mean "strange," but most people only use it to mean "homosexual" now.

Queer As A Three-Dollar Bill
USED WITH EXTREME CAUTION

Homosexual.

EXAMPLE 1

"Cheryl wanted to date Andrew, but he's queer as a three-dollar bill."

EXAMPLE 2

"My doctor is queer as a three-dollar bill. He's always talking about his boyfriend."

○ Learn more...

- You may also hear "gay as a three-dollar bill."

- "Three-dollar bills" don't exist, so it would be strange ("queer") to find one.

Quickie
USED WITH ANYONE

A brief session of sex.

EXAMPLE 1

"I have ten minutes before I have to leave for work. Let's have a quickie!"

EXAMPLE 2

"Delf and I work together, so sometimes we meet in the supply closet for a quickie."

R IS FOR **RAT-BASTARD**

Rack
USED WITH FRIENDS

Breasts.

EXAMPLE 1
"Those women have the nicest racks I've ever seen."

EXAMPLE 2
"She has a big rack, but she wants it to be bigger."

Rack Salesman
USED WITH FRIENDS

A person who finds customers for prostitutes; a pimp (p. 145).

EXAMPLE 1
"What price did the rack salesman give you for two hours?"

EXAMPLE 2
"I'm so lonely! I'm going to visit the rack salesman so I don't have to sleep alone."

Racy
USED WITH ANYONE

More sexual than is appropriate for the situation.

EXAMPLE 1
"You look racy in that dress! Let's go have sex!"

EXAMPLE 2
"This movie is too racy for me. I don't like to think about sex very much."

Ralph
USED WITH FRIENDS

To vomit.

EXAMPLE 1

"When that guy hit me in the stomach, I ralphed all over him."

EXAMPLE 2

"Dina ralphed on my favorite shirt last night. I hate that girl."

Ramrod
USED WITH FRIENDS

Penis.

EXAMPLE 1

"I can't think when Faye touches my ramrod. It feels so good!"

EXAMPLE 2

"My ramrod and I haven't had sex in two months."

o Learn more...

- You may also hear "rammer."

Rat
USED WITH ANYONE

A very bad person.

EXAMPLE 1

"That rat has been selling drugs for years."

EXAMPLE 2

"Only a rat would try to steal money from old people."

o Learn more...

- To "rat on someone" is "to report someone to the authorities."

Rat-bastard
USED WITH FRIENDS

A nasty or cruel man.

EXAMPLE 1

"That rat-bastard kicked my dog!"

EXAMPLE 2

"My last boyfriend was a rat-bastard. He stole my stereo while I was sleeping!"

Raunchy
USED WITH ANYONE

Sexually nasty.

EXAMPLE 1

"I'm not dating Ted anymore. He likes raunchy sex!"

EXAMPLE 2

"I like looking at naked women, but this magazine is too raunchy for me."

Raw Sex
USED WITH FRIENDS

Sex without a condom.

EXAMPLE 1

"I won't have raw sex with anyone. It's too dangerous."

EXAMPLE 2

"Jake caught three diseases from having raw sex. Now he uses condoms."

Reach Around
USED WITH EXTREME CAUTION

During anal sex between two men, the man penetrating his partner also masturbates his partner with his hands.

EXAMPLE 1

"If we have anal sex later, I demand a reach around! It's not fair otherwise."

EXAMPLE 2

"Charles never gives me a reach around during anal sex. He's so selfish!"

Rear End
USED WITH ANYONE

Butt.

EXAMPLE 1

"He makes me so angry! I want to kick him in the rear end. "

EXAMPLE 2

"The doctor gave me an injection in my rear end. It really hurt!"

Red-light District
USED WITH ANYONE

The area of town containing prostitutes and places of prostitution.

EXAMPLE 1
"If you want to find a prostitute, we need to go to the red-light district."

EXAMPLE 2
"I met my new girlfriend in the red-light district. I have to pay her $100 an hour to date her."

Retard
USED WITH EXTREME CAUTION

A stupid or mentally damaged person.

EXAMPLE 1
"That retard is trying to climb into the trash."

EXAMPLE 2
"Only a retard would play golf in a storm. You could be struck by lightning!"

o **Learn more...**

* It's considered very rude to call a person with real learning problems "retarded." The most common phrases used now are "mentally-challenged" and "learning-disabled."

Retch
USED WITH ANYONE

To vomit.

EXAMPLE 1
"Hospital food makes me retch. I won't eat it."

EXAMPLE 2
"I'm going to retch if you try to kiss me again. I promise!"

Ridden Hard And Put Away Wet
USED WITH FRIENDS

To look tired and sick, like a person who has had a difficult life.

EXAMPLE 1
"Those older women at the end of the bar look like they've been ridden hard and put away wet."

EXAMPLE 2
"Most men I know look like they've been ridden hard and put away wet. I can't meet any attractive guys!"

DIALOGUE
"THE RAT-BASTARD"

Here is a short dialogue between two Americans.

KAREN
"Charles got ripped and had sex with a girl from the red-light district. He didn't even use a rubber!"

HANK
"Yeah, he should be more careful if he's going to run around like that. That rat-bastard has a wife and kids!"

KAREN
"Men like him make me want to retch."

Ripped (p. 162)
Red-light district (p. 161)
Rubber (p. 164)

Run around (p. 165)
Rat-bastard (p. 160)

Retch (p. 161)

o Learn more...

- You may also hear "ridden hard and put away sweaty."

- A horse that has been ridden a long time (until it's covered in sweat) must be brushed and walked afterwards. If the horse is "put away wet" (or "put away sweaty"), it can get very sick and die.

Ride Bareback
USED WITH FRIENDS

To have sex without a condom.

EXAMPLE 1
"If Dave keeps riding bareback, he's going to get a sexual disease."

EXAMPLE 2
"Only a fool would ride bareback with the threat of so many sexual diseases around."

o Learn more...

- Most people who use the phrase "riding bareback" are talking about riding a horse without a saddle.

Ride The Red Tide
USED WITH FRIENDS

To menstruate.

EXAMPLE 1
"I stay away from my girlfriend when she is riding the red tide."

EXAMPLE 2
"All three of my sisters ride the red tide at the same time each month."

Rimming
USED WITH FRIENDS

Licking or sucking a person's anus for sexual pleasure.

EXAMPLE 1
"Carl was rimming me for an hour last night. I wouldn't let him stop because it felt so good."

EXAMPLE 2
"Rimming feels great, but shower before you try it!"

o Learn more...

- You may also hear "rim job" or "ream job."

Rip Someone A New Asshole
USED WITH FRIENDS

To yell at someone.

EXAMPLE 1
"The boss just ripped me a new asshole because I missed the meeting."

EXAMPLE 2
"If you're not home by midnight, your father will rip you a new asshole!"

o Learn more...

- You may also hear "rip someone a new one" to avoid using the word "asshole."

Ripped
USED WITH ANYONE

Drunk.

EXAMPLE 1
"I always get ripped on Friday night. It's my reward for surviving the week at work!"

EXAMPLE 2
"Are you ripped? You can barely walk!"

o Learn more...

- "Ripped" can also mean "muscular."

Roaring Drunk
USED WITH ANYONE

Very drunk.

EXAMPLE 1
"Gail got roaring drunk at the Christmas party and I had to drive her home."

EXAMPLE 2
"The only time I go to the library is when I'm roaring drunk."

o Learn more...

- You may also hear "rip-roaring drunk."

Rocked

USED WITH ANYONE

Drunk.

EXAMPLE 1

"My mother got really rocked after my dad died. She wouldn't stop drinking vodka."

EXAMPLE 2

"I've never been so rocked in my entire life. My head will hurt tomorrow!"

Rod

USED WITH FRIENDS

Penis.

EXAMPLE 1

"My rod is so big, most girls are afraid to have sex with me."

EXAMPLE 2

"I have to stop masturbating. My rod is starting to get sore."

o Learn more...

- You may also hear "rod of love" as in "Come back home with me and I'll let you touch my rod of love!"

AT THE MOVIES
"RISKY BUSINESS" (1983)

In *Risky Business*, a young Tom Cruise stars as a good boy named Joel who wants to have some fun while his parents are away.

MILES

"My daddy used to spank my bare bottom. Now he's gone. Will you take his place?"

—

Bottom (p. 21)

JOEL

"College women can smell ignorance... like dog shit."

Shit (p. 174)

—

MILES

"I don't believe this! I've got a trig midterm tomorrow, and I'm being chased by Guido the killer pimp."

Pimp (p. 145)

—

JOEL

"Porsche. There is no substitute."

MILES

"Fuck you."

"Fuck you" (p. 76)

—

MILES

"Sometimes you gotta say "What the fuck," make your move. Joel, every now and then, saying "What the fuck" brings freedom."

"What the fuck?"
(p. 213)

—

JOEL

"If there were any logic to our language, 'trust' would be a four-letter word."

Four-letter word
(p. 70)

Roll In The Hay
USED WITH ANYONE

A session of sex.

EXAMPLE 1

"I had a little roll in the hay with two women from my office. I hope my boss doesn't find out!"

EXAMPLE 2

"We've been friends for a long time. A roll in the hay won't change that."

o **Learn more...**

- Books and movies often show people having sex on a pile of hay, usually in a barn or a stable.

Roll The Fuzzy Dice
USED WITH FRIENDS

To masturbate.

EXAMPLE 1

"After a hard day at work, I like to relax and roll the fuzzy dice at home."

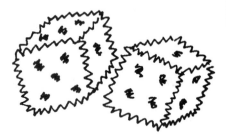

EXAMPLE 2

"All men masturbate! I roll the fuzzy dice at least once a day!"

o **Learn more...**

- In this phrase, "fuzzy dice" refers to "testicles," which are usually covered in pubic hair.

Rub The Rod
USED WITH FRIENDS

To masturbate.

EXAMPLE 1

"When I was seven years old, I learned how to rub the rod. Since then, masturbating is my favorite thing to do."

EXAMPLE 2

"Since my girlfriend never wants to have sex, I'm always rubbing the rod."

Rubber
USED WITH FRIENDS

A condom.

EXAMPLE 1

"Did you bring any rubbers? We can't have sex without them."

EXAMPLE 2

"I don't like rubbers. They make it difficult for me to have an orgasm."

Rump
USED WITH ANYONE

Butt.

EXAMPLE 1

"Look at the rump on that girl! That's the biggest rump I've ever seen."

EXAMPLE 2

"My rump is too big for those small seats on airplanes."

Rump Ranger
USED WITH EXTREME CAUTION

A homosexual man.

EXAMPLE 1

"That rump ranger tried to get my brother to go on a date with him, but my brother isn't gay."

EXAMPLE 2

"Luke and Ryan are dating? I didn't know they were rump rangers."

o **Learn more...**

- To homosexual men, a "rump ranger" is a homosexual man who enjoys anal sex, not just any homosexual man.

Run Around

USED WITH ANYONE

To have sex with many different people.

EXAMPLE 1

"Marilyn ran around with every guy on the basketball team."

EXAMPLE 2

"That guy is always running around with some woman from his office."

Runt

USED WITH ANYONE

A very small and weak person.

EXAMPLE 1

"Keith is the runt of the family. Everyone else is over six feet tall."

EXAMPLE 2

"Adam wants to fight me? He's a runt! I'll beat him easily."

○ **Learn more...**

- When animals have many babies at once, the smallest one is called the "runt" and often dies.

S IS FOR SCREWED UP

S. And M.
USED WITH ANYONE

Sadism (pleasure from giving pain to others) and masochism (pleasure from receiving pain).

EXAMPLE 1
"I love S. and M., but I'm worried that other people will discover my secret."

EXAMPLE 2
"Be careful with S. and M.! My last girlfriend was too rough with me and I had to go to the hospital."

Sack
USED WITH FRIENDS

❶ **The skin around the testicles.**

EXAMPLE 1
"The doctor was squeezing my sack during the examination. Is that normal?"

EXAMPLE 2
"I had hair on my sack when I was 12 years old."

❷ **Courage or strength.**

EXAMPLE 1
"Will you grow some sack? Don't be afraid of those little spiders!"

EXAMPLE 2
"Larry will never try to challenge me because he doesn't have the sack."

Sadist
USED WITH ANYONE

A person who gets pleasure from giving pain to others.

EXAMPLE 1

"I'm definitely a sadist. I get excited whenever my lovers scream in pain."

EXAMPLE 2

"I think my new boyfriend is a sadist. He slapped me last night and seemed to enjoy it."

Sadomasochist
USED WITH ANYONE

A person who gets pleasure from both receiving and giving pain.

EXAMPLE 1

"My wife is a sadomasochist. As long as there is blood, she has an orgasm."

EXAMPLE 2

"I'm a sadomasochist. Anything you want to do is fine with me!"

o **Learn more...**

- This is a combination of the words "sadist" (p. 167) and "masochist" (p. 124).

Salami
USED WITH FRIENDS

Penis.

EXAMPLE 1

"My salami doesn't look good. I wonder if I have a sexual disease!"

EXAMPLE 2

"Kelly will lick any guy's salami. You just have to ask."

o **Learn more...**

- You may also hear "sausage."

Satisfy
USED WITH ANYONE

To fulfill one's sexual needs.

EXAMPLE 1

"Curtis is a great guy, but he just doesn't satisfy me in the bedroom."

EXAMPLE 2

"I am having my penis surgically enlarged so I can finally satisfy the women I have sex with."

o **Learn more...**

- "Satisfy" also means "to fulfill one's (non-sexual) needs" as in "I'm satisfied with my new job. It makes me happy."

Sauced
USED WITH ANYONE

Drunk.

EXAMPLE 1

"That girl is so sauced! I think she would have sex with any guy right now."

EXAMPLE 2

"I won't be able to drive home if I get too sauced."

Scam
USED WITH ANYONE

To flirt or try to attract another person.

EXAMPLE 1

"Claud has been scamming all the girls in the club, but no one seems interested."

EXAMPLE 2

"That cute guy at the other end of the bar is scamming you. You should go over there and talk to him."

Scare The Shit Out Of Someone
USED WITH FRIENDS

To scare someone a lot.

EXAMPLE 1

"The boy ran when the police arrived. They scared the shit out of him!"

EXAMPLE 2

"That loud noise scared the shit out of me!"

Scared Shitless
USED WITH FRIENDS

Very scared.

EXAMPLE 1

"I was scared shitless by that horror movie."

EXAMPLE 2

"Tony dressed as a ghost, jumped out, and yelled at me. I was scared shitless!"

Scaredy-cat
USED WITH ANYONE

A person who is easily scared.

EXAMPLE 1
"Beth is a scaredy-cat. She screamed during the whole movie!"

EXAMPLE 2
"I won't go into that dark room. I'm a scaredy-cat!"

○ **Learn more...**

- Cats are surprised and scared by almost anything.

- Children use this phrase more often than adults.

Scatterbrain
USED WITH ANYONE

A person who forgets a lot.

EXAMPLE 1
"I'm a scatterbrain today. I forgot to put on underwear!"

EXAMPLE 2
"Brian drove to the mall instead of the movie theater. What a scatterbrain!"

○ **Learn more...**

- A person can also be "scatterbrained" as in "I'm scatterbrained today. I forgot to put on a shirt!"

Schizo
USED WITH FRIENDS

A crazy person.

EXAMPLE 1
"My boss is a schizo. He wants me to work 20 hours every day."

EXAMPLE 2
"You schizo! I told you to meet me here at 3:00pm, not 4:00pm!"

○ **Learn more...**

- "Schizo" comes from "schizofrenia," a type of insanity.

- You may also hear "schizoid" as in "That schizoid stole my shopping cart."

Score
USED WITH FRIENDS

To have sex.

EXAMPLE 1
"You're an ugly, short, smelly little man, and you have no chance of scoring with me!"

EXAMPLE 2
"I scored with Danielle last night. She's great in bed."

○ **Learn more...**

- "Score" also means "to obtain" as in "Eddie scored some drugs at last night's party. He's so lucky!"

- In sports, you need to "score" points in order to win. The word "score" often means "to succeed."

Screamer
USED WITH FRIENDS

A person who screams during sex or orgasm.

EXAMPLE 1
"I really enjoy having sex with Fannie because she's a screamer. I love it when she yells my name!"

EXAMPLE 2
"The girl I had sex with last night was such a screamer that my neighbors called the police."

Screaming Fairy
USED WITH EXTREME CAUTION

A very feminine homosexual man.

EXAMPLE 1
"Jacob's a screaming fairy. He is the most gay person I have ever met."

EXAMPLE 2
"That screaming fairy is an excellent cook."

Screw
USED WITH FRIENDS

❶ To have sex.

EXAMPLE 1

"Kenny and I finally screwed last night. He was really good!"

EXAMPLE 2

"My wife likes me to screw her while she watches Mel Gibson movies. Mel really is sexy."

❷ To cheat or lie to someone.

EXAMPLE 1

"I got screwed by my boss. He promised me a raise and then fired me!"

EXAMPLE 2

"Brad owes me money but he moved out of the country. He totally screwed me!"

❍ Learn more...

- "Screw" can be used in most of the same ways as the more offensive word "fuck" (p. 72).

Screw Around
USED WITH ANYONE

❶ To spend time without doing much.

EXAMPLE 1

"I don't feel like seeing a movie. I'm going to stay home and screw around the house for a while."

IN OTHER WORDS...
"HAVE SEX"

Is there anything that people like to talk about more than sex? Well, we can't think of anything. If you want to be romantic, use "make love" or "have sex." If you want to be cute, use "roll in the hay" or "make whoopee."

USED WITH ANYONE

Go all the way (p. 85)

Hop in the sack (p. 103)

Hump (p. 105)

Make love (p. 123)

Make whoopee (p. 123)

Roll in the hay (p. 164)

Sleep together (p. 180)

Sow one's oats (p. 184)

USED WITH FRIENDS

Boink (p. 19)

Bone (p. 19)

Bump and grind (p. 24)

Bump uglies (p. 25)

Dick (p. 46)

Do it (p. 48)

Do the deed (p. 48)

Do the do (p. 48)

Do the nasty (p. 48)

Do the wild thing (p. 49)

Get into someone's pants (p. 82)

Get it on (p. 82)

Get laid (p. 82)

Get some (p. 83)

Grind (p. 88)

Jump someone's bones (p. 110)

Lay pipe (p. 116)

Make the beast with two backs (p. 123)

Play bouncy-bouncy (p. 148)

Play "Hide the sausage" (p. 149)

Score (p. 168)

Screw (p. 169)

Screw someone's brains out (p. 170)

Shag (p. 174)

Shtup (p. 178)

USED WITH EXTREME CAUTION

Ball (p. 9)

Bang (p. 11)

Fuck (p. 72)

Fuck someone's brains out (p. 74)

Get a piece of ass (p. 81)

Get some ass (p. 83)

Nail (p. 132)

Tap that ass (p. 195)

Throw one in her (p. 199)

EXAMPLE 2

"We screwed around the mall for a few hours and then came home."

❷ **To have sexual contact.**

EXAMPLE 1

"Gwen and I were screwing around all night, but we never had sex."

EXAMPLE 2

"I won't screw around with a guy I'm not dating."

"Screw off!"
USED WITH FRIENDS

Phrase indicating anger or dislike.

EXAMPLE 1

"Screw off! I don't need your help!"

EXAMPLE 2

"You want to borrow my car? Screw off! You got in an accident last time you borrowed it."

Screw Someone Over
USED WITH FRIENDS

To cheat or betray someone.

EXAMPLE 1

"My lawyer screwed me over. I paid him a lot of money, and I still went to jail!"

EXAMPLE 2

"I screwed my business partner over. When he wasn't looking, I stole money from the cash box."

○ **Learn more...**

• You may also hear "screw over someone" as in "My boss likes to screw over his employees. He promises them vacations, then makes them work weekends instead."

Screw Someone's Brains Out
USED WITH FRIENDS

To have a lot of sex.

EXAMPLE 1

"I'd love to screw Paul's brains out. He's so sexy!"

EXAMPLE 2

"Michelle and I screwed each other's brains out last night. We just couldn't get enough sex."

Screw the Pooch
USED WITH FRIENDS

To fail badly.

EXAMPLE 1

"Burt got lost and didn't deliver the package. He really screwed the pooch!"

EXAMPLE 2

"I need to study or I'll screw the pooch on tomorrow's test."

○ **Learn more...**

• "Pooch" is another word for "dog," so to "screw the pooch" is to "have sex with a dog"!

Screw-up
USED WITH ANYONE

A stupid or unpopular person.

EXAMPLE 1

"That screw-up burned the contracts in the fireplace when he was cleaning."

EXAMPLE 2

"I am such a screw-up! I can't do anything right."

Screw Up Someone
USED WITH ANYONE

To harm someone emotionally.

EXAMPLE 1

"The Hendersons really screwed up their sons. Both boys are in their thirties and they still live at home!"

EXAMPLE 2

"I'm afraid I screwed up my daughter by yelling at her too much. Now, she only dates men who are mean to her."

o Learn more...

• You may also hear "screw someone up" as in "That horror movie really screwed me up. I had nightmares for weeks!"

Screw Up Something
USED WITH ANYONE

❶ To ruin something.

EXAMPLE 1

"I screwed up the pie I was baking. It tastes terrible!"

EXAMPLE 2

"Jeff screwed up his knee in a skiing accident. He needs an operation or he'll be walking with a cane the rest of his life."

❷ To make a mistake.

EXAMPLE 1

"If you screw up again, you're fired!"

EXAMPLE 2

"I screwed up and bought my wife the wrong earrings. She's going to be very disappointed."

o Learn more...

• You may also hear "screw something up" as in "Stop pulling my arm! You're going to screw my wrist up."

Screw With Someone
USED WITH ANYONE

To tease or annoy someone.

EXAMPLE 1

"Don't screw with me. I know karate!"

EXAMPLE 2

"I was just screwing with Wally about his car, but he got angry."

Screw With Something
USED WITH ANYONE

To play with something, usually in order to fix it.

EXAMPLE 1

"Stop screwing with my television. You're just going to make it worse!"

EXAMPLE 2

"The microwave stopped working? I'll screw with it after work and try to fix it."

"Screw you!"
USED WITH FRIENDS

Phrase indicating anger or dislike.

EXAMPLE 1

"You don't like my haircut? Screw you!"

EXAMPLE 2

"Screw you, Donald. I hope I never see you again!"

o Learn more...

• You may also hear "screw her," "screw him," "screw them," etc.

• You may also hear "screw you and the horse you rode in on" for emphasis.

Screwed
USED WITH FRIENDS

In trouble.

EXAMPLE 1

"I borrowed my mother's diamond earrings and lost them at the party. I'm screwed!"

EXAMPLE 2

"You forgot to study for today's test? You're screwed! I heard it's really hard."

Screwed In The Head
USED WITH FRIENDS

Crazy or strange.

EXAMPLE 1

"That man just jumped onto the subway tracks. He must be screwed in the head!"

EXAMPLE 2

"You're screwed in the head if you think I would kiss Darrell. He's so ugly!"

Screwed Up
USED WITH ANYONE

Crazy or strange.

EXAMPLE 1

"Joe smoked marijuana so much when he was young, that he's really screwed up now."

EXAMPLE 2

"That guy is really screwed up. He tried to eat my lunch!"

o **Learn more...**

- You may also hear "screwy" or "screwball" as in "My sister is screwy. She sleeps 18 hours a day. Her husband is a screwball, too. He sleeps 19 hours a day."

Scrooge
USED WITH ANYONE

A person who hates spending money.

EXAMPLE 1

"My husband didn't buy me a Christmas present. What a scrooge!"

EXAMPLE 2

"I don't want to be a scrooge, but I don't have enough money to buy lunch for you."

o **Learn more...**

- In Charles Dicken's book *A Christmas Carol*, Ebeneezer Scrooge is a mean person who hates spending money, even at Christmas.

- This expression is used more often around Christmas (December 25th).

Scum
USED WITH ANYONE

A worthless or nasty person.

EXAMPLE 1

"I feel like scum! I borrowed my sister's sneakers and ruined them."

EXAMPLE 2

"You're scum! You've been lying to me for years."

o **Learn more...**

- You may also hear "scummy" as in "That was a scummy thing to do. You really hurt Naoko."

- You may also hear "scumbag" or "scum of the earth."

Seat
USED WITH ANYONE

Butt.

EXAMPLE 1

"I need big jeans because I have a big seat."

EXAMPLE 2

"His seat is so big he looks like two people from far away."

Second Base
USED WITH FRIENDS

Touching a girl's or woman's breast.

EXAMPLE 1

"Tonight I'm going to second base with Katie. I can't wait to touch her breasts!"

EXAMPLE 2

"I went to second base with my girlfriend's mother. I hope my girlfriend doesn't find out!"

See A Man About A Horse

USED WITH ANYONE

To urinate or defecate.

EXAMPLE 1

"Billy will be back in a minute. He had to see a man about a horse."

EXAMPLE 2

"Excuse me, please. I have to see a man about a horse."

o Learn more...

- This is an old phrase still used today, often as a joke.

Service Station

USED WITH FRIENDS

A place of prostitution.

EXAMPLE 1

"The only way Franklin can get sex is from a service station."

EXAMPLE 2

"My new girlfriend used to work at a service station. She knows a lot about sex!"

Sex Appeal

USED WITH ANYONE

Sexual attractiveness.

EXAMPLE 1

"I need to buy some clothes that give me more sex appeal. I want to have sex, but guys don't even notice me now."

EXAMPLE 2

"That girl has more sex appeal than any other girl I have ever seen."

Sex Drive

USED WITH ANYONE

The desire to have sex.

EXAMPLE 1

"My husband has an overactive sex drive. He wants to have sex all the time."

EXAMPLE 2

"Margie's sex drive is missing! She never wants to have sex."

Sex Symbol

USED WITH ANYONE

A person who represents the ideal of sex and sexuality.

EXAMPLE 1

"Brad Pitt is one of the biggest sex symbols in the world."

DIALOGUE
"CINDY SWALLOWS!"

Here is a short dialogue between two Americans.

EDDIE
"I scored with Cindy last night. She's has been in a few skin flicks, so she's a sleaze. But the girl swallows, and that's all I care about!"

Score (p. 168)
Skin flick (p. 180)
Sleaze (p. 180)
Swallow (p. 192)

LEO
"You lucky son of a bitch! I asked Cindy to go skinny-dipping with me once, but she said no."

Son of a bitch (p. 184)
Skinny-dip (p. 180)

EDDIE
"Maybe your shlong wasn't big enough for her."

Shlong (p. 177)

LEO
"Smart ass."

Smart ass (p. 182)

EXAMPLE 2

"Marilyn Monroe is an amazing sex symbol. A lot of people try to dress and act like she did."

Shack Up With Someone
USED WITH ANYONE

To live (and have sex) with someone.

EXAMPLE 1

"Darla and I decided to shack up. She's moving into my apartment next week."

EXAMPLE 2

"I would rather shack up with an elephant than live with you."

Shag
USED WITH FRIENDS

To have sex.

EXAMPLE 1

"I usually don't like British people, but I love to shag British women."

EXAMPLE 2

"That crazy European girl was asking me to shag her all night long."

❶ **Learn more...**

- We took this phrase from the British.

- Mike Myers' character Austin Powers uses "shag" all the time. In the 1997 movie *Austin Powers: International Man of Mystery*, he says "Shall we shag now, or shall we shag later?" The second Austin Powers movie is even called *The Spy Who Shagged Me*.

Shake Hands With The Governor
USED WITH FRIENDS

To masturbate.

EXAMPLE 1

MELANIE: "Where's Greg?"

FRANK: "He's in the bathroom shaking hands with the governor again."

EXAMPLE 2

"I like to shake hands with the governor before every basketball game. It keeps me relaxed."

Shattered
USED WITH ANYONE

Drunk.

EXAMPLE 1

"Mom's been drinking wine since noon. She's shattered!"

EXAMPLE 2

"No one should fly a plane if they're shattered."

Shit
USED WITH FRIENDS

❶ **One's belongings.**

EXAMPLE 1

"Pack your shit and get out of my apartment. Now!"

EXAMPLE 2

"Is that your shit? You have some cool things!"

❷ **Nothing.**

EXAMPLE 1

"Jeb used to be rich, but now he has shit."

EXAMPLE 2

"I worked here for two years and I have shit to show for all my hard work."

❸ **A nasty person.**

EXAMPLE 1

"You shit! You hurt me!"

EXAMPLE 2

"Ronnie is mean to women. He's a real shit."

❹ **Excrement.**

EXAMPLE 1

"There's dog shit all over my lawn. The neighbor should keep his dog on a leash!"

EXAMPLE 2

"Don't walk on the carpet if you have shit on your shoes."

❺ **To defecate.**

EXAMPLE 1

"If I don't shit soon, I'm going to explode."

EXAMPLE 2

"Remember to shit before we leave. You won't get another chance until we get to Kansas."

⊙ Any unidentified substance.

EXAMPLE 1

"What is that shit on your clothes? Did you spill something?"

EXAMPLE 2

"There's some kind of shit all over the stereo."

Shit a Brick
USED WITH FRIENDS

To become very scared.

EXAMPLE 1

"When I heard Dave screaming, I almost shit a brick!"

EXAMPLE 2

"You look like you're going to shit a brick. Why are you so scared?"

Shit-eating Grin
USED WITH FRIENDS

A smile used by someone who feels that he or she is better than other people.

EXAMPLE 1

"Lose that shit-eating grin, Sara. You won the contest, but you shouldn't make us feel bad about it!"

EXAMPLE 2

"Hans always wears a shit-eating grin when he's dating a beautiful woman."

Shit-faced
USED WITH FRIENDS

Drunk.

EXAMPLE 1

"I got shit-faced last night and had sex with Jacob!"

EXAMPLE 2

"You can't drive, Ted. You're totally shit-faced!"

Shit-for-brains
USED WITH FRIENDS

A stupid person.

EXAMPLE 1

"That shit-for-brains is trying to sell hot chocolate in the summer!"

EXAMPLE 2

"Hey, shit-for-brains! You can't park on the bridge!"

"Shit happens."
USED WITH FRIENDS

"Bad things happen, but there's nothing we can do about it."

EXAMPLE 1

"My cat got out of the house two weeks ago and hasn't come back. Shit happens, I guess."

EXAMPLE 2

AL: "You lost your job? That's terrible!"

TOM: "Yeah, shit happens."

Shit List
USED WITH FRIENDS

A mental list of people one is angry at.

EXAMPLE 1

"Carol is on my shit list because she won't pay me the money she owes me."

EXAMPLE 2

"If you forget my birthday, you'll be on my shit list!"

Shit On Someone
USED WITH FRIENDS

To abuse someone.

EXAMPLE 1

"The boss always shits on his employees. He makes them work hard for very little money."

EXAMPLE 2

"I'm tired of getting shit on by my girlfriend. She's always yelling at me for no reason."

Shit Or Get Off The Pot
USED WITH FRIENDS

To make a decision.

EXAMPLE 1
"I can't decide if I should date Thad. I need to shit or get off the pot!"

EXAMPLE 2
"Martin can't decide which college to attend. He should shit or get off the pot."

o **Learn more...**

- In this phrase, "shit" means "to defecate" and "pot" means "toilet," so this phrase means "defecate or get off the toilet."

Shit Out Of Luck
USED WITH FRIENDS

To be unlucky; to have a problem.

EXAMPLE 1
"We're shit out of luck. They just sold the last ticket for the show!"

EXAMPLE 2
"We'll be shit out of luck if I can't find my car keys!"

o **Learn more...**

- You may also hear "S-O-L," which can be used with anyone.

Shit Someone
USED WITH FRIENDS

To lie to someone; to tease.

EXAMPLE 1
"Are you shitting me? You got us seats in the front row? That's great!"

EXAMPLE 2
WADE: "I'm going to Harvard!"

SUKI: "You're shitting me!"

Shitbox
USED WITH FRIENDS

A bad, almost broken car.

EXAMPLE 1
"Val's shitbox will never get us safely to Las Vegas. We should ride the bus."

EXAMPLE 2
"My last car was a shitbox. It only lasted two months before I had to buy a new one."

Shithead
USED WITH FRIENDS

A rude, mean, or irritating person.

EXAMPLE 1
"That man took our parking space! What a shithead!"

EXAMPLE 2
"Mack is a shithead for stealing my girlfriend."

Shithouse
USED WITH FRIENDS

Toilet or bathroom.

EXAMPLE 1
"Who built this shithouse so far away from everything else?"

EXAMPLE 2
"No matter where you are, all shithouses smell the same."

o **Learn more...**

- You may also hear "outhouse," which can be used with anyone.

Shitload
USED WITH FRIENDS

A lot.

EXAMPLE 1
"Eve bought a shitload of groceries. We have enough to eat for a month!"

EXAMPLE 2
"I have a shitload of work to do before I can go home tonight."

Shitter
USED WITH FRIENDS

Toilet or bathroom.

EXAMPLE 1
"John is still in the shitter. I hope he's okay. He's been in there for an hour."

EXAMPLE 2
"You really need to clean the shitter. It's a mess in there."

Shitty
USED WITH FRIENDS

Terrible.

EXAMPLE 1

"I feel shitty today. I think I'm getting sick."

EXAMPLE 2

"Punching Gillian was a shitty thing to do."

○ **Learn more...**

- You may also hear "shittiest" as in "Lance is driving the shittiest car I've ever seen. It's so ugly!"

Shlong
USED WITH FRIENDS

Penis.

EXAMPLE 1

"Dave didn't know it, but his schlong was sticking out of his pants."

EXAMPLE 2

"I have the longest schlong in my gym class."

○ **Learn more...**

- This word is Yiddish for "penis."

Shmuck
USED WITH ANYONE

A stupid or irritating person.

EXAMPLE 1

"You shmuck! You left your shoes at the bar!"

EXAMPLE 2

"Hank wants to have sex with me. What a shmuck! I'd never date him!"

○ **Learn more...**

- This word is Yiddish for "penis."

- Men are called "shmucks" more often than women.

"Shoot!"
USED WITH ANYONE

Indicates surprise or frustration.

EXAMPLE 1

"Shoot! I forgot to walk the dog!"

EXAMPLE 2

"Shoot! I can't go to the party because I have to work late."

○ **Learn more...**

- This is a nicer way to say "shit" (p. 174).

Shoot One's Mouth Off
USED WITH ANYONE

To speak rudely.

EXAMPLE 1

"I shot my mouth off last night and yelled at my boss!"

EXAMPLE 2

"Edith shoots her mouth off at her mother too much."

Shoot One's Wad
USED WITH FRIENDS

To ejaculate.

EXAMPLE 1

"Todd got so excited when he kissed Liselle that he shot his wad in his pants!"

EXAMPLE 2

"I was supposed to have sex with Alyssa last night, but I shot my wad too early."

Shoot The Shit
USED WITH FRIENDS

To talk.

EXAMPLE 1

"I'm late because Trudy and I were shooting the shit."

EXAMPLE 2

"Do you want to get coffee with me later? I'd love to shoot the shit with you for a while."

○ **Learn more...**

- You may also hear the more polite version "shoot the breeze."

Shout At One's Shoes
USED WITH FRIENDS

To vomit.

EXAMPLE 1

"Adam had some bad sushi. He has been shouting at his shoes all afternoon."

EXAMPLE 2

"Drinking whiskey always makes me shout at my shoes later. I'll never drink it again!"

Shrimp
USED WITH ANYONE

A very small person.

EXAMPLE 1

"You're a shrimp! You can fight me, but I'll beat you easily."

EXAMPLE 2

"Gina is dating a shrimp! Ted is only five feet tall!"

Shtup
USED WITH FRIENDS

To have sex.

EXAMPLE 1

"Larry tried to shtup me last night. I had to hit him in the head so he would stop."

EXAMPLE 2

"Jill and I were dating for six months before we shtupped. Kids today can't wait for more than two dates."

o **Learn more...**

• This is a Yiddish word.

Shucks
USED WITH ANYONE

Indicates disappointment.

EXAMPLE 1

"Shucks! I lost the contest."

EXAMPLE 2

"I don't have enough money to go to the restaurant tonight. Shucks."

o **Learn more...**

• This is a nicer way to say "shit" (p. 174).

Sicko
USED WITH ANYONE

A person who likes or does strange sexual things.

EXAMPLE 1

"My old girlfriend is a sicko. She always wanted me to urinate on her."

EXAMPLE 2

"Susan's math teacher is a sicko. He's always rubbing his arm against her breasts."

o **Learn more...**

• You may also hear "sickie" as in "That old man is a real sickie. He touched my breasts on the train."

Silent But Deadly
USED WITH FRIENDS

Flatulence that you do not hear, but smells very bad.

EXAMPLE 1

"The silent but deadly ones smell the worst, and you can never hear them coming."

EXAMPLE 2

"Get ready! A silent but deadly one is coming at you. You should smell it soon."

o **Learn more...**

• You may also hear "S-B-D," although it's not very common.

Sissy
USED WITH EXTREME CAUTION

❶ **A coward.**

EXAMPLE 1

"Willy cried at school today. What a sissy!"

EXAMPLE 2

"I don't want to be a sissy, but I'm afraid of the dark!"

❷ A homosexual man.

EXAMPLE 1
"You like the color pink? You must be a sissy!"

EXAMPLE 2
"Tom's a sissy. He likes other boys."

o Learn more...

- Men are called "sissies" more often than women.

- The second definition is always used as an insult, and makes this word very dangerous to use.

68 (Sixty-eight)
USED WITH EXTREME CAUTION

Oral sex performed on one person now, and the other person later. ("Perform oral sex on me now, and I'll owe you one.")

EXAMPLE 1
"Hey, lover, why don't we do a 68? You give me oral sex now, and I'll give you oral sex tomorrow."

EXAMPLE 2
"My boyfriend never wants to perform oral sex on me when I do it to him. I hate 68s."

o Learn more...

- This is based on the more common phrase "69" (see next entry).

- This phrase is not used often.

69 (Sixty-nine)
USED WITH EXTREME CAUTION

To perform oral sex on someone while that person performs oral sex on you.

EXAMPLE 1
"Whenever my girlfriend and I 69, she's on top of me."

EXAMPLE 2
"I videotaped my friend's sister 69ing with me yesterday. You want to see the video?"

o Learn more...

- In the 1989 movie *Bill and Ted's Big Adventure*, the two heroes (played by Keanu Reaves and Alex Winter) say "Excellent!" every time they hear the number "69."

Size Queen
USED WITH EXTREME CAUTION

A homosexual man who prefers men with large penises.

EXAMPLE 1
"Mack's really handsome, but he would never date me. I hear he's a size queen."

EXAMPLE 2
"Size queens love me and my 9-inch penis."

Skank
USED WITH FRIENDS

A woman who has sex often with different people; a prostitute.

EXAMPLE 1
"Jessica is a total skank! I saw her with Tim last week, and Ed last night!"

EXAMPLE 2
"You're having sex with four different men? You skank!"

o Learn more...

- You may also hear "skanky" as in "Do I look skanky in this dress?"

- You may also hear "skanky ho" as in "You're sister is a skanky ho!"

- Women are called "skanks" more often than men.

Skin And Bones
USED WITH ANYONE

Very skinny.

EXAMPLE 1
"You need to eat more. You're just skin and bones!"

EXAMPLE 2
NANCY: "I'm fat."

CELIA: "No, you're not! You're skin and bones!"

o Learn more...

- You may also hear someone is "nothing but skin and bones."

Skin Flick
USED WITH FRIENDS

A movie featuring naked people (usually women).

EXAMPLE 1

"Let's go see the new skin flick. I heard it's really exciting."

EXAMPLE 2

"This skin flick is great! The women are so amazing."

o Learn more...

- "Flick" is slang for "movie."

Skinny-dip
USED WITH ANYONE

To swim naked outdoors.

EXAMPLE 1

"Sue and I went skinny-dipping last week, so I finally got to see her naked."

EXAMPLE 2

"Skinny-dipping can be fun as long as the water is warm."

Slap The Snake
USED WITH FRIENDS

To masturbate.

EXAMPLE 1

"I usually slap the snake five or six times a week, just before I get out of bed."

EXAMPLE 2

"My penis is so big I need two hands to slap the snake."

Slaphappy
USED WITH ANYONE

Silly.

EXAMPLE 1

"I'm sorry if I seem slaphappy, but I haven't slept in three days."

EXAMPLE 2

"Kim drank so much coffee, she started to get slaphappy."

Sleaze
USED WITH FRIENDS

A person who likes or does things that most people would find disgusting or wrong.

EXAMPLE 1

"That guy at the next table is a real sleaze. I just saw him looking at pictures of naked children."

EXAMPLE 2

"The man who owns my apartment is a sleaze. He asked me to have sex with him instead of paying my monthly rent!"

o Learn more...

- You may also hear "sleazy," "sleazeball," or "sleaze bucket."

Sleep Around
USED WITH ANYONE

To have sex with many different people.

EXAMPLE 1

"Donna sleeps around with guys in Alaska. There aren't many women there, so she's always busy!"

EXAMPLE 2

"Ed sleeps around a lot. He's probably got five sexual diseases by now."

Sleep Together
USED WITH ANYONE

To have sex.

EXAMPLE 1

"George and Barbara have been sleeping together for two months now."

EXAMPLE 2

"I don't want to sleep together until we're married."

Slimeball
USED WITH FRIENDS

A person who likes or does things that most people would find disgusting or wrong.

EXAMPLE 1
"I think lawyers are slimeballs. I never know if I can trust them."

EXAMPLE 2
"That guy standing on the street corner looks like a slimeball. He's probably a criminal."

○ **Learn more...**

• You may also hear "slime," "slimy," or "slime bucket."

Sloshed
USED WITH ANYONE

Drunk.

EXAMPLE 1
"Let's go to the bar and get sloshed. I had a terrible day and I want to forget all about it!"

EXAMPLE 2
"Dirk's dad is always sloshed when he gets home from school. Poor Dirk!"

Slow On The Draw
USED WITH ANYONE

Stupid.

EXAMPLE 1
"You need to explain everything to Mary twice. She's really slow on the draw."

EXAMPLE 2
"Terrence has been slow on the draw ever since he hit his head last month."

○ **Learn more...**

• You may also hear "slow on the uptake" as in "Kyle is really slow on the uptake. I had to explain it to him three times."

Slut
USED WITH EXTREME CAUTION

A person (usually a woman) who has sex often with different people.

EXAMPLE 1
"My wife is a slut. She's having sex with the mailman and the neighbor!"

DIALOGUE
"JOHN GOT SHIT-FACED"

Here is a short dialogue between two Americans.

TERRY
"John got so shit-faced at the party that he did a striptease in front of everyone!"

Shit-faced (p. 175)
Striptease (p. 189)

LUKE
"Whenever he gets stupid drunk, he starts asking girls if they can suck the chrome off a trailer hitch. He's a shmuck."

Stupid drunk (p. 190)
Suck the chrome off a trailer hitch (p. 191)
Shmuck (p. 177)

TERRY
"That snot! I don't want to be around him when he gets that sloshed again."

Snot (p. 183)
Sloshed (p. 181)

EXAMPLE 2

"Bob called me a slut because he saw me talking to another man. He's too jealous and cruel for me."

o **Learn more...**

• You may also hear "slutty" as in "That short skirt makes you look slutty."

Smart-ass

USED WITH FRIENDS

A person who says rude things because he or she feels smarter than everyone else.

EXAMPLE 1

"I tried to tell a story, but Eddie kept making rude comments. What a smart-ass!"

EXAMPLE 2

"My daughter is a smart-ass. Whenever I ask her to do something, she makes a joke."

Smashed

USED WITH ANYONE

Drunk.

EXAMPLE 1

"My girlfriend gets smashed after one glass of wine. She's a cheap date!"

EXAMPLE 2

"I always get smashed on my birthday. It's the best way to celebrate!"

Smut

USED WITH ANYONE

Sexual material.

EXAMPLE 1

"I'm bored. I want to read some smut!"

EXAMPLE 2

"They shouldn't show that smut on television!"

o **Learn more...**

• You may also hear "smutty" as in "This story is smutty. The priest and the teacher have had sex six times so far!"

Snake

USED WITH ANYONE

A person who can't be trusted.

EXAMPLE 1

"Paul is a snake! He'll say anything to get sex."

EXAMPLE 2

"My ex-husband is a snake. He took all of my money when we got divorced."

o **Learn more...**

• You may also hear "snake in the grass."

Snap

USED WITH ANYONE

To become crazy.

EXAMPLE 1

"My father is going to snap when he sees that the television is missing."

EXAMPLE 2

"If one more person asks me what time it is, I'm going to snap! Why don't they get their own watches?"

o **Learn more...**

• A similar phrase, to "snap at someone," refers to speaking to someone in an angry voice. For example: "Linda snapped at me for being late to work again."

Snatch
USED WITH EXTREME CAUTION

Vagina.

EXAMPLE 1

"Ron saw Isabelle's snatch while she was changing clothes."

EXAMPLE 2

"I hate that girl. I want to kick her in the snatch."

○ Learn more...

- You may also hear "snatch" used politely to mean "to steal," as in "That man snatched my purse. Someone stop him!" It's safer to just use "steal."

- The 2000 movie *Snatch*, starring Brad Pitt, is about a stolen diamond and the people trying to recover it.

Snot
USED WITH ANYONE

❶ Mucus from the nose.

EXAMPLE 1

"Yuck! There's snot on my notebook!"

EXAMPLE 2

"My little brother likes to eat his own snot."

❷ A disgusting or irritating person.

EXAMPLE 1

"You little snot! You stole my homework!"

EXAMPLE 2

"Paul is a snot. He found my wallet and threw it in the lake."

❸ An arrogant person.

EXAMPLE 1

"Erin is a snot. She won't be friends with people like us."

EXAMPLE 2

"My dad is such a snot. He's always making people feel bad because they don't know as much as he does."

○ Learn more...

- You may also hear "snotty" as in "My piano teacher is very snotty. She only teaches me classical music."

Snowball
USED WITH EXTREME CAUTION

To swallow one's own ejaculation after it has been in someone else's mouth, vagina, or anus.

EXAMPLE 1

"Paul likes to snowball, so I save his semen in my mouth after oral sex so he can drink it."

EXAMPLE 2

"Henry really likes to snowball, but I think it's disgusting."

○ Learn more...

- You may also hear "snowballing."

- There is a character in Kevin Smith's 1994 movie *Clerks* called "Snowball" because he enjoys "snowballing." Most people hadn't heard the word before they saw this movie.

Sodomist
USED WITH ANYONE

A person who has anal sex.

EXAMPLE 1

"Bill just told me he loves anal sex. I didn't know he was a sodomist."

EXAMPLE 2

"Being a sodomist is illegal in many American states. That old law should be changed!"

Softcore Porn
USED WITH ANYONE

Sexual material that doesn't show every detail.

EXAMPLE 1

"You can watch softcore porn movies on television late at night."

EXAMPLE 2

"Softcore porn won't show a man's penis, but I love penises!"

○ Learn more...

- You may also hear this shortened to just "softcore."

Someone's Ass Is Grass
USED WITH FRIENDS

Someone is in trouble.

EXAMPLE 1

"Be home by eleven or your ass is grass!"

EXAMPLE 2

"My ass is grass if my mother sees that I crashed the car!"

o **Learn more...**

- You may also hear "Your ass is grass, and I'm the lawnmower."

- You may also hear "someone's ass is toast" as in "Brad's ass is toast if he tries to fight me."

Son Of A Bitch
USED WITH FRIENDS

❶ **A nasty person.**

EXAMPLE 1

"Ralph lied to us and kept the money for himself. That son of a bitch!"

EXAMPLE 2

"You had sex with my sister? You son of a bitch!"

❷ **Indicates anger or frustration.**

EXAMPLE 1

"Son of a bitch! I just cut my finger with the knife!"

EXAMPLE 2

"Son of a bitch! I didn't get the job I wanted."

o **Learn more...**

- You may also hear "S-O-B."

- You may see this written as "sonuvabitch."

Sow One's Oats
USED WITH ANYONE

To have sex with many different people.

EXAMPLE 1

"Before I marry Nick, I want to sow my oats with some other men."

EXAMPLE 2

"I would sow my oats from here to China if I could."

o **Learn more...**

- You may also hear "sow one's wild oats."

- Some people believe that if you have sex with a lot of people before you get married, you'll be able to stay faithful.

Space Cadet
USED WITH ANYONE

A person who is not focused on the current situation.

EXAMPLE 1

"William is a space cadet. He always forgets to bring a pen to class."

EXAMPLE 2

"Our waitress is a real space cadet. We ordered water 20 minutes ago, and we still don't have it!"

o **Learn more...**

- You may also hear "spacey" or "space case."

Spanish Fly
USED WITH FRIENDS

A drug that is supposed to make someone want to have sex.

EXAMPLE 1

"I bought some Spanish fly when I was in Mexico, but I'm afraid to use it. It doesn't seem right."

EXAMPLE 2

"I gave my girlfriend three Spanish flies but she still doesn't want to have sex with me."

o **Learn more...**

- This drug doesn't actually exist.

Spare Tire
USED WITH ANYONE

Extra fat around one's waist.

EXAMPLE 1
"I saw Bill at the baseball game. He's getting a spare tire from eating all those hotdogs."

EXAMPLE 2
"I got a spare tire from drinking beer. I guess three bottles of beer every night before bed is too much."

o **Learn more...**

• Men have "spare tires" more often than women.

Spaz
USED WITH ANYONE

A person who is too loud, stupid, or energetic.

EXAMPLE 1
"Peter broke my glasses when we were dancing. What a spaz!"

EXAMPLE 2
"You're a spaz when you drink coffee. You should stop!"

o **Learn more...**

• You may also hear "spastic" as in "Don't give Celia candy or she'll go spastic!"

• When the body or part of the body shakes uncontrollably, it "spasms."

Spermicide
USED WITH ANYONE

A chemical that kills sperm.

EXAMPLE 1
"I tried to buy condoms with spermicide, but the store didn't have any."

EXAMPLE 2
"Jill prefers when I buy vaginal lubricant with spermicide."

Spew
USED WITH FRIENDS

To vomit.

EXAMPLE 1
"There must be something wrong with the chicken we had for dinner. I feel like I'm going to spew."

EXAMPLE 2
"This movie is so bad, it makes me want to spew."

Spike
USED WITH ANYONE

To add alcohol to something.

EXAMPLE 1
"Rudy spiked my drink when I wasn't looking! Now I'm drunk!"

EXAMPLE 2
"I'm going to spike the drinks. I want people to have fun!"

Spineless
USED WITH ANYONE

A coward; a person who isn't strong.

EXAMPLE 1
"My mother is spineless. She let's my father tell her what to do."

EXAMPLE 2
"I'm so spineless! Jerry wanted to see that terrible movie, and I didn't say no!"

Learn more...

- The backbone (or spine) helps humans stand tall and appear strong. If you don't have a backbone, you are considered weak.

- You may also hear "spineless wonder" (a person who is such a coward that it's amazing).

Spinster
USED WITH ANYONE

An older woman who never married.

EXAMPLE 1

"Jessica is waiting for the perfect guy, but she'll be a spinster if she doesn't start dating people soon!"

EXAMPLE 2

"My sister is a spinster. She never found anyone she wanted to marry."

Spit
USED WITH EXTREME CAUTION

To spit out the sperm ejaculated into one's mouth during oral sex.

EXAMPLE 1

"I'll give you oral sex for $25, but I spit. If you want me to swallow your sperm, the price is $50."

EXAMPLE 2

"I always have to spit after oral sex with Henry. I hate the thought of eating his sperm."

Learn more...

- If someone asks you "Do you spit or swallow?" they are referring to your oral sex practices. It's a very rude question to ask!

Spit Up
USED WITH ANYONE

To vomit.

EXAMPLE 1

"Mom, Billy spit up on the television again."

EXAMPLE 2

"I think the cat is ill. She keeps spitting up."

Learn more...

- This phrase is often used with children and animals.

Spoon
USED WITH ANYONE

For two people to lie on their sides, facing the same direction and holding each other tightly (the way two spoons fit together when you stack them).

EXAMPLE 1

"Mike and Rachel like to spoon when they watch movies at home."

EXAMPLE 2

"Carrie is sad that she can't spoon when her boyfriend is away."

Spunk
USED WITH EXTREME CAUTION

Sperm.

EXAMPLE 1

"I love the taste of spunk! I don't understand why some people spit it out."

EXAMPLE 2

"I got spunk in my girlfriend's hair last night, but she didn't notice."

Learn more...

- We took this phrase from the British.

- Samantha, from HBO's "Sex and the City," once complained that a man's sperm tasted bad by saying he had "funky spunk." ("Funky" means "strange.")

- "Spunk" can also mean "full of energy" and can be used with anyone. Be careful of the context.

Squat
USED WITH FRIENDS

To defecate.

EXAMPLE 1

"Greg will be ready to go to the party after he squats."

EXAMPLE 2

"I don't see a bathroom, so I'm going to squat right here."

o Learn more...

- Literally, to "squat" means to "sit in a crouching position (knees bent and the butt on or near the heels)."

Stacked
USED WITH FRIENDS

Said of a woman with large breasts.

EXAMPLE 1

"My girlfriend is so stacked! She can hide an apple under one of her breasts."

EXAMPLE 2

"That girl is really stacked. Her breasts must be fake."

Staff
USED WITH FRIENDS

Penis.

EXAMPLE 1

"Gino is playing with his staff again. Will he ever stop masturbating?"

EXAMPLE 2

"Get your staff over here! I'm ready for sex."

o Learn more...

- You may also hear "spear" or "sword." (Ouch!)

IN OTHER WORDS...
"STUPID"

There are a lot of ways to call someone "a stupid person."

USED WITH ANYONE

Airhead (p. 2)

Bimbo (p. 15)

Birdbrain (p. 15)

Blockhead (p. 18)

Bonehead (p. 20)

Dimwit (p. 47)

Dipstick (p. 47)

Dode (p. 49)

Dolt (p. 50)

Doofus (p. 52)

Dummy (p. 56)

Dunce (p. 56)

Dweeb (p. 56)

Goon (p. 88)

Lam-o (p. 116)

Loser (p. 121)

Meathead (p. 126)

Nincompoop (p. 133)

Nitwit (p. 133)

Numbskull (p. 136)

Pinhead (p. 146)

Putz (p. 156)

Screw-up (p. 170)

Shmuck (p. 177)

Twit (p. 204)

Yo-yo (p. 219)

USED WITH FRIENDS

Ass clown (p. 5)

Asshead (p. 6)

Asswipe (p. 7)

Boob (p. 20)

Booger (p. 20)

Bung hole (p. 25)

Crackhead (p. 38)

Dipshit (p. 47)

Douche bag (p. 52)

Dumb-ass (p. 55)

Dumb-shit (p. 56)

Fat-head (p. 64)

Jack-off (p. 108)

Jerk-off (p. 109)

Numb-nuts (p. 135)

Shit-for-brains (p. 175)

USED WITH EXTREME CAUTION

Butt fuck (p. 26)

Chucklefuck (p. 32)

Dumb-fuck (p. 56)

Fuck-up (p. 75)

Fuckface (p. 77)

Fucknut (p. 77)

Fuckstick (p. 78)

Retard (p. 161)

Staggering Drunk
USED WITH ANYONE

Very drunk.

EXAMPLE 1

"I couldn't walk back to my apartment after the party. I was staggering drunk."

EXAMPLE 2

"My girlfriend needs to get staggering drunk before she'll have sex with me."

S-T-D
USED WITH ANYONE

Sexually Transmitted Disease.

EXAMPLE 1

"You should wear a condom when you have sex with her. She has several S-T-Ds."

EXAMPLE 2

"Ken didn't tell me he had any S-T-Ds. My doctor had to tell me."

Steamy
USED WITH ANYONE

Sexy.

EXAMPLE 1

"I just had a steamy date with Phil! We kissed for almost three hours."

EXAMPLE 2

"The love scene in the movie is really steamy. I need to have sex tonight!"

Stick Figure
USED WITH ANYONE

A skinny person.

EXAMPLE 1

"Walter's new wife is a stick figure! She needs to gain some weight."

EXAMPLE 2

"Lee is a stick figure. He needs more muscle!"

○ **Learn more...**

• A "stick figure" is a picture of a person drawn with thin lines.

Stick Something Where The Sun Don't Shine
USED WITH FRIENDS

To put something up one's butt.

EXAMPLE 1

"Either eat the sandwich the way I made it, or stick it where the sun don't shine."

EXAMPLE 2

"I quit my job yesterday and told my boss to stick that job where the sun don't shine."

Stiffy
USED WITH FRIENDS

An erect penis.

EXAMPLE 1

"I got a stiffy when I saw Charlene in her new dress."

EXAMPLE 2

"I hate getting a stiffy at work. It's hard to hide from my co-workers."

Stinking Drunk
USED WITH FRIENDS

Very drunk.

EXAMPLE 1

"Every time I see Charles, he's stinking drunk and smells like cheap wine."

EXAMPLE 2

"My latest goal is to get stinking drunk every Monday, Tuesday, Wednesday, Thursday, and Friday night."

Straight
USED WITH ANYONE

Heterosexual.

EXAMPLE 1

"I thought I was straight until I met Tina. Now I know I'm a lesbian!"

EXAMPLE 2

"Straight men are so rude! They wear ugly clothes and say terrible things."

Strap-on
USED WITH EXTREME CAUTION

A penis-shaped object worn on the crotch that gives women the ability to penetrate their partners during sex.

EXAMPLE 1

"Cheryl owns a strap-on. She and her husband like to take turns penetrating each other."

EXAMPLE 2

"A lot of lesbians don't buy strap-ons. They enjoy using their tongues, fingers, and hands instead."

Streak
USED WITH ANYONE

To run naked through a public place.

EXAMPLE 1

"Let's get drunk and streak across campus!"

EXAMPLE 2

"I'll give you ten dollars to streak through class tomorrow."

Learn more...

• "Streakers" are often found at sporting events.

Streetwalker
USED WITH ANYONE

A prostitute.

EXAMPLE 1

"Let's go talk to those streetwalkers. Maybe they'll have sex with us for free!"

EXAMPLE 2

"If I don't find a job soon, I'll have to become a streetwalker!"

Strip
USED WITH ANYONE

To take off one's clothing.

EXAMPLE 1

"I hate stripping at the doctor's office. It's so cold!"

EXAMPLE 2

"My girlfriend said she would strip for me if I bought her some diamond earrings."

Learn more...

• You may also hear "strip down" as in "Strip down to your underwear. I want to look at your body."

Stripper
USED WITH ANYONE

A person who takes off his or her clothes for money.

EXAMPLE 1

"I used to work as a stripper. I made a lot of money!"

EXAMPLE 2

"Hire a stripper for Jerry's party. He needs to see a naked woman before he gets married!"

Striptease
USED WITH ANYONE

A performance where someone takes off his or her clothing in a slow, sexual way.

EXAMPLE 1

"Ginger does a great striptease! I'll drive fifty miles to see her!"

EXAMPLE 2

"Their striptease show is terrible. The men are all fat!"

Learn more...

• A person who performs a "striptease" is called a "striptease artist."

• Actress Demi Moore played a stripper in the 1996 movie *Striptease*.

• In the 1997 British film *The Full Monty*, six unemployed men become strippers to make money. "The full monty" means "complete nudity" in British English.

Stuck Up
USED WITH ANYONE

Arrogant.

EXAMPLE 1
"Alice thinks she is better than us. She's so stuck up!"

EXAMPLE 2
"Wade isn't stuck up, he's just proud."

Stud
USED WITH ANYONE

A sexy man.

EXAMPLE 1
"You're a stud, Rick. Everyone I know wants to have sex with you!"

EXAMPLE 2
"That police officer is a stud! I'd let him handcuff me any day!"

o **Learn more...**

• You may also hear "stud muffin."

Stupid Drunk
USED WITH FRIENDS

Very drunk.

EXAMPLE 1
"I was stupid drunk last night. I woke up on a park bench!"

EXAMPLE 2
"She was so stupid drunk that she called her parents at 3:00 a.m. just to say hello."

Submissive
USED WITH FRIENDS

A person who enjoys being controlled or dominated by his or her sexual partner.

EXAMPLE 1
"My girlfriend is a submissive. She likes it when I tie her to the bed and tell her what to do."

EXAMPLE 2
"You're a submissive? Then come over here and take off all your clothes. I want to see you naked."

Suck
USED WITH FRIENDS

To be terrible.

EXAMPLE 1
"It sucks that we don't have enough money for a new T.V."

EXAMPLE 2
"You suck! I wanted to buy that car but you bought it first!"

Suck A Golf Ball Through A Garden Hose
USED WITH FRIENDS

To perform oral sex on a man very well.

EXAMPLE 1
"Alyse can suck a golf ball through a garden hose! She performs oral sex better than any woman I've ever dated."

EXAMPLE 2
"I won't marry a woman unless she can suck a golfball through a garden hose. I expect a lot from my wife."

Suck Ass
USED WITH FRIENDS

To be terrible.

EXAMPLE 1
"That movie sucked ass. We shouldn't have paid money to see something so bad."

EXAMPLE 2
"This food really sucks ass. Let's leave this restaurant."

Suck Face
USED WITH FRIENDS

To kiss.

EXAMPLE 1
"If we don't suck face soon, I'm going to find a new boyfriend!"

EXAMPLE 2
"Did you suck face with Kelly last night?"

Suck Someone Off
USED WITH EXTREME CAUTION

To perform oral sex on a man.

EXAMPLE 1

"That girl has really big lips. I imagine she would be great at sucking me off."

EXAMPLE 2

"The woman that sucked me off at the party had really hairy legs and a deep voice. Oh no!"

○ Learn more...

- You may also hear "suck off someone" as in "I heard that Cheryl sucked off Jon last night!"

Suck The Chrome Off A Trailer Hitch
USED WITH FRIENDS

To perform oral sex on a man very well.

EXAMPLE 1

"Everyone knows Heather can suck the chrome off a trailer hitch. That's why we always invite her to our parties."

EXAMPLE 2

"Keisha isn't smart or pretty, but she can suck the chrome off a trailer hitch."

AT THE MOVIES
"SCENT OF A WOMAN" (1992)

The Academy Award-winning movie *Scent of a Woman*, starring Al Pacino and Chris O'Donnell, tells the story of a college student who agrees to take care of a blind man for some much-needed money. But the blind man, Lieutenant Colonel Frank Slade, is nothing but trouble.

FRANK
"Women. What could you say? Who made them? God must have been a fucking genius."

Fucking (p. 77)

—

FRANK
"When in doubt, fuck."

Fuck (p. 72)

—

FRANK
"There are only two syllables in this whole wide world worth hearing: pussy."

Pussy (p. 155)

—

FRANK
"Harry, Jimmy, Trent — wherever you are out there, fuck you, too."

"Fuck you" (p. 76)

—

RANDY
"You want to know the truth? The truth is, he was an asshole before. Now he's just a blind asshole."

Asshole (p. 6)

—

FRANK
"Take the fucking wax out of your ears! Grow up! It's fuck your buddy, cheat on your wife, call your mother on Mother's Day....Charlie, it's all shit."

Fucking (p. 77)
Fuck (p. 72)
Shit (p. 174)

Swallow
USED WITH EXTREME CAUTION

To swallow the sperm ejaculated into one's mouth during oral sex.

EXAMPLE 1

"Don says his perfect girlfriend will have a great body, won't speak, and will love to swallow."

EXAMPLE 2

"Kendra always swallows when she performs oral sex. She says she likes the taste."

o **Learn more...**

- If someone asks you "Do you spit or swallow?" they are referring to your oral sex practices. It's a very rude question to ask!

Swap Spit
USED WITH FRIENDS

To kiss.

EXAMPLE 1

"Let's find a dark room and swap spit!"

EXAMPLE 2

"Kim and I swapped spit during the movie. She's a great kisser!"

o **Learn more...**

- To "swap" means to "trade."

Swing Both Ways
USED WITH ANYONE

To be bisexual (attracted to both men and women).

EXAMPLE 1

"Tom swings both ways. He'll have sex with almost anyone!"

EXAMPLE 2

"I know three people who swing both ways, and they're all really cool. I wish I liked both men and women!"

Swinger
USED WITH ANYONE

A person who is willing to try many different sexual activities.

EXAMPLE 1

"Are you a swinger? If you are, we can have a lot of fun!"

EXAMPLE 2

"I used to trade wives with my friend Larry, but I'm not a swinger anymore."

Switch Hitter
USED WITH FRIENDS

A bisexual (a person who is attracted to both men and women).

EXAMPLE 1

"Wesley is a switch hitter. He's dating Paul, Sheila, and Lisette!"

EXAMPLE 2

"I have a boyfriend, but I might be a switch hitter. I think Sarah is really cute!"

o **Learn more...**

- In baseball, a "switch hitter" can bat either right- or left-handed.

Sympathy Fuck
USED WITH EXTREME CAUTION

To have sex with someone because you feel sorry for him or her.

EXAMPLE 1

"When my pet rabbit died, my friend Katie gave me a sympathy fuck."

EXAMPLE 2

"Malcolm hasn't had sex in over a year. I think I'll give him a sympathy fuck to make him happy."

Syphilis
USED WITH ANYONE

A sexually transmitted disease.

EXAMPLE 1

"The Europeans gave syphilis to the Indians when they came to America."

EXAMPLE 2

"Jessica has syphilis. Be careful if you kiss her!"

o **Learn more...**

- You may also hear the shortened version pronounced "sif."

T IS FOR TANKED

T. And A.
USED WITH FRIENDS

Women's breasts and butts.

EXAMPLE 1
"I don't like football, but I love watching the cheerleaders for the T. and A."

EXAMPLE 2
"This movie has a lot of T. and A. You're going to love it!"

○ **Learn more...**

- Literally, this means "Tits" (p. 201) and "Ass" (p. 4).

Ta-tas
USED WITH FRIENDS

Breasts.

EXAMPLE 1
"Tina let me touch her ta-tas this morning. I'm so happy!"

EXAMPLE 2
"Brenda has some beautiful ta-tas. She should be on T.V."

Tail
USED WITH FRIENDS

Butt.

EXAMPLE 1
"Can you see the nice tail on that woman across the street? I'd love to touch that!"

EXAMPLE 2

"I'm only attracted to men with nice tails."

Take A Dump
USED WITH FRIENDS

To defecate.

EXAMPLE 1

"You're walking funny. Did you take a dump in your pants again?"

EXAMPLE 2

"I have to take a huge dump, but the toilet is broken."

Take A Leak
USED WITH FRIENDS

To urinate.

EXAMPLE 1

"Wait here. I'm going to take a leak."

EXAMPLE 2

"Jack went into the forest to take a leak, but that was six days ago."

Take A Shit
USED WITH FRIENDS

To defecate.

EXAMPLE 1

"I need to take a shit. Where's the bathroom?"

EXAMPLE 2

"Rod likes to take a shit before going to class."

Take A Squirt
USED WITH FRIENDS

To urinate.

EXAMPLE 1

"I have to take a squirt. Where is the bathroom?"

EXAMPLE 2

"Lenny took a squirt all over the toilet seat again. I hate him."

Take It Up the Ass
USED WITH EXTREME CAUTION

❶ To have anal sex.

EXAMPLE 1

"I heard that Marc takes it up the ass."

EXAMPLE 2

"Kelly won't take it up the ass. I need a new girlfriend."

❷ To accept abuse.

EXAMPLE 1

"I paid too much for my car. I really took it up the ass!"

EXAMPLE 2

"Sandra lies to Evan all the time. He's really taking it up the ass."

Take Shit
USED WITH FRIENDS

To accept abuse.

EXAMPLE 1

"I hate my job! I take shit from my boss all the time."

EXAMPLE 2

"I'm leaving! I won't take your shit anymore."

Talk To Huey On The Big White Phone
USED WITH FRIENDS

To vomit.

EXAMPLE 1

"I feel terrible. I'm going to talk to Huey on the big white phone and see if that helps."

EXAMPLE 2

"What's that noise? Sounds like someone is talking to Huey on the big white phone."

o Learn more...

- "The big white phone" represents the toilet when the lid is open, and "Huey" is a man's name, as well as the sound people make when they vomit.

Tanked
USED WITH ANYONE

Drunk.

EXAMPLE 1

"Janet fell off the sofa! She's completely tanked."

EXAMPLE 2

"Paul got tanked last night and took his pants off at the bar."

Tap That Ass
USED WITH EXTREME CAUTION

To have sexual contact or sex.

EXAMPLE 1
GERARD: "What do I have to do to tap that ass?"

NATALIE: "First, try cleaning your teeth."

EXAMPLE 2
"I would love to tap that woman's ass. She's so sexy!"

Teabag
USED WITH EXTREME CAUTION

To place one's testicles in the mouth of another person.

EXAMPLE 1
"My mother walked in my room when I was teabagging my girlfriend last night. I've never seen her so angry."

EXAMPLE 2
"Wilson had to get stitches last night! His boyfriend Todd accidentally bit into Wilson's testicles when they were teabagging."

Technicolor Yawn
USED WITH FRIENDS

Vomit.

EXAMPLE 1
"You should go home now before I show you my technicolor yawn."

EXAMPLE 2
"Paul's technicolor yawn was three minutes long. Yuck!"

Than Shit
USED WITH FRIENDS

To the extreme.

EXAMPLE 1
"Invite Chelsea to the party. She's funnier than shit!"

EXAMPLE 2
"My brother is dumber than shit. He can't even buy his own clothes!"

That Time Of The Month
USED WITH ANYONE

The time of the month when a woman menstruates.

EXAMPLE 1
"I really want to eat ice cream today. It must be that time of the month again."

EXAMPLE 2
"Whenever I get angry, my boyfriend assumes it's that time of the month. "

The Back Door
USED WITH FRIENDS

The anus.

EXAMPLE 1
"Regular sex is fun, but sometimes I like to enter through the back door."

EXAMPLE 2
"Victor's back door is too tight. We need to use a lot of lubrication to have anal sex."

The Big "O"
USED WITH FRIENDS

An orgasm.

EXAMPLE 1
"Carmen is never going to have an orgasm. Her husband thinks the big 'O' is a famous basketball player."

EXAMPLE 2
"If you want the big 'O,' you need to find a man with a big penis."

The Birds And The Bees
USED WITH ANYONE

How sex and sexual relationships work.

EXAMPLE 1
"No one explained the birds and the bees to me until I was 23 years old, and then it was too late."

EXAMPLE 2

"My mother gave me the talk about the birds and the bees yesterday. She was really embarrassed."

The Clap
USED WITH ANYONE

Gonorrhea, a sexually transmitted disease.

EXAMPLE 1

"I heard that Nelson has the clap. Did you have sex with him last night?"

EXAMPLE 2

"I'd pay for a prostitute, but I don't want to get the clap."

The Curse
USED WITH FRIENDS

Menstruation.

EXAMPLE 1

"Greta can't go swimming because she has the curse."

EXAMPLE 2

"Sarah doesn't like to have sex with me when she gets the curse."

The F-word
USED WITH ANYONE

The word "fuck" (p. 72).

EXAMPLE 1

"If you use the F-word, I'll wash your mouth with soap!"

EXAMPLE 2

"Jane is very innocent. She never uses the F-word."

The High Hard One
USED WITH FRIENDS

An erect penis.

EXAMPLE 1

"That girl is so cute! She gives me the high hard one."

EXAMPLE 2

"I took off her panties and gave her the high hard one in the elevator."

The Pill
USED WITH ANYONE

The "birth control pill," a pill taken each day to prevent pregnancy.

EXAMPLE 1

"Amy started taking the pill when she was dating Hank. She doesn't want to get pregnant."

EXAMPLE 2

"I won't date a woman unless she's taking the pill."

The Red Flag's Up
USED WITH FRIENDS

That woman is menstruating.

EXAMPLE 1

"Arlene cancelled our date on Friday. I think the red flag is up."

EXAMPLE 2

"Paula looks really tired today. I wonder if the red flag is up."

○ Learn more...

• You may also hear "the Red Sea is in."

The Runs
USED WITH FRIENDS

Diarrhea.

EXAMPLE 1

"Kyle can't play volleyball with you today. He has the runs."

EXAMPLE 2

"Jerry has gone to the bathroom three times in 45 minutes. He must have the runs."

The Shit
USED WITH FRIENDS

Awesome or important.

EXAMPLE 1

"Now that Nancy's dating a famous actor, she thinks she's the shit!"

EXAMPLE 2

"My new car is the shit! I paid a lot of money for it, but it was worth it!"

"The shit rolls downhill."
USED WITH FRIENDS

"The blame is placed on the person with the least power."

EXAMPLE 1
"The boss fired that new secretary Jean for the mistake, even though she wasn't responsible. I guess the shit rolls downhill."

EXAMPLE 2
"If something goes wrong, the shit will roll downhill and I'll get in trouble. No one else will accept the blame."

"The shit's going to hit the fan!"
USED WITH FRIENDS

"Something bad is going to happen!"

EXAMPLE 1
"If you don't finish this project, the shit's going to hit the fan tomorrow!"

EXAMPLE 2
"The shit will hit the fan when Mom sees my bad grades in school!"

o **Learn more...**

• Americans often shorten "going to" to "gonna," as in "The shit's gonna hit the fan!"

The Trots
USED WITH FRIENDS

Diarrhea.

EXAMPLE 1
"I hate it when I have the trots. I have to stay so close to the bathroom all day."

EXAMPLE 2
"My vacation was terrible because I had the trots all week. I was in the bathroom more than I was at the beach."

The Y
USED WITH EXTREME CAUTION

Vagina.

EXAMPLE 1
"Terry is coming to my house tonight, so I can spend some time down at the Y."

EXAMPLE 2
"I am taking my penis to the Y tonight when I see Marta."

o **Learn more...**

• "The Y" is also a nickname for the "YMCA," a popular community center.

DIALOGUE
"TOMMY WANTS TITS"

Here is a short dialogue between two Americans.

TOMMY
"Let's go to a topless bar tonight. I want to see some tits and get toasted."

CLETUS
"No way. Last time, you were three sheets to the wind and spent all night in the can."

TOMMY
"Okay, I promise not to get tanked this time."

CLETUS
"Tough shit. I'm not going."

Topless (p. 202)
Tits (p. 201)
Toasted (p. 201)

Three sheets to the wind (p. 198)
Can (p. 29)

Tanked (p. 194)

Tough shit (p. 202)

Thick
USED WITH ANYONE

Stupid.

EXAMPLE 1

"My mom is really thick if she thinks I like her cooking. It's terrible!"

EXAMPLE 2

"I tried to help Sean with his math homework, but he was too thick to understand."

○ **Learn more...**

• You may also hear "thick-headed" or "thick in the head" as in "Wow! You must be thick in the head if you dont' like that joke."

Thin As A Rail
USED WITH ANYONE

Very skinny.

EXAMPLE 1

"My son is as thin as a rail. He just won't eat!"

EXAMPLE 2

"I don't want to be as thin as a rail, but I do need to lose weight."

Thing
USED WITH FRIENDS

Penis.

EXAMPLE 1

"Tom wants me to touch his thing, but I don't think I can do it without laughing."

EXAMPLE 2

"Mort's thing is so small, he's too embarrassed to date anyone."

Think One's Shit Doesn't Stink
USED WITH FRIENDS

To think one is better than other people.

EXAMPLE 1

"Lafe thinks his shit doesn't stink, but he's just like us."

EXAMPLE 2

"Shae thinks her shit doesn't stink because she's rich."

Third Base
USED WITH FRIENDS

Touching genitals.

EXAMPLE 1

"I would pay any amount of money to get to third base with a girl like Jennise."

EXAMPLE 2

"I used to think that going to third base was the best until I had sex."

○ **Learn more...**

• In baseball, "third base" is the last base you must touch before you "score a run" (which means "have sex").

Third Leg
USED WITH FRIENDS

Penis.

EXAMPLE 1

"Douglas is always talking about his third leg, but I heard it isn't that big."

EXAMPLE 2

"Be careful! You might hurt your third leg if you keep jumping around like that."

○ **Learn more...**

• You may also hear "middle leg."

Three Sheets To The Wind
USED WITH ANYONE

Very drunk.

EXAMPLE 1

"I only had one drink, but I'm already three sheets to the wind!"

EXAMPLE 2

OZ: "Where's Ginny?"

MICKY: "She's three sheets to the wind and talking to the dog. Let's leave without her."

Threesome
USED WITH ANYONE

Sex between three people at the same time.

EXAMPLE 1

"All I want for Christmas is to have a threesome with my girlfriend and her cousin."

EXAMPLE 2

"Threesomes, sex with animals, drugs...Joseph will do anything!"

Throne

USED WITH ANYONE

Toilet.

EXAMPLE 1

"Sorry, Lucy can't come to the phone now. She's on the throne."

EXAMPLE 2

"Bob cleans the throne every day because his roommate always urinates on the seat."

Throw One In Her

USED WITH EXTREME CAUTION

To have sex.

EXAMPLE 1

"I usually don't like women with small breasts, but I'd throw one in her."

EXAMPLE 2

"That girl is so ugly, you'd have to pay me to throw one in her."

o **Learn more...**

- In this phrase, "one" refers to the man's penis.

AT THE MOVIES
"TITANIC" (1997)

The Academy Award-winning movie *Titanic*, starring Kate Winslet and Leonardo DiCaprio, is a love story set during the disasterous first voyage of the Titanic, a ship that was supposed to be unsinkable. The story is told by an old woman who was on the ship when it sank.

JACK
"We are the luckiest sons of bitches in the world, you know that?"

Son of a bitch (p. 184)

—

TOMMY
"Ah, forget it, lad. You'd like as have angels fly out of your arse as get next to the likes of her."

Arse (p. 4)

—

TOMMY
"That's typical. First class dogs come down here to take a shit."

Dog (p. 49)
Take a shit (p. 194)

—

ROSE
"I'd rather be a whore to him than your wife!"

Whore (p. 214)

—

ROSE
"You unimaginable bastard!"

Bastard (p. 11)

—

LEWIS
"Incredible. There's Smith, and he's standing there, and he's got the iceberg warning in his fucking hand — excuse me — in his hand, and he's ordering *more speed*."

Fucking (p. 77)

Throw Up
USED WITH ANYONE

To vomit.

EXAMPLE 1

"I made dinner for my mom, but it made her throw up. I'm not a good cook."

EXAMPLE 2

"Donald threw up during gym class today. They shouldn't have made him run so far."

Tickle The Tiger
USED WITH FRIENDS

To masturbate.

EXAMPLE 1

"I like to tickle the tiger on the balcony as I watch my neighbor take her clothes off."

EXAMPLE 2

"You should always tickle the tiger before you go on a date. Then you won't think about having sex too much."

Tight-ass
USED WITH FRIENDS

A person who is unable to have fun.

EXAMPLE 1

"Robert really needs a vacation. He's such a tight-ass!"

EXAMPLE 2

"Are you coming to the party, or are you going to be a tight-ass?"

Tight-fisted
USED WITH ANYONE

Not willing to spend money.

EXAMPLE 1

"Eddie's too tight-fisted to buy dinner for me."

EXAMPLE 2

"Can you pay for our train tickets, or are you too tight-fisted?"

o **Learn more...**

- When you hold your money in your hand and squeeze so that it can't leave your hand for spending, you are "tight-fisted."

- You may also hear "close-fisted."

Tightwad
USED WITH ANYONE

A person unwilling to spend money.

EXAMPLE 1

"John is a tightwad! He never spends money on anything fun."

EXAMPLE 2

"You never buy me flowers. You're a tightwad!"

Tinkle
USED WITH ANYONE

To urinate.

EXAMPLE 1

"Daddy, I have to go tinkle. Can you take me to the toilet?"

EXAMPLE 2

"The dog tinkled in my shoes again. I'm going to kill him!"

o **Learn more...**

- This phrase is used most often by children and adults talking to children.

Tipsy
USED WITH ANYONE

A little drunk.

EXAMPLE 1

"Ned is getting tipsy. He's laughing like a little girl!"

EXAMPLE 2

"That wine made me tipsy! I need to sit down."

Tit Fuck
USED WITH EXTREME CAUTION

To rub a man's penis between a woman's breasts, usually until the man orgasms.

EXAMPLE 1

"Lisa's breasts are too small to tit fuck."

EXAMPLE 2

"Wendy likes tit fucking better than regular sex. She knows she can't get pregnant that way."

o **Learn more...**

- You may also hear "titty fuck."

Tits
USED WITH EXTREME CAUTION

Breasts.

EXAMPLE 1

"Your wife has the nicest tits I've ever seen. You're a lucky man!"

EXAMPLE 2

"All tits are different and beautiful in their own way. Don't listen to anyone who says there's one perfect size and shape."

o **Learn more...**

- You may also hear "titties."

Toasted
USED WITH ANYONE

Drunk.

EXAMPLE 1

"Mom only had one beer, but she looks really toasted."

EXAMPLE 2

"To celebrate my new job, I'm going to the bar to get toasted."

Tool
USED WITH ANYONE

❶ **A person who is easily controlled by other people.**

EXAMPLE 1

"You're such a tool, Fred. You always do what you're told."

EXAMPLE 2

"I used to be a tool, but now I do what I want instead of listening to my friends."

❷ **Penis.**

EXAMPLE 1

"Arthur has a small tool, but he knows how to use it! We have great sex."

EXAMPLE 2

"Mark is always playing with his tool. He needs to find a different hobby."

o **Learn more...**

- A tool (like a hammer) doesn't do anything unless it's used by someone.

- You may also hear "toolbox," as in "Harry is helping the teacher clean her erasers. What a toolbox!"

Toot
USED WITH FRIENDS

To expel gas from the anus; to flatulate.

EXAMPLE 1

"Devon toots whenever he wants. His mom is horrified!"

EXAMPLE 2

"I've been tooting ever since I ate that Mexican food last night. Sorry if it smells in here."

o **Learn more...**

- A popular American rhyme is "Beans, beans, the magical fruit, the more you eat, the more you toot."

Top
USED WITH FRIENDS

❶ **The dominant person in a sexual situation.**

EXAMPLE 1

"Yurgi is a great top! He's always in control, and I love to do whatever he says!"

EXAMPLE 2

"I'm not a good top. I love to tie Melissa to the bed, but then I don't know what to do!"

❷ **For homosexual men, the man who penetrates the other man with his penis.**

EXAMPLE 1

"Fred is cute, but I think he's a top. I'm not looking for one of those."

EXAMPLE 2

"I am surprised to hear that Gary and Dave are still dating. I thought they were both tops."

Topless
USED WITH ANYONE

Naked above the waist.

EXAMPLE 1

"We went to a topless bar for Quico's birthday, and we all got really drunk."

EXAMPLE 2

"Once I saw a woman riding the train topless. Every man on the train was looking at her breasts."

Toss One's Cookies
USED WITH ANYONE

To vomit.

EXAMPLE 1

"What could be worse than our President going to Japan and tossing his cookies on the Japanese Prime Minister?"

EXAMPLE 2

"Brady's dinner was so bad, I tossed my cookies as soon as I left his house."

Tough Shit
USED WITH FRIENDS

A nasty way of saying that someone else's problem or opinion isn't important.

EXAMPLE 1

"You don't like my shirt? Tough shit! I don't care what you think."

EXAMPLE 2

"If Lynn isn't happy with the new president, that's tough shit. She should have voted."

o **Learn more...**

• You may also hear "tough titty" or "tough titties." A "tit" (p. 201) is a "breast."

Tramp
USED WITH FRIENDS

A person who has sex often with different people.

EXAMPLE 1

"I want to date Melissa, but I heard she's a tramp."

EXAMPLE 2

"Natalie had sex with every man on the football team. She's a tramp!"

o **Learn more...**

• Women are called "tramps" more often than men.

• Literally, a "tramp" is a homeless person who sleeps in a different place every night.

Trannie
USED WITH FRIENDS

A transsexual (see next entry).

EXAMPLE 1

"Your sister is now your brother? I didn't know she was a trannie!"

EXAMPLE 2

"Why are you wearing that dress, Noah? Are you a trannie?"

Transsexual
USED WITH ANYONE

❶ **A person who has had an operation to become a person of the opposite sex.**

EXAMPLE 1

"I'm a transsexual. My parents named me George, but after my operation, you'll have to call me Georgette!"

EXAMPLE 2

"Your date is pretty, but she has a very low voice. Is she a transsexual?"

❷ **A person who wants to be recognized by society as a person of the opposite sex.**

EXAMPLE 1

"Barnaby is a transsexual. He likes to wear makeup and pantyhose with his dresses."

EXAMPLE 2

"Jane keeps her hair really short and wears suits. She's a transsexual — she wants to be treated like a man."

Transvestite
USED WITH ANYONE

A person who dresses and acts like a person of the opposite sex.

EXAMPLE 1

"I thought our waiter was a woman, but he's a transvestite."

EXAMPLE 2

"I can never tell if I'm talking to a woman or a transvestite."

Treat Someone Like Shit
USED WITH FRIENDS

To behave badly towards someone.

EXAMPLE 1

"Ned treated me like shit, so I left him."

EXAMPLE 2

"I used to treat my mom like shit, but I really love her now."

Trick
USED WITH FRIENDS

A sexual act performed for money.

EXAMPLE 1

"Joy had four tricks tonight. She made more than two hundred dollars."

EXAMPLE 2

"Leena hasn't had a trick in a week. She needs to lower her prices!"

○ **Learn more...**

• You may also hear "turn tricks" as in "I turned tricks for a few years to earn money for college."

Trouser Snake
USED WITH FRIENDS

Penis.

EXAMPLE 1

"My trouser snake and I are looking for a sexy woman."

EXAMPLE 2

"I had three girls sucking on my trouser snake, and then I woke up from my dream."

○ **Learn more...**

• You may also hear "one-eyed trouser snake" or "trouser trout."

Tub
USED WITH FRIENDS

A fat person.

EXAMPLE 1

"That tub at the next table tried to eat my food when I went to the bathroom!"

IN OTHER WORDS... "TOILET"

If you want to be polite, say "restroom," "bathroom," or "facilities." Everything else is too graphic for polite company!

USED WITH ANYONE

Facilities (p. 61)

Head (p. 96)

Potty (p. 153)

Throne (p. 199)

USED WITH FRIENDS

Andy Gump (p. 3)

Can (p. 29)

Crapper (p. 39)

Pot (p. 152)

Shithouse (p. 176)

Shitter (p. 176)

EXAMPLE 2

"Monica's a tub! She'll never finish the marathon."

o **Learn more...**

- You may also hear "tub of lard" or "tubby."

Tune One's Organ
USED WITH FRIENDS

To masturbate.

EXAMPLE 1

"We were supposed to go see a movie, but Kip decided to stay home and tune his organ all night. He really needs a girlfriend!"

EXAMPLE 2

"I like to tune my organ at least once a day."

Turd
USED WITH FRIENDS

Excrement.

EXAMPLE 1

"I'm so mad! Someone put a turd on top of my car while I was in the bank."

EXAMPLE 2

"When I was young, I tried to make my brother eat dog turds."

Turned On
USED WITH FRIENDS

To become sexually aroused.

EXAMPLE 1

"My teacher turns me on so much, I can't think about anything but sex during math class."

EXAMPLE 2

"I love wearing this dress! It really turns on all the guys."

Tush
USED WITH ANYONE

Butt.

EXAMPLE 1

"My husband has hair all over his tush."

EXAMPLE 2

"Ruppert falls on his tush whenever he tries to ski."

o **Learn more...**

- You may also hear "tushy."

Twat
USED WITH EXTREME CAUTION

Vagina; a woman's pubic area.

EXAMPLE 1

"Bobby Jo shaved her twat, so she could swim faster in the competition."

EXAMPLE 2

"Mitch says his new girlfriend has an amazing twat. He'd rather perform oral sex on her than have sex!"

Twelve-step
USED WITH FRIENDS

A drunk person.

EXAMPLE 1

"Hey, twelve-step! I'm going to call a taxi for you. You shouldn't be driving home."

EXAMPLE 2

"That twelve-step at the end of the bar is going to vomit."

o **Learn more...**

- You enter a "Twelve-Step Program" when you want to stop drinking alcohol. Calling someone a "Twelve-step" implies that they need the program because they are obviously drinking too much.

Twit
USED WITH ANYONE

A stupid person.

EXAMPLE 1

"Elizabeth forgot about the meeting and went home. What a twit!"

EXAMPLE 2

BRAD: "I can't find my shoes."

SHEILA: "You twit! They're under your bed."

U IS FOR UPCHUCK

Ugs

USED WITH ANYONE

Ugly.

EXAMPLE 1
"Those curtains are ugs. You need to get new ones."

EXAMPLE 2
"Sam is totally ugs. I hate to even look at him."

o **Learn more...**

- This is a shortened version of "ugly."

Undies

USED WITH ANYONE

Underwear.

EXAMPLE 1
"I took Melissa's undies from her bedroom and sold them on the Internet for $20."

EXAMPLE 2
"I'm wearing purple undies for my date with Paul tonight. Purple is his favorite color."

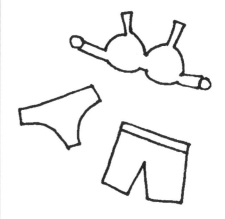

IN OTHER WORDS...
"UGLY"

Most Americans like to be creative when they call someone "ugly."

USED WITH FRIENDS

A face only a mother could love (p. 1)

Beaten with the ugly stick (p. 13)

Butt ugly (p. 27)

Coyote ugly (p. 37)

Dog (p. 49)

Eaten by wolves and shit over a cliff (p. 58)

Fell out of the ugly tree and hit every branch on the way down (p. 64)

Fugly (p. 78)

Gross (p. 88)

Hard on the eyes (p. 91)

Hit in the face with a hot bag of nickels (p. 100)

Ugs (p. 205)

Unit
USED WITH FRIENDS

Penis.

EXAMPLE 1
"I lifted up the blanket while Anthony was sleeping and looked at his unit."

EXAMPLE 2
"Quinn's unit was much bigger than I expected. I can't wait until we have sex!"

Unmentionables
USED WITH ANYONE

Underwear; very private clothes.

EXAMPLE 1
"Tim just walked into my bedroom and saw all my unmentionables in a pile on the floor. I'm so embarrassed!"

EXAMPLE 2
"Don't go in the bathroom! Wendy is only wearing her unmentionables."

○ **Learn more...**

• This phrase is used by older people.

Up Shit Creek
USED WITH FRIENDS

To be in trouble.

EXAMPLE 1
"We'll be up shit creek if we don't find Jannie's dog!"

EXAMPLE 2
"I have to finish this project tonight, and I haven't started yet! I'm really up shit creek."

○ **Learn more...**

• This is a more offensive way to say "up the creek without a paddle" (see next entry).

Up The Creek Without A Paddle
USED WITH ANYONE

To be in trouble without any options.

EXAMPLE 1
"Jeff can't pay his rent this month. He's up the creek without a paddle."

EXAMPLE 2
"If I don't find a job soon, I'll be up the creek without a paddle."

○ **Learn more...**

• A "creek" is a small river.

Up The Wazoo

USED WITH ANYONE

A lot.

EXAMPLE 1

"I have homework up the wazoo. I'll never finish!"

EXAMPLE 2

"Stacy has breasts up the wazoo! How can that girl even walk with such big breasts?"

Up The Yin-yang

USED WITH ANYONE

A lot.

EXAMPLE 1

"Nate's got money up the yin-yang. He bought two cars last year!"

EXAMPLE 2

"I have faults up the yin-yang. I drink too much, I smoke, and I lie to everyone."

"Up yours!"

USED WITH EXTREME CAUTION

Phrase indicating anger or dislike.

EXAMPLE 1

ALEX: "Move your car. You're blocking the road!"

SHEILA: "Up yours!"

EXAMPLE 2

"Hey, Mayor Thompson! Up yours! You're the worst mayor this city has ever seen."

o Learn more...

• The soda company *7-Up* ran a very successful advertising campaign with "Make 7" on the front of a T-shirt, and "Up Yours!" on the back.

Upchuck

USED WITH ANYONE

To vomit.

EXAMPLE 1

"I thought the guy on the train was going to upchuck all over me."

EXAMPLE 2

"Someone upchucked in the street and I stepped in it."

IN OTHER WORDS... "URINATE"

Because most Americans don't like to talk about urination, they often use funny or polite phrases when they need to "urinate." The most common is probably "Please excuse me. I need to use the restroom."

USED WITH ANYONE

Go (p. 85)

Go check the plumbing (p. 85)

Go wee (p. 86)

Make a pit stop (p. 123)

Pee (p. 143)

Pee-pee (p. 143)

Piddle (p. 144)

Powder one's nose (p. 153)

See a man about a horse (p. 173)

Tinkle (p. 200)

Void (p. 210)

USED WITH FRIENDS

Drain the lizard (p. 54)

Piss (p. 146)

Take a leak (p. 194)

Take a squirt (p. 194)

Whiz (p. 214)

V IS FOR VIRGIN

V.D.
USED WITH ANYONE

Venereal Disease, a disease involving sex or the genitals.

EXAMPLE 1
"I've been having sex since I was 14 years old, but I don't have any V.D.s."

EXAMPLE 2
"What kind of V.D. did Bradford get? I hope it's nothing bad!"

Vertical Smile
USED WITH EXTREME CAUTION

Vagina.

EXAMPLE 1
"If I don't see Chelsea's vertical smile tonight, I'm going to find another girlfriend. I've been waiting for over four months!"

EXAMPLE 2
"My wife's vertical smile is much nicer than her actual smile!"

Vibrator

USED WITH FRIENDS

A machine (often shaped like a penis) that vibrates, used for sexual pleasure.

EXAMPLE 1

"The best orgasm I ever had was from my big green vibrator."

EXAMPLE 2

"Never buy your girlfriend a vibrator because she won't want to have sex with you anymore."

Virgin

USED WITH ANYONE

A person who has never had sex.

EXAMPLE 1

"Cheryl is still a virgin? I thought she had sex with Mick last year. I guess I was wrong."

EXAMPLE 2

"My father was a virgin until he got married. I really respect that."

o Learn more...

- The most famous virgin is Mary. According to the *Bible*, she had a son but never had sex!

IN OTHER WORDS...
"VOMIT"

Vomiting is very unpleasant. Americans have responded by creating a lot of funny ways to describe it.

USED WITH ANYONE	USED WITH FRIENDS
Be sick (p. 12)	Barf (p. 11)
Frab (p. 70)	Blow chunks (p. 18)
Lose one's lunch (p. 120)	Boot (p. 20)
Pray to the porcelain god (p. 153)	Buick (p. 23)
Retch (p. 161)	Chum (p. 32)
Spit up (p. 186)	Chunder (p. 33)
Throw up (p. 200)	Decorate the pavement (p. 45)
Toss one's cookies (p. 202)	Deliver street pizza (p. 45)
Upchuck (p. 207)	Dishonorable discharge (p. 48)
	Drive the porcelain bus (p. 54)
	Heave (p. 97)
	Holler at the toilet (p. 101)
	Hurl (p. 105)
	Laugh at the lawn (p. 116)
	Puke (p. 155)
	Ralph (p. 160)
	Shout at one's shoes (p. 178)
	Spew (p. 185)
	Talk to Huey on the big white phone (p. 194)
	Technicolor yawn (p. 195)
	Yak (p. 218)
	York (p. 219)
	Yuke (p. 219)

Void

USED WITH ANYONE

To urinate or defecate.

EXAMPLE 1

"Do you know where the bathroom is? I have to void."

EXAMPLE 2

"If you drink too much water before you go to sleep, you'll have to void in the middle of the night."

Voyeur

USED WITH ANYONE

A person who enjoys watching other people have sex.

EXAMPLE 1

"Kyle is a voyeur. He asked if he could watch me have sex with my husband."

EXAMPLE 2

"I don't know if I'm a voyeur, but I like to watch women touching each other's bodies."

IN OTHER WORDS...
"VAGINA"

Most of the words for "vagina" are crude rather than romantic. A lot of people just avoid referring to that body part completely!

USED WITH FRIENDS

C-U-Next-Tuesday (p. 28)

Cha-cha (p. 30)

Honey pot (p. 102)

Wonder-down-under (p. 216)

USED WITH EXTREME CAUTION

Beaver (p. 14)

Box (p. 22)

Cooch (p. 36)

Cooter (p. 36)

Crack (p. 38)

Cunt (p. 42)

Fur pie (p. 78)

Furburger (p. 78)

Hole (p. 101)

Love dungeon (p. 121)

Muff (p. 130)

Muffin (p. 130)

Poonani (p. 150)

Poontang (p. 150)

Pussy (p. 155)

Snatch (p. 183)

The Y (p. 197)

Twat (p. 204)

Vertical smile (p. 208)

W IS FOR WHACKO

Washroom
USED WITH ANYONE

The bathroom.

EXAMPLE 1
"Excuse me, sir. Where is the washroom?"

EXAMPLE 2
"My boss has a huge house. The washroom is bigger than my whole apartment!"

Wasted
USED WITH ANYONE

Drunk.

EXAMPLE 1
"Marc was so wasted! He doesn't even remember kissing my brother."

EXAMPLE 2
"The party was so great, even the dog got wasted!"

Water Sports
USED WITH FRIENDS

Sexual activity involving urine or urination.

EXAMPLE 1
"Emily enjoys water sports, but I don't think I can urinate on her."

EXAMPLE 2
"Julia and Mike enjoy water sports. She said they urinate on each other in the shower every morning."

o Learn more...

- Literally, "water sports" are activities like water-skiing, sailboating, and riding jet skis.

Weirdo
USED WITH ANYONE

A strange person.

EXAMPLE 1

"Look at that weirdo over there. I think he's wearing underwear on his head!"

EXAMPLE 2

"My sister is a weirdo. She goes to work dressed up like a character from *Star Trek*."

Wet
USED WITH FRIENDS

Sexually aroused (women only).

EXAMPLE 1

"Brian's so strong and handsome! I get wet just looking at him."

EXAMPLE 2

"Katie gets so wet that we never have to use other lubrication when we have sex."

o **Learn more...**

• When a woman gets sexually aroused, her vagina becomes wet.

Wet Dream
USED WITH FRIENDS

An orgasm that occurs during sleep.

EXAMPLE 1

"I never had a wet dream, but I wish I did! I would love to dream about sex."

EXAMPLE 2

"Luke had another wet dream last night. I found sperm in the sheets again this morning."

Whack Off
USED WITH FRIENDS

To masturbate.

EXAMPLE 1

"I think Jack just whacked off in the kitchen. The floor is really sticky!"

EXAMPLE 2

"My girlfriend saw me whacking off yesterday. I told her that it feels better than having sex with her."

Whacko
USED WITH ANYONE

A crazy person.

EXAMPLE 1

"I just saw some whacko on television trying to juggle kittens."

EXAMPLE 2

"Only a real whacko would drink gasoline."

o **Learn more...**

• You may also hear "wacky" or "whack job" as in "Look at that whack job running into traffic. I haven't seen anything that wacky for years."

• Singer Michael Jackson has been called "Whacko Jacko."

Whale
USED WITH FRIENDS

A fat person.

EXAMPLE 1

"That whale is eating a piece of pizza while jogging! He'll never get thin like that."

EXAMPLE 2

"Martina's a whale, but I like big women. We're in love!"

o **Learn more...**

• You may also hear "beached whale" which means "a person so fat that he or she can't even move."

Wham Bam, Thank You, Ma'am
USED WITH FRIENDS

To have sex with a woman quickly.

EXAMPLE 1

"She came back to my apartment, then wham bam, thank you ma'am, and she left."

EXAMPLE 2

"I did a little wham bam, thank you ma'am with Seiko last night."

o **Learn more...**

• You may also hear "Slam bam, thank you, ma'am."

What The Fuck
USED WITH EXTREME CAUTION

Indicates surprise or disbelief.

EXAMPLE 1
"What the fuck is on top of that car? It looks like a naked woman!"

EXAMPLE 2
"What the fuck! Katrina was supposed to be here an hour ago!"

o **Learn more...**

• You may also hear "W-T-F" as in "There's a huge elephant in the sky! W-T-F?"

What The Hell
USED WITH FRIENDS

Indicates surprise or disbelief.

EXAMPLE 1
"There's a strange light in the sky. What the hell?"

EXAMPLE 2
"What the hell is that shirt you're wearing? You look like a clown."

Whip The Weenie
USED WITH FRIENDS

To masturbate.

EXAMPLE 1
"My professor gets me so excited! I'm going to leave class early, so I can whip the weenie."

EXAMPLE 2
"Last night I saw a guy whipping his weenie in a parking lot. I called the police and he was arrested."

o **Learn more...**

• You may also hear "whip the worm" as in "I didn't whip the worm until I was 20 years old."

DIALOGUE
"RAOUL WAS A WUSS"

Here is a short dialogue between two Americans.

RAOUL
"My new girlfriend likes water sports. She asked me to take a whiz on her last night."

WILLIAM
"What the fuck! Did you do it?"

RAOUL
"Yeah, I was really wasted. And I didn't want her to think I was a wuss. But I'm really embarrassed about it now."

WILLIAM
"That's what you get for dating a white trash whore."

Water sports (p. 211)
Whiz (p. 214)

What the fuck (p. 213)

Wasted (p. 211)
Wuss (p. 216)

White trash (p. 214)
Whore (p. 214)

White Trash
USED WITH FRIENDS

Poor white people considered stupid.

EXAMPLE 1
"Patty is white trash! Her family is very poor, and she doesn't know how to be polite to anyone."

EXAMPLE 2
"The other kids at school think I'm white trash just because I wear old clothes every day."

Whiz
USED WITH FRIENDS

To urinate.

EXAMPLE 1
"Your apartment looks like someone whizzed all over it. Do you have dogs?"

EXAMPLE 2
"I can whiz more than five feet. How far can you whiz?"

Whore
USED WITH FRIENDS

❶ A woman who trades sex for money; a prostitute.

EXAMPLE 1
"That whore is pretty, but she's too expensive for me. I only have $50."

EXAMPLE 2
"Alice has been a whore for years. That's how she earned enough money for college."

❷ A woman who has sex with a lot of people.

EXAMPLE 1
"Is your sister dating her teacher now? She's a total whore!"

EXAMPLE 2
"That whore Veronica will sleep with any guy that breathes."

❸ A nasty woman.

EXAMPLE 1
"When did Tina become such a whore? She used to be so nice!"

EXAMPLE 2
MANDY: "I've been dating your brother for months. I love him more than you."

GREG: "You whore!"

○ Learn more...

- "Whore" is another word for "prostitute," but is often used as a general insult for women.

Whorehouse
USED WITH FRIENDS

A place of prostitution.

EXAMPLE 1
"Sandra looks like she's working at a whorehouse. She should wear a longer skirt to work!"

EXAMPLE 2
"Do you know any good whorehouses in Nevada? I need sex!"

○ Learn more...

- There is a popular movie called *The Best Little Whorehouse In Texas* (starring Burt Reynolds and Dolly Parton) about a sheriff who tries to keep a place of prostitution open.

Wiener
USED WITH FRIENDS

Penis.

EXAMPLE 1
"My wiener needs sex! I'm tired of masturbating all the time."

EXAMPLE 2
"Francine tried to cut off Dan's wiener when they were fighting last night!"

○ Learn more...

- You may also hear "weenie."

- A "wiener" is also a "hot dog."

Willie
USED WITH FRIENDS

Penis.

EXAMPLE 1

"P.J. is so strange. He loves to run through the school with his willie hanging out of his pants."

EXAMPLE 2

"With a willie that small, no woman will want to have sex with Winthrop."

Windbag
USED WITH ANYONE

A person who talks too much.

EXAMPLE 1

"My teacher is a windbag. It took him ten minutes to explain the test!"

EXAMPLE 2

"Tim's mother always talks about her childhood. What a windbag!"

o **Learn more...**

• You may also hear "long-winded" as in "Your boyfriend is really long-winded. I thought he'd never stop talking about his new car!"

Witch
USED WITH ANYONE

A nasty woman.

EXAMPLE 1

"My mother is a witch. She hates it when I have fun."

AT THE MOVIES
"WHAT WOMEN WANT" (2000)

What Women Want, starring Mel Gibson and Helen Hunt, is about an executive who gets hit on the head and can suddenly understand what women are thinking. The experience helps him to understand women.

NICK
"What's the difference between a wife and a job? After 10 years, a job still sucks."

Suck (p. 190)

—

LOLA
"You talk to me like a woman, you think like a woman. Nick, come on, admit it. You're totally and completely gay!"

Gay (p. 80)

—

DARCY
"Before I came here, I heard that you were a tough chauvinistic prick."

Prick (p. 154)

—

DARCY
"I'm the man-eating bitch Darth Vader of the ad world."

Bitch (p. 16)

—

DARCY
"You wore control-top pantyhose? And how did you look in them?"

NICK
"Hot."

Hot (p. 104)

—

NICK
"What the hell's wrong with me?"

What the hell (p. 213)

EXAMPLE 2

"You're such a witch today, Callie! Why are you being so mean?"

o **Learn more...**

- Literally, a "witch" is also a "person who practices Witchcraft or Wicca as a religion."

- Women are called "witches" more often than men.

Womanizer
USED WITH ANYONE

A man who likes to have sex with many women, but may not care about them.

EXAMPLE 1

"Don't date Val! He's a womanizer. As soon as you have sex, he'll find someone else."

EXAMPLE 2

"If you don't care about the women you date, you're just a womanizer!"

Wonder-down-under
USED WITH FRIENDS

Vagina.

EXAMPLE 1

"I visited Celia's wonder-down-under last night!"

EXAMPLE 2

"Peter doesn't like my wonder-down-under. He never performs oral sex on me."

Woody
USED WITH FRIENDS

An erect penis.

EXAMPLE 1

"Dave always gets a woody when he sees the cheerleaders from the basketball team."

EXAMPLE 2

"I've had a woody all day. I can't get my penis to relax."

o **Learn more...**

- You may also hear "wood" or "sporting wood" as in "Ernie started sporting wood during the middle of his lecture. He must have been thinking about sex!"

Working Girl
USED WITH ANYONE

A prostitute.

EXAMPLE 1

"That's the tallest working girl I've ever seen. I can't imagine having sex with her."

EXAMPLE 2

"Working girls have to worry about sexual diseases every time they get a customer. It's a difficult life."

o **Learn more...**

- A "working girl" can also mean "a woman who works" like it does in the 1988 film *Working Girl*, starring Melanie Griffith, Harrison Ford, and Sigourney Weaver, although this meaning is less common.

Wuss
USED WITH ANYONE

A coward.

EXAMPLE 1

"If you can't dive into the pool, you're a wuss!"

EXAMPLE 2

"You're a wuss! You're too scared to play soccer with us!"

o **Learn more...**

- You may also hear "wussy."

IS FOR
X-RATED

X-rated

USED WITH ANYONE

Very sexual.

EXAMPLE 1
"This T.V. show should be X-rated! You can see the man's penis!"

EXAMPLE 2
"Maya's dress should be X-rated. You can see her vagina!"

o Learn more...

- Movies with very sexual material are "X-rated," so people under 18 can't watch.

- The sign or rating "XXX" means the show or movie is extremely sexual.

Y IS FOR
YO-YO

Yabbos
USED WITH FRIENDS

Breasts.

EXAMPLE 1
"Yabbos are my favorite part of a woman's body. They're so much fun to touch!"

EXAMPLE 2
"A woman with nice yabbos is worth the world to me."

Yak
USED WITH FRIENDS

To vomit.

EXAMPLE 1
"The bacon made me yak all night long. It must have been bad."

EXAMPLE 2
"When I saw what the fire did to that helpless man, I had to yak."

Yank The Yak
USED WITH FRIENDS

To masturbate.

EXAMPLE 1
"The new swimsuit catalog is here! I'm going to yank the yak. I'll see you in five minutes."

EXAMPLE 2
"The airplane was so empty that I yanked the yak in my seat and no one noticed."

Yellow

USED WITH ANYONE

A coward.

EXAMPLE 1
"If you can't walk alone at night, you must be yellow."

EXAMPLE 2
"Isabelle is yellow! She's afraid to ask Ned for a date."

o Learn more...

- You may also hear "yellow-bellied" as in "Barth is too yellow-bellied to go rock-climbing with us."

- The color yellow has been linked to cowardice for hundreds of years, even back to the ancient Greeks.

Yo-yo

USED WITH ANYONE

A stupid person.

EXAMPLE 1
"You yo-yo! You parked in the wrong place again!"

EXAMPLE 2
"Don't be a yo-yo! Get over here and help me!"

York

USED WITH FRIENDS

To vomit.

EXAMPLE 1
"Samantha was about to york, but then she just fell down."

EXAMPLE 2
"The food at that Indian restaurant makes me york every time I eat it."

"You bet your sweet ass!"

USED WITH FRIENDS

"Yes, of course!"

EXAMPLE 1
CARRIE: "Do you like apple pie?"

JERRY: "You bet your sweet ass I do!"

EXAMPLE 2
"You bet your sweet ass I'm going to ask for more money! Everyone else in the company got more."

You-know-what

USED WITH ANYONE

A phrase used instead of a bad word.

EXAMPLE 1
"Melissa has sex with everyone! She's a you-know-what."

EXAMPLE 2
"Paula kicked Mike in the you-know-what when he tried to kiss her!"

Yuke

USED WITH FRIENDS

To vomit.

EXAMPLE 1
"Ed yuked all over the table, which made everyone else yuke. It was terrible."

EXAMPLE 2
"As soon as I got pregnant, I started yuking every morning."

Z IS FOR ZIT

Zit
USED WITH FRIENDS

Pimple.

EXAMPLE 1
"I don't want to have my picture taken today. I have a big zit on my nose."

EXAMPLE 2
"I am 39 years old and I still get zits. I was hoping that after high school, I wouldn't get them anymore."

MAIN INDEX

A Face Only A Mother Could Love
. . . . 1
A Face That Could Crack A Mirror
see: *A Face Only A*
Mother Could Love . . . 1
A Face That Could Stop A Clock
see: *A Face Only A*
Mother Could Love . . . 1
A Few Sandwiches Short
Of A Picnic 1
A-hole
see: *Asshole* 6
A Talker. 2
Abso-fucking-lutely 2
AC/DC 2
AIDS 2
Airhead 2
All Over Each Other 2
Androgynous 3
Andy Gump 3
Anorexic 3
Apeshit 3
Aphrodisiac 3
Around The World 4
Arse 4
As Shit 4
Asexual. 4
Ass 4
Ass Backwards 4
Ass Clown. 5
Ass-fuck 5
Ass-kisser 6
Ass-licker
see: *Ass-kisser* 6
Ass Man. 6
Ass-peddler 6
Ass-ream 6
Asshead 6
Asshole 6
Asswipe 7
Au Natural 7
Aunt Flo Is Visiting 7
"Aw, hell!"
see: *"Oh, hell!"* 138
B. And D. 8
B.M. 8
B-F-D
see: *"Big fucking deal.".* . . 15
B-S
see: *Bullshit* 24
Baby
see: *Crybaby* 41
Back 9
Back Door
see: *The Back Door* 195
Badass 9
Bag It. 9
Ball 9
Ball And Chain 9
Ball-buster. 10
Ball-breaker
see: *Ball-buster* 10
Balloons 10
Balls. 10
Balls Deep 10
Ballsy 10
Baloney 10
Bang 11
Bare-assed 11
Bare-assed naked. . . . .
see: *Bare-assed* 11
Barf 11
Bass Ackwards
see: *Ass Backwards* 4
Bastard 11
Bats In The Belfry
see: *Have Bats In The Belfry* 94
Battering Ram 12
Batty 12

Bazongas
see: *Balloons* 10
Bazooka 12
Bazookas
see: *Balloons* 10
Bazooms
see: *Balloons* 10
Be On The Rag. 12
Be Regular. 12
Be Sick 12
Beached Whale
see: *Whale* 212
Bean Pole 12
Beard Burn 13
Beat Off 13
Beat One's Meat 13
Beat The Shit Out Of Someone 13
Beatch 13
Beaten With The Ugly Stick. . 13
"Beats the shit out of me." . . 13
Beaver. 14
Beaver-eater. 14
Behind. 14
Bestiality 14
Between The Sheets 14
Bi 14
Bicycle
see: *Bi* 14
Big Backyard. 14
Big-boned 14
"Big fucking deal." 15
Big "O"
see: *The Big "O"* 195
Big Red Dropped In 15
Bimbo 15
Birdbrain 15
Birds And The Bees
see: *The Birds And The*
Bees 195
Birth Control 16
Birthday Suit
see: *In One's Birthday Suit* 106
B-I-T-C-H 16
Bitch 16
Bitch On Wheels 16
Bitch Session 16
Bitch Slap 17
Bitchin' 17
Blabbermouth 17
Bleed The Weasel 17
Bleeping 17
Blimp 17
Blitzed. 18
Blockhead 18
Blow. 18
Blow Chunks 18
Blow Job. 18
Blow One's Load
see: *Blow* 18
Blow One's Wad
see: *Blow* 18
Blowhard 18
Blue Balls 19
Blue-veined Throbber 19
B.O. 19
Boink 19
Bombed 19
Bone 19
Bonehead 20
Boner 20
Bonk
see: *Boink* 19
Bonkers 20
Boob 20
Boobies
see: *Boob* 20
Booger 20
Boot. 20
Booty 21

Booty Call 21
Bordello 21
Bottom 21
Bow-wow
see: *Dog* 49
Box 22
Box Lunch 22
Bowel Movement
see: *B.M.* 8
Boytoy. 22
Break Wind 22
Breast Fuck 22
Breast Man 22
Breeder 22
Broad 23
Brothel 23
Buck Naked 23
Buffalo Chips. 23
Bug Up One's Ass
see: *Have A Bug Up One's*
Ass 92
Buick 23
Bulldyke 23
Bullshit 24
Bum 24
Bum-fuck 24
Bumble-fuck
see: *Bum-fuck* 24
Bump And Grind 24
Bump Pussy 24
Bump Uglies 25
Bun In The Oven
see: *Have A Bun In The*
Oven 92
Bung Hole 25
Bunnyfuck
see: *Fuck Like Bunnies* . . . 74
Buns. 25
Bush. 25
Bust. 26
Bust A Nut 26
Bust Ass 26
Butch 26
Butt Fuck 26
Butt Naked
see: *Buck Naked* 23
Butt Pirate 27
Butt Plug 27
Butt Ugly 27
Butthead. 27
Button. 27
Buzzed 27
C-U-Next-Tuesday 28
C-Y-A
see: *Cover Your Ass* 37
Caboose 28
Cajones 29
Call Boy 29
Call Girl 29
Camel Toe 29
Can 29
Candy-ass 29
Canned Fruit 29
Cans. 30
Carnal Knowledge
see: *Have Carnal Knowledge*
Of Someone 94
Carpet-muncher
see: *Munch Carpet* 131
Castrate 30
Catch Shit 30
Catcher 30
Cathouse 30
Cha-cha 30
Change Of Life 31
Cheapskate 31
Cherry. 31
Chick 31

Chicken
see: *Chicken-shit* 32
Chicken Hawk 31
Chicken Ranch 31
Chickie
see: *Chick* 31
Chicken-shit 32
Chocolate Speedway 32
Choke The Chicken. 32
"Christ!"
see: *"Jesus Christ!"* 109
Chubby-chaser. 32
Chucklefuck 32
Chum 32
Chump 32
Chunder 33
Circle Jerk 33
Clap
see: *The Clap.* 196
Clean 33
Climax. 33
Clit 33
Close-fisted
see: *Tight-fisted* 200
Closet Case 34
Closet Queen 34
Closet Queer
see: *Closet Queen* 34
Closeted
see: *Come Out Of*
The Closet 36
Clusterfuck 34
Cock 34
Cock-block. 34
Cock Ring 35
Cocksucker 35
Cocktease 35
Coconuts
see: *Melons* 126
Cold Fish 35
Collar The Cock 35
Come Hell Or High Water . . . 36
Come On To Someone 36
Come Out Of The Closet. . . . 36
Convertible
see: *Bi* 14
Cooch 36
Cooter 36
Cop A Feel 36
Cornhole. 37
Cover Your Ass. 37
Cow 37
Cow Patty 37
Coyote Ugly 37
Crabs 38
Crack 38
Cracked 38
Crackhead 38
Crackpipe
see: *Crackhead* 38
Crackpot. 38
Crap. 38
Crapper 39
Crater-face 40
Cream. 40
Cream One's Jeans 40
Creep 40
Crock Of Shit 40
Crocked 40
Crop-Dusting 40
Crybaby 41
Cuckoo 41
Cucumber 41
Cum 41
Cunnilingus 42
Cunt 42
Curse
see: *The Curse* 196
Cuss. 42

Cut One 42
Cut The Cheese 42
Cyclops 42
"D'oh!" 43
Daddy 43
Daisy Chain 44
Dammit
   see: *Damn* 44
Damn 44
Darn 44
Date Rape 44
Date Rosy Palm And Her
   Five Sisters 44
Decorate The Pavement . . . 45
Deep Throat 45
Deliver Street Pizza 45
Den Of Iniquity 45
Dental Dam 45
Derriere 46
Diarrhea Of The Mouth
   see: *Have Diarrhea Of The*
    Mouth 94
Dick 46
Dick With Someone 46
Dickie And The Boys 46
Dickhead
   see: *Dick* 46
Dicktease
   see: *Cocktease* 35
Dickweed
   see: *Dick* 46
Diesel Dyke
   see: *Bulldyke* 23
Dildo 46
Dimwit 47
Dinosaur 47
Dip
   see: *Dipstick* 47
Dipshit 47
Dipstick 47
Dirtbag 47
Dirty 47
Dirty Mind
   see: *Have A Dirty Mind* . . 92
Dirty Old Man 48
Dishonorable Discharge . . . 48
Diving Suit 48
Do It 48
Do One's Business 48
Do The Deed 48
Do The Do 48
Do The Nasty 48
Do The Wild Thing 49
Dode 49
"Does a bear shit in the
   woods?" 49
Dog 49
Doggie-style 50
Dolt 50
Dominant 50
Dominatrix 50
"Don't get your panties in
   a bunch." 50
Don't Give A Flying Fuck
   see: *Don't Give A Fuck* . . . 51
Don't Give A Fuck 51
Don't Have A Backbone . . . 51
Don't Have A Snowball's
   Chance In Hell 51
Don't Have Much Upstairs
   see:*Have Nothing Upstairs* . 94
Don't Know Jack
   see: *Don't Know Jack Shit* . . 51
Don't Know Jack Shit 51
Don't Know One's Ass From A
   Hole in the Ground
   see: *Don't Know One's*
    Ass From One's Elbow . 51
Don't Know One's Ass From
   One's Elbow 51
Don't Know Shit
   see: *Don't Know Jack Shit* . 51
Don't Know Shit From Shinola 51
Dong 52
Doo-doo 52

Doof
   see: *Doofus* 52
Doofus 52
Dork 52
Double Bag It 52
Douche 52
Douche Bag 52
Down There 53
Drag Queen 53
Dragging Ass 54
Drain The Lizard 54
Drain The Vein
   see: *Drain The Lizard* . . . 54
Drat 54
Drive The Porcelain Bus . . 54
Drop One's Load 54
Drop Some Thunder 54
Drop The Kids Off At The Pool 54
Drunk As A Skunk 54
Dry Fuck 55
Dry Hump
   see: *Dry Fuck* 55
Duff 55
Dum-dum
   see: *Dummy* 56
Dumb As A Sack Of Rocks . . 55
Dumb As A Sack Of Wet Mice
   see: *Dum As A Sack Of*
    Rocks. 55
Dumb As An Ox 55
Dumb-ass 55
Dumb-fuck 56
Dumb-shit 56
Dummy 56
Dumper 56
Dunce 56
Dweeb 56
Dyke 56
East Bum-fuck
   see: *Bum-fuck* 24
Easy 57
Easy Lay
   see: *Easy* 57
Eat My Shorts 57
"Eat shit!" 58
"Eat shit and die!"
   see: *"Eat shit!"* 58
Eat Someone Out 58
Eaten By Wolves And Shit
   Over A Cliff 58
Effeminate 58
80 (Eighty) 58
88 (Eighty-eight) 58
86'd (Eighty-six'd) 59
Equipment 59
Erotica 60
Escort Service 60
Eunuch 60
Exhibitionist 60
F'd
   see: *Fucked* 76
F'd In The A
   see: *Fucked In The Ass* . . 76
F-ing 61
F-nut
   see: *Fucknut* 77
F-U
   see: *"Fuck you!"* 76
F-word
   see: *The F-word* 196
Facilities 61
Facts Of Life 61
Fag
   see: *Faggot* 62
Fag Hag 62
Faggot 62
Fairy 62
Fake It 62
Family Jewels 62
Fanny 62
Fart 63
Fat Pig
   see: *Pig* 145
Fat Slob 63
Fat-head 64
Fatso 64

Fatty
   see: *Fatso* 64
Feel Like Ass 64
Feeling No Pain 64
Fell Out Of The Ugly Tree And
   Hit Every Branch On The
   Way Down 64
Fellatio 64
Fetishist 65
Filth 65
Finger
   see: *Finger-fuck* 65
Finger-fuck 65
Fist-fuck
   see: *Fisting* 65
Fisting 65
Flagellation 65
Flake 66
Flamer 66
Flaming
   see: *Flamer* 66
Flasher 66
Flat 66
Flatsy Patsy 66
Flesh Peddler 66
Flip One's Lid 67
Flip One's Wig
   see: *Flip One's Lid* 67
Flip Out
   see: *Flipped* 68
Flip Someone Off
   see: *Flip Someone The Bird* . 67
Flip Someone The Bird . . . 67
Flipped 68
Float An Air Biscuit 68
Flog The Bishop 68
Floozy 68
Fluffer 68
Fooey 68
Fool Around 69
For Shit 69
For The Hell Of It 69
Foreplay 69
Foul Language 69
Foul Mouth 70
Four-eyes 70
Four-letter Word 70
Fox 70
Foxy Lady
   see: *Fox* 70
Frab 70
Fraidy-cat 70
Freak 71
Freak Out
   see: *Freak* 71
French Kiss 71
French Tickler 71
Friend Of Dorothy 71
Friggin' 72
Frigid 72
Frottage 72
Fruit 72
Fruitcake 72
Fuck 72
"Fuck a duck!" 73
Fuck Around 73
Fuck Buddy 73
Fuck Friend
   see: *Fuck Buddy* 73
Fuck Like Bunnies 74
"Fuck no!" 74
"Fuck off!" 74
Fuck Someone Over 74
Fuck Someone's Brains Out . 74
"Fuck that noise!" 74
Fuck-up 75
Fuck Up Someone 75
Fuck Up Something 76
Fuck With Someone 76
Fuck With Something 76
"Fuck yes!" 76
"Fuck you!" 76
"Fuck you and the horse you
   rode in on!"
   see: *"Fuck you!"* 76
Fucked 76
Fucked In The Ass 76

Fucked In The Head 77
Fucked-up 77
Fucker 77
Fuckface 77
Fuckhead
   see: *Fuckface* 77
Fucking 77
"Fucking A!" 77
Fucking Ugly
   see: *Fugly* 78
Fucknut 77
Fuckstick 78
Fuckwad
   see: *Fuckstick* 78
Fudgepacker 78
Fugly 78
Full Of Baloney
   see *Full Of Shit* 78
Full Of Crap
   see *Full Of Shit* 78
Full Of It
   see *Full Of Shit* 78
Full Of Piss And Vinegar . . 78
Full Of Shit 78
Fur Pie 78
Furburger 78
G Spot 79
G-string 79
Gang Bang 80
Gay 80
Gay As A Three-dollar Bill
   see: *Queer As A Three-*
    dollar Bill 158
Gay Bashing 80
Gay For Pay 80
Gaydar 80
Gee Whillikers
   see: *Geez* 81
Gee Whiz
   see: *Geez* 81
Geek 80
Geez 81
Geez Louise
   see: *Geez* 81
Gerbiling 81
Get A Little Action 81
Get A Piece Of Ass 81
Get Into Someone's Pants . . 82
Get It On 82
Get It Up 82
Get Laid 82
Get Off 82
Get One's Ass in Gear . . . 82
Get One's Rocks Off 82
Get One's Shit Together . . . 83
Get Some 83
Get Some Action
   see: *Get A Little Action* . . 81
Get Some Ass 83
Get Some Sack
   see: *Grow Some Sack* . . 89
Get The Lead Out Of One's Ass 83
Gigolo 84
Give A Shit 84
Give Head 84
"Give me some sugar." . . . 84
Give Someone Shit 84
Give Someone The Bird
   see: *Flip Someone The Bird* . 67
Give Someone The Eye . . . 84
Glory Hole 85
Go 85
Go All The Way 85
Go Bananas 85
Go Bonkers
   see: *Bonkers* 20
Go Check The Plumbing . . . 85
Go Down
   see: *Go Down On Someone* . 85
Go Down On Someone . . . 85
Go Down The Dirt Road . . . 85
Go Downtown
   see: *Go Down On Someone* . 85
Go On And On 86
"Go to hell!" 86

Go To The Pisser
  see: *Piss* 146
Go Wee 86
"God!" 86
God Damn 86
Golden Shower 86
Gonads 86
Gonorrhea 87
"Good gravy!"
  see: "*Good grief!*" . . . 87
"Good grief!" 87
Good Lay 87
Goof Ball 88
Goon 88
Goose 88
Gourds
  see: *Melons* 126
Grapefruit
  see: *Melons* 126
Grease the Bayonet 88
Grind 88
Gross 88
Group Grope 89
Grow Some Sack 89
Guns 89
Guppie 89
Gutless 89
Gutless Wonder
  see: *Gutless* 89
Gutter
  see: *Have One's Mind In
    The Gutter* 95
Gym Queen 89
Half-assed 90
Hammered 90
Hand Job 90
Handballing 91
Hanky-panky 91
Happy As A Pig In Shit . . . 91
Hard-ass 91
Had Hard Miles 91
Hard On The Eyes 91
Hard-on 91
Hardbody 92
Hardcore 92
Haul Ass 92
Have A Bug Up One's Ass . . 92
Have A Bun In The Oven . . . 92
Have A Dirty Mind 92
Have A Headache 93
Have A Nooner 93
Have A One-night Stand . . . 93
Have A Screw Loose 93
Have A Shit Fit 94
Have A Stick Up One's Ass
  see: *Have A Bug Up
    One's Ass* 92
Have Bats In The Belfry . . . 94
Have Carnal Knowledge Of
  Someone 94
Have Diarrhea Of The Mouth . 94
Have No Lead In One's Pencil . 94
Have Nothing Upstairs . . . 94
Have One's Back Teeth Floating 95
Have One's Head Up One's Ass 95
Have One's Mind In The Gutter 95
Have One's Thumb Up One's
  Ass 96
Have Relations 96
Have Shit For Brains 96
Have Someone By The Balls . 96
Have Someone By The
  Short Hairs 96
Have Someone's Ass 96
Have The Hots For Someone . 96
Head 96
Head Up One's Ass
  see: *Have One's Head Up
    One's Ass* 96
Headcase 97
Headlights 97
Hang A Heat Stick 97
Heave 97
Heck 97
Heinie 97
Hell 97
Hell On Something 98

Hell-raiser 98
Hell To Pay 98
"Hell's bells!" 98
Hella 98
Helluva 98
Helmet 99
Hermaphrodite 99
Herpes 100
Hershey Highway 100
Hershey Squirts 100
Hickey 100
High Hard One
  see: *The High Hard One* . 196
Highbeams 100
Hippo 100
Hit In The Face With A
  Hot Bag Of Nickles . . . 100
Hit On 101
H-I-V 101
Ho 101
Hog 101
Hole 101
Holler At The Toilet . . . 101
Holy Christ
  see: *Holy Cow* 101
"Holy Cow" 101
Holy Crap
  see: *Crap* 38
Holy Cripes
  see: "*Holy shit!*" . . . 102
Holy Moley
  see: *Holy Cow* 101
Holy Moses
  see: *Holy Cow* 101
"Holy shit!" 102
Home Base 102
Homo 102
Honey Pot 102
Hook Shop 102
Hook Up 102
Hooker 102
Hooters 103
Hop In The Sack 103
Horn Dog 103
Horny 104
Horse Around 104
Horse Shit
  see: *Bullshit* 24
Hose 104
Hot 104
Hot And Bothered 104
Hot Shit 104
Hot To Trot 104
"Hot Damn!" 104
Hots
  see: *Have The Hots For
    Someone* 96
House Of Delight
  see: *House Of Ill Repute* . 105
House Of Ill Fame
  see: *House Of Ill Repute* . 105
House Of Ill Repute 105
House Of Joy
  see: *House Of Ill Repute* . 105
Hummer 105
Hump 105
Hung 105
Hung Like A Horse
  see: *Hung* 105
Hurl 105
Hustle 105
Impotent 106
In Deep Shit 106
In One's Birthday Suit . . . 106
In The Buff 107
In The Mood 107
In The Raw 107
Incest 107
Indecent Exposure 107
Jack Off 108
Jack-off 108
Jackass 108
Jail Bait 109
Jerk 109
Jerk Off 109
Jerk-off 109
Jerkin' The Gherkin 109

"Jesus Christ !" 109
Jesus-freak 110
Jism 110
Jiz
  see: *Jism* 110
Jock Strap 110
John 110
Johnson 110
Joy House
  see: *House Of Ill Repute* . 105
Joystick 110
Jugs 110
Jump Someone
  see: *Jump Someone's Bones* 110
Jump Someone's Bones . . . 110
Junior 111
Junk 111
Junk In The Trunk
  see: *Junk* 111
"Keep your panties on." . . . 112
Keester 112
Kick Ass 112
Kick-ass 113
Kick Someone's Ass 113
King Shit
  see: *Hot Shit* 104
Kinky 113
Kiss Ass 113
Kiss-ass 114
Knocked Up 114
Knockers 114
Knock Up Someone
  see: *Knockup Up* . . . 114
Know-it-all 114
Kook 114
Kweef
  see: *Queef* 157
La Petite Mort 115
Ladies' Man 115
Lady Of The Evening . . . 116
Lady Of The Night
  see: *Lady Of The Evening* . 116
Lam-o 116
Lamebrain
  see: *Lam-o* 116
Lame 116
Lard-ass 116
Laugh At The Lawn 116
Laugh One's Ass Off 116
Laugh One's Butt Off
  see: *Laugh One's Ass Off* . 116
Lay A Log 116
Lay Pipe 116
Leather Queen 117
Lech
  see: *Lecher* 117
Lecher 117
Les-be-friends 117
Lesbian 117
Lesbo 117
Let One Fly 118
Let One Go
  see: *Let One Fly* . . . 118
Lewd 118
Lezzie
  see: *Lesbo* 117
Light In The Loafers 118
"The lights are on, but
  nobody's home." 118
Like Hell 118
Limp-wrist 118
Lip-lock 118
Lipstick Lesbian 119
Lit 119
Little Black Book 119
Little Shit 119
Live In Sin 120
LMAO
  see: *Laugh One's Ass Off* . 116
Loaded 120
Long-winded
  see: *Windbag* 215
Look Like Death Warmed Over 120
Loon 120
Loony-tune
  see: *Loon* 120
Looped 120

Loose 120
Lose One's Lunch 120
Lose One's Marbles 120
Loser 121
Loudmouth 121
Love Button
  see: *Button* 27
Love Dungeon 121
Love Handles 121
Love Muscle 121
Low-down, No-good 121
Low-life 121
Mack 122
Mack Daddy
  see: *Mack* 122
Maggot 122
Make A Pit Stop 123
Make An Anal Announcement 123
Make Eyes At Someone
  see: *Give Someone The Eye* 84
Make Love 123
Make Out 123
Make The Beast With Two
  Backs 123
Make Whoopee 123
Man Juice 123
Man Pussy 124
Man-hater 124
Manhole Inspector 124
Maracas 124
Mary 124
Masochist 124
Massage Parlor 125
Master 125
Matinee 126
Meat 126
Meat And Two Vegetables . . 126
Meathead 126
Melons 126
Menage A Trois 126
Mercy Fuck 127
Middle Leg
  see: *Third Leg* 198
Milf 127
Milk Bottles 127
Milk The Chicken 127
Mind In The Gutter
  see: *Have One's Mind In
    The Gutter*
Mindfuck 127
Missionary Position 127
Mistress 128
Mofo
  see: *Motherfucker* . . . 130
Molest 128
Money Shot 128
Montezuma's Revenge . . . 128
Monthly Visitor 128
Moon 128
Morning-after Pill 128
Mosquito Bites 129
Mother 129
Motherfucker 130
Motherfucking 130
Motormouth 130
Move Ass
  see: *Haul Ass* 92
Mr. Happy 130
Muff 130
Muff-diver 130
Muffin 130
Munch Box 131
Munch Carpet 131
Munch Rug
  see: *Munch Carpet* . . . 131
Muscle Mary 131
Nads
  see: *Gonads* 86
Nail 132
Naked As A Jaybird 132
"Nature is calling" 132
Neck 133
Necrophiliac 133
Nellie 133
Nerd 133
Nincompoop 133
Nipple Clips 133

Nitwit 133
No Lead In One's Pencil
    see: *Have No Lead In One's*
       Pencil. 94
"No shit!". 134
"No shit, Sherlock!"
    see: *"No shit!"* 134
No Spring Chicken 134
Nocturnal Emission 134
Nookie 134
Nooner
    see: *Have A Nooner* 93
Not All There 134
Not Cooking On All Four
    Burners 134
Not Playing With A Full Deck. 135
Not To Have A Pot To Piss In 135
Nothing But Skin And Bones
    see: *Skin And Bones* . . . 179
Numb-nuts 135
Number One 135
Number Two 136
Numbskull 136
Nut Case 136
Nut Job
    see: *Nut Case* 136
Nuts 136
Nutty
    see: *Nuts.* 136
Nympho
    see: *Nymphomaniac* . . . 136
Nymphomaniac 136
O-T-R
    see: *Be On The Rag* 12
Off One's Rocker 137
Off The Deep End. 137
Off The Wagon 137
Off-color 138
"Oh, hell!" 138
Old Ball And Chain
    see: *Ball And Chain* 9
Old Maid 138
On Someone's Ass 138
On The Make 138
On The Sauce. 138
On The Wagon 138
One-eyed Monster 138
One-eyed Trouser Snake
    see: *Trouser Snake* 203
One-eyed Wonder
    see: *One-eyed Monster* . . 138
One-night Stand
    see: *Have A One-night*
       Stand. 93
Open A Can Of Whoop-ass . 138
Opposite Sex 139
Orgy 139
Out Of It 139
Out Of One's Gourd
    see: *Out Of One's Mind* . . 139
Out Of One's Head
    see: *Out Of One's Mind* . . 139
Out Of One's Mind 139
Out Of One's Skull
    see: *Out Of One's Mind* . . 139
Out There 139
Out To Lunch 140
Outhouse
    see: *Shithouse* 176
Over The Hill 140
Overcoat 140
P.O.'d 141
Package 141
Packing Fudge
    see: *Fudgepacker* 78
Pain In The Ass 141
Party Hat 142
Pass Gas 142
Pat. 142
Pearl Necklace 142
Pecker 142
Peckerhead 142
Peddle Some Ass
    see: *Ass-peddler* 6
Pederast 142
Pedophile 143
Pee. 143

Pee-pee 143
Peeping Tom 144
Period 144
Perv
    see: *Pervert* 144
Pervert 144
Peter. 144
Peter-eater 144
Pick Up 144
Piddle 144
Piece Of Crap
    see: *Crap* 38
Piece Of Shit 144
Pig 145
Pigfuck 145
Pill
    see: *The Pill* 196
Pillow-biter 145
Pimp 145
Pimp Slap 145
Pinch A Loaf 145
Pinhead 146
Pipsqueak 146
Piss 146
Piss Away. 146
Piss Hard-on 146
"Piss on that!" 146
Piss-poor 146
Pissant 146
Pissed
    see: *Pissed Off* 146
Pissed Off 146
Pisser 147
Pistol 147
Pitch A Tent 148
Pitcher 148
Pitches For The Other Team
    see: *Plays For The Other*
       Team 149
Pity Fuck
    see: *Mercy Fuck* 127
Pizza-face 148
Plant One On Someone . . . 148
Plastered 148
Platonic. 148
Play Bouncy-Bouncy . . . 148
Play Doctor. 148
Play "Hide The Sausage" . . 149
Play The Skin Flute . . . 149
Play Tonsil Hockey 149
Play With Oneself 149
Plays For The Other Team . 149
P-M-S 149
Pocket Pool 150
Poke 150
Poke In The Hay
    see: *Poke* 150
Pole 150
Polish The Knob. 150
Polish The Lance
    see: *Polish The Knob* . . 150
Polluted 150
Poo-Poo 150
Poon
    see: *Poontang* 150
Poonani 150
Poontang 150
Poop 151
Poop Chute 152
Pop Someone's Cherry . . 152
Porker
    see: *Pig* 145
Porn 152
Pornographic 152
Pornography 152
Pot 152
Potty 153
Powder One's Nose . . . 153
Powder Room 153
Pray To The Porcelain God. . 153
Precum. 154
Premature Ejaculation. . . 154
Prick 154
Private Parts 154
Privates
    see: *Private Parts* . . . 154
Psycho 154

Puke 155
Pull Shit 155
Punch The Clown 155
Punk-ass 155
Punk-ass Bitch
    see: . . . . *Punk-ass*
    155
Purple Helmet
    see: *Helmet* 99
Pussy. 155
Pussy-whipped 156
"Put a sock in it." 156
Put Out. 156
Put The Moves On Someone . 156
Putz 156
Queef 157
Queen 157
Queer 158
Queer As A Three-Dollar Bill. 158
Quickie 158
Rack 159
Rack Salesman 159
Racy 159
Ralph. 160
Rammer
    see: *Ramrod* 160
Ramrod 160
Rat. 160
Rat-bastard 160
Rat On Someone
    see: *Rat* 160
Raunchy 160
Raw Sex 160
Reach Around. 160
Ream Job
    see: *Rimming.* 162
Ream Someone's Ass
    see: *Ass-ream* 6
Rear End 160
Red Flag
    see: *The Red Flag's Up* . 196
Red Sea
    see: *The Red Flag's Up* . 196
Red-light District 161
Rent Boy
    see: *Call Boy* 29
Retard 161
Retch. 161
Ridden Hard And Put Away
    Wet 161
Ride Bareback 162
Ride The Red Tide. . . . 162
Rim Job
    see: *Rimming.* 162
Rimming 162
Rip Ass
    see: *Bust Ass* 26
Rip Someone A New Asshole 162
Rip Someone A New One
    see: *Rip Someone A New*
       Asshole 162
Ripped 162
Roaring Drunk 162
Rocked 163
Rod 163
Rod Of Love
    see: *Rod* 163
Roll In The Hay 164
Roll The Fuzzy Dice . . . 164
Rub The Rod 164
Rubber 164
Rug-muncher
    see: *Munch Carpet* . . . 131
Rump 164
Rump Ranger 164
Run Around. 164
Runs
    see: *The Runs* 196
Runt 165
S. And M.. 166
S-B-D
    see: *Silent But Deadly.* . . . 178
S-O-L
    see: *Shit Out Of Luck* . . . 176
Sack 166
Sadist 167
Sadomasochist 167

Salami 167
Satisfy 167
Sauced 167
Sausage
    see: . . . . *Salami*
    167
Scam 167
Scare The Shit Out Of
    Someone 167
Scared Shitless 167
Scaredy-cat 168
Scatterbrain 168
Schizo 168
Schizoid
    see: *Schizo.* 168
Score. 168
Screamer. 168
Screaming Fairy 168
Screw 169
Screw Around. 169
"Screw off!" 170
Screw Someone Over . . . 170
Screw Someone's Brains Out 170
Screw the Pooch 170
Screw-up 170
Screw Up Someone . . . 170
Screw Up Something . . . 171
Screw With Someone . . . 171
Screw With Something . . 171
"Screw you!" 171
"Screw you and the horse
    you rode in on!!"
    see: *"Screw you!".* . . . 171
Screwball
    see: *Screwed Up* 172
Screwed 171
Screwed In The Head . . . 171
Screwed Up. 172
Screwy
    see: *Screwed Up.* 172
Scrooge 172
Scum. 172
Scumbag
    see: *Scum.* 172
Scummy
    see: *Scum.* 172
Seat 172
Second Base 172
See A Man About A Horse . 173
Service Station 173
Sex Appeal 173
Sex Drive. 173
Sex Friend
    see: *Fuck Buddy* 73
Sex Symbol. 173
Shag 174
Shake Hands With The
    Governor 174
Shattered. 174
Shit 174
Shit a Brick 175
Shit-eating Grin. 175
Shit-faced 175
Shit Fit
    see: *Have A Shit Fit* 94
Shit-for-brains 175
"Shit happens." 175
Shit List 175
Shit On Someone 175
Shit Or Get Off The Pot . . . 176
Shit Out Of Luck 176
Shit Someone. 176
Shit Someone Pulls
    see: *Pull Shit.* 155
Shitbox. 176
Shithead 176
Shithouse 176
Shittiest
    see: *Shitty.* 177
Shitload 176
Shitter 176
Shitty 177
Shlong 177
Shmuck 177
"Shoot!" 177
Shoot
    see: *Blow* 18

     THE SLANGMAN GUIDE TO DIRTY ENGLISH

Shoot One's Mouth Off . . . 177
Shoot One's Wad 177
Shoot The Shit 177
Short Hairs
   see: *Have Someone By*
     The Short Hairs 96
Shout At One's Shoes 178
Shrimp 178
Shtup 178
Shucks 178
Sickie
   see: *Sicko* 178
Sicko 178
Sif
   see: *Syphilis* 192
Silent But Deadly 178
Sissy 178
68 (Sixty-eight) 179
69 (Sixty-nine) 179
Size Queen 179
Skank 179
Skanky
   see: *Skank* 179
Skanky Ho
   see: *Skank* 179
Skin And Bones 179
Skin Flick 180
Skinny-dip 180
Slap The Snake 180
Slaphappy 180
Sleaze 180
Sleaze Bucket
   see: *Sleaze* 180
Sleazeball
   see: *Sleaze* 180
Sleazy
   see: *Sleaze* 180
Sleep Around 180
Sleep Together 180
Slime
   see: *Slimeball* 181
Slime Bucket
   see: *Slimeball* 181
Slimeball 181
Slimy
   see: *Slimeball* 181
Sloshed 181
Slow On The Draw 181
Slow On The Uptake
   see: *Slow On The Draw* . 181
Slut 181
Slutty
   see: *Slut* 181
Smart-ass 182
Smashed 182
Smut 182
Smutty
   see: *Smut* 182
Snake 182
Snake In The Grass
   see: *Snake* 182
Snap 182
Snap At Someone
   see: *Snap* 182
Snatch 183
Snot 183
Snotty
   see: *Snot* 183
Snowball 183
Sodomist 183
Softcore Porn 183
Someone's Ass Is Grass . . . 184
Someone's Ass Is Toast
   see: *Someone's Ass Is*
     Grass 184
Son Of A Bitch 184
South Of The Border
   see: *Down There* 53
Sow One's Oats 184
Space Cadet 184
Space Case
   see: *Space Cadet* 184
Spacey
   see: *Space Cadet* 184
Spanish Fly 184
Spare Tire 185

Spastic
   see: *Spaz* 185
Spaz 185
Spear
   see: *Staff* 187
Spermicide 185
Spew 185
Spike 185
Spineless 185
Spineless Wonder
   see: *Spineless* 185
Spinster 186
Spit 186
Spit Up 186
Spoon 186
Sporting Wood
   see: *Woody* 216
Spunk 186
Squat 186
Stacked 187
Staff 187
Staggering Drunk 188
S-T-D 188
Steamy 188
Stick Figure 188
Stick Something Where The
   Sun Don't Shine 188
Stiffy 188
Stinking Drunk 188
Straight 188
Strap-on 189
Streak 189
Streetwalker 189
Strip 189
Strip Down
   see: *Strip* 189
Stripper 189
Striptease 189
Stroke Oneself
   see: *Play With Oneself* . . 149
Stuck Up 190
Stud 190
Stud Muffin
   see: *Stud* 190
Stupid Drunk 190
Submissive 190
Suck 190
Suck A Golf Ball Through A
   Garden Hose 190
Suck Ass 190
Suck Face 190
Suck Someone Off 191
Suck The Chrome Off A
   Trailer Hitch 191
Sugar Daddy
   see: *Daddy* 43
Swallow 192
Swap Spit 192
Swing Both Ways 192
Swinger 192
Switch Hitter 192
Sword
   see: *Staff* 187
Sympathy Fuck 192
Syphilis 192
T. And A. 193
Ta-ta's 193
Tail 193
Take A Dump 194
Take A Leak 194
Take A Shit 194
Take A Squirt 194
Take Shit 194
Talk To Huey On The Big
   White Phone 194
Tang
   see: *Poontang* 150
Tanked 194
Tap That Ass 195
Teabag 195
Tear Ass
   see: *Bust Ass* 26
Technicolor Yawn 195
Than Shit 195
That Time Of The Month . . . 195
The Back Door 195
The Big "O" 195

The Birds And The Bees . . . 195
The C-word
   see: *Cunt* 42
The Clap 196
The Curse 196
The F-word 196
The High Hard One 196
The Hots
   see: *Have The Hots For*
     Someone 96
The Pill 196
The Red Flag's Up 196
The Red Sea Is In
   see: *The Red Flag's Up* . . 196
The Runs 196
The Shit 196
"The shit rolls downhill." . . 197
"The shit's going to hit the
   fan!" 197
The Trots 197
The Y. 197
Thick 198
Thick-headed
   see: *Thick* 198
Thick In The Head
   see: *Thick* 198
Thin As A Rail 198
Thing 198
Think One's Shit Doesn't Stink 198
Third Base 198
Third Leg 198
Three Sheets To The Wind . . 198
Threesome 198
Throne 199
Throw One In Her 199
Throw Up 200
Thumb Up One's Ass
   see: *Have One's Thumb*
     Up One's Ass 96
Tickle The Tiger 200
Tight-ass 200
Tight-fisted 200
Tightwad 200
Tinkle 200
Tipsy 200
Tit Fuck 200
Tits 201
Titties
   see: *Tits* 201
Titty Fuck
   see: *Tit Fuck* 200
Toasted 201
Tool 201
Toolbox
   see: *Tool* 201
Toot 201
Top 201
Topless 202
Toss One's Cookies 202
Tough Shit 202
Tough Titties
   see: *Tough Shit* 202
Tough Titty
   see: *Tough Shit* 202
Toyboy
   see: *Boytoy* 22
Tramp 202
Trannie 202
Transsexual 202
Transvestite 202
Treat Someone Like Shit . . . 203
Trick 203
Trots
   see: *The Trots* 197
Trouser Snake 203
Trouser Trout
   see: *Trouser Snake* . . . 203
Tub 203
Tub Of Lard
   see: *Tub* 203
Tubby
   see: *Tub* 203
Tune One's Organ. 204
Turd 204
Turn Tricks
   see: *Trick* 203
Turned On 204

Tush 204
Tushy
   see: *Tush* 204
Twat 204
12-step 204
Twit 204
Ugs 205
Undies 205
Unit 206
Unmentionables 206
Up Shit Creek 206
Up The Creek Without A Paddle
   206
Up The Wazoo 207
Up The Yin-yang 207
"Up yours!" 207
Upchuck 207
V.D. 208
Vertical Smile 208
Vibrator 209
Virgin 209
Void 210
Voyeur 210
W-T-F
   see: *What The Fuck* . . . 213
Washroom 211
Wasted 211
Water Sports 211
Watermelons
   see: *Melons* 126
Weirdo 212
Wet 212
Wet Dream 212
Whack Job
   see: *Whacko* 212
Whack Off 212
Whacko 212
Whacky
   see: *Whacko* 212
Whale 212
Wham Bam, Thank You,
   Ma'am 212
What The Fuck 213
What The Hell 213
Whip The Weenie 213
Whip The Worm
   see: *Whip The Weenie* . . 213
White Trash 214
Whiz 214
Whore 214
Whorehouse 214
Wiener 214
Wienie
   see: *Wiener* 214
Willie 215
Windbag 215
Witch 215
Womanizer 216
Wonder-down-under 216
Wood
   see: *Woody* 216
Woody 216
Working Girl 216
Wuss 216
Wussy
   see: *Wuss* 216
X-rated 217
Yabbos 218
Yak 218
Yank The Yak 218
Yellow 219
Yellow-bellied
   see: *Yellow* 219
Yo-yo 219
York 219
"You bet your sweet ass!" . . 219
You-know-what 219
"Your ass is grass, and I'm
   the lawnmower."
   see: *Someone's Ass is*
     Grass 184
Yuke 219
Zit 220

INDEX BY USE

USED WITH ANYONE

A Few Sandwiches Short Of A
   Picnic 1
A Talker. 2
AIDS 2
Airhead 2
All Over Each Other 2
Androgynous 3
Anorexic 3
Aphrodisiac 3
Asexual 4
Au Natural 7
B.M. 8
Ball And Chain 9
Baloney 10
Batty 12
Be Regular. 12
Be Sick 12
Bean Pole 12
Behind. 14
Between The Sheets 14
Bi 14
Big-boned 14
Bimbo 15
Birdbrain 15
Birth Control 16
Blabbermouth 17
Bleeping 17
Blitzed. 18
Blockhead 18
Blowhard 18
B.O. 19
Bombed 19
Bonehead 20
Bonkers 20
Bordello 21
Brothel 23
Buck Naked 23
Bulldyke 23
Bum. 24
Bust 26
Buzzed 27
Caboose 28
Castrate 30
Change Of Life 31
Cheapskate 31
Chump 32
Clean 33
Climax 33
Cold Fish 35
Come On To Someone 36
Cop A Feel 36
Cow Patty 37
Cracked 38
Crackpot. 38
Creep 40
Crocked 40
Crybaby 41
Cuckoo 41
Cuss. 42
"D'oh!" 43
Darn. 44
Date Rape 44
Den Of Iniquity 45
Derriere 46
Dimwit. 47
Dinosaur 47
Dipstick 47
Dirty. 47
Dirty Old Man 48
Do One's Business 48
Dode 49
Dolt 50
Don't Have A Backbone. . . . 51
Doo-doo 52
Doofus 52
Dork. 52
Down There 53
Drat 54

Drunk As A Skunk 54
Duff 55
Dumb As A Sack of Rocks . . 55
Dumb As An Ox 55
Dummy 56
Dunce 56
Dweeb 56
Effeminate. 58
86'd (Eighty-six'd) 59
Erotica. 60
Escort Service 60
Exhibitionist 60
Facilities. 61
Facts Of Life 61
Fake It 62
Family Jewels 62
Fanny 62
Fat Slob 63
Feeling No Pain 64
Fellatio 64
Fetishist 65
Filth 65
Flake 66
Flasher 66
Flip One's Lid 67
Flip Someone The Bird 67
Flipped 68
Fooey 68
Fool Around 69
Foul Language 69
Foul Mouth. 70
Four-eyes 70
Four-letter Word 70
Fox 70
Frab 70
Fraidy-cat 70
Freak 71
French Kiss 71
G-string 79
Gay 80
Gay Bashing 80
Gay For Pay 80
Gaydar 80
Geek 80
Geez 81
Gigolo 84
"Give me some sugar." 84
Give Someone The Eye . . . 84
Go. 85
Go All The Way 85
Go Bananas 85
Go Check The Plumbing . . . 85
Go On And On 86
Go Wee 86
Gonorrhea 87
"Good grief!" 87
Goof Ball. 88
Goon 88
Goose 88
Gross 88
Gutless 89
Hammered. 90
Hanky-panky 91
Hardbody 92
Have A Bun In The Oven . . 92
Have A Dirty Mind 92
Have A Headache 93
Have A One-Night Stand . . 93
Have A Screw Loose 93
Have Bats In The Belfry . . . 94
Have Carnal Knowledge
   Of Someone. 94
Have Nothing Upstairs 94
Have One's Mind In The Gutter 95
Have Relations 96
Have The Hots For Someone . 96
Head 96
Headcase 97

Heck. 97
Heinie 97
Hella 98
Hermaphrodite. 99
Herpes 100
Hickey 100
Hit On 101
H-I-V. 101
Holy Cow 101
Hook Up 102
Hop In The Sack 103
Horse Around 104
Hot. 104
Hot To Trot 104
House Of Ill Repute 105
Hump 105
Hustle 105
Impotent 106
In One's Birthday Suit. . . . 106
In The Buff 107
In The Mood 107
In The Raw 107
Incest 107
Indecent Exposure 107
Jerk 109
Jock Strap 110
John 110
Keester. 112
Kinky. 113
Know-it-all 114
Kook 114
Ladies' Man 115
Lady Of The Evening 116
Lam-o 116
Lame. 116
Lecher 117
Lesbian. 117
Lewd 118
Light In The Loafers. 118
"The lights are on, but
   nobody's home." 118
Lit 119
Little Black Book 119
Live In Sin 120
Loaded 120
Loon 120
Looped 120
Lose One's Lunch 120
Lose One's Marbles 120
Loser. 121
Loudmouth 121
Love Handles 121
Low-down, No-good. 121
Low-life 121
Mack 122
Make A Pit Stop. 123
Make Love 123
Make Out 123
Make Whoopee 123
Masochist 124
Meathead. 126
Mistress 128
Molest 128
Montezuma's Revenge . . . 128
Moon 128
Morning-after Pill 128
Motormouth 130
Naked As A Jaybird 132
"Nature is calling". 132
Neck 133
Necrophiliac 133
Nerd 133
Nincompoop 133
Nitwit 133
No Spring Chicken 134
Not All There 134
Not Cooking On All Four
   Burners 134

Not Playing With A Full Deck. 135
Number One 135
Number Two 136
Numbskull 136
Nut Case 136
Nuts 136
Nymphomaniac 136
Off One's Rocker 137
Off The Deep End 137
Off The Wagon 137
Off-color 138
Old Maid 138
On The Make 138
On The Sauce. 138
On The Wagon 138
Opposite Sex 139
Orgy 139
Out Of It 139
Out Of One's Mind 139
Out There 139
Out To Lunch 140
Over The Hill 140
P.O.'d 141
Pass Gas 142
Pederast 142
Pedophile. 143
Pee. 143
Pee-pee 143
Peeping Tom 144
Period 144
Pervert 144
Pick Up 144
Piddle 144
Pig 145
Pimp 145
Pinhead 146
Pipsqueak 146
Plant One On Someone . . . 148
Plastered 148
Platonic. 148
Plays For The Other Team . . 149
P-M-S 149
Polluted 150
Poo-Poo 150
Poop 151
Porn 152
Pornographic 152
Pornography 152
Potty 153
Powder One's Nose 153
Powder Room. 153
Pray To The Porcelain God. 153
Premature Ejaculation. . . . 154
Private Parts 154
Psycho 154
"Put a sock in it." 156
Put The Moves On Someone. 156
Putz 156
Quickie 158
Racy 159
Rat. 160
Raunchy 160
Rear End 160
Red-light District 161
Retch. 161
Ripped 162
Roaring Drunk 162
Rocked 163
Roll In The Hay 164
Rump 164
Run Around. 164
Runt 165
S. And M. 166
Sadist 167
Sadomasochist 167
Satisfy 167
Sauced 167
Scam. 167

Scaredy-cat 168
Scatterbrain 168
Screw Around. 169
Screw-up. 170
Screw Up Someone 170
Screw Up Something 171
Screw With Someone . . . 171
Screw With Something . . . 171
Screwed Up. 172
Scrooge 172
Scum. 172
Seat. 172
See A Man About A Horse . 173
Sex Appeal 173
Sex Drive. 173
Sex Symbol. 173
Shattered. 174
Shmuck 177
"Shoot!" 177
Shoot One's Mouth Off . . 177
Shrimp 178
Shucks 178
Sicko 178
Skin And Bones 179
Skinny-dip 180
Slaphappy 180
Sleep Around 180
Sleep Together 180

Sloshed 181
Slow On The Draw 181
Smashed 182
Smut. 182
Snake 182
Snap 182
Snot 183
Sodomist 183
Softcore Porn 183
Sow One's Oats 184
Space Cadet 184
Spare Tire 185
Spaz 185
Spermicide 185
Spike 185
Spineless 185
Spinster 186
Spit Up 186
Spoon 186
Staggering Drunk 188
S-T-D 188
Steamy. 188
Stick Figure. 188
Straight 188
Streak 189
Streetwalker 189
Strip 189
Stripper 189

Striptease 189
Stuck Up 190
Stud 190
Swing Both Ways 192
Swinger 192
Syphilis. 192
Tanked 194
That Time Of The Month. . 195
The Birds And The Bees . . 195
The Clap 196
The F-word 196
The Pill 196
Thick 198
Thin As A Rail. 198
Three Sheets To The Wind. . 198
Threesome 198
Throne 199
Throw Up 200
Tight-fisted 200
Tightwad 200
Tinkle 200
Tipsy 200
Toasted 201
Tool 201
Topless 202
Toss One's Cookies 202
Transsexual 202
Transvestite 202

Tush 204
Twit 204
Ugs 205
Undies 205
Unmentionables. 206
Up The Creek Without A
  Paddle. 206
Up The Wazoo 207
Up The Yin-yang 207
Upchuck 207
V.D. 208
Virgin 209
Void 210
Voyeur 210
Washroom 211
Wasted 211
Weirdo 212
Whacko. 212
Windbag 215
Witch. 215
Womanizer 216
Working Girl 216
Wuss 216
X-rated. 217
Yellow 219
Yo-yo. 219
You-know-what 219

USED WITH FRIENDS

A Face Only A Mother Could
  Love 1
AC/DC 2
Andy Gump 3
Apeshit 3
Around The World 4
Arse 4
As Shit 4
Ass 4
Ass Backwards 4
Ass Clown. 5
Ass-kisser. 6
Ass Man. 6
Ass-peddler 6
Ass-ream 6
Asshead 6
Asshole 6
Asswipe. 7
Aunt Flo Is Visiting 7
B. And D. 8
Back 9
Badass 9
Bag It. 9
Ball-buster. 10
Balloons 10
Balls 10
Balls Deep 10
Ballsy 10
Bare-assed 11
Barf 11
Bastard 11
Battering Ram 12
Bazooka 12
Be On The Rag. 12
Beard Burn 13
Beat Off 13
Beat One's Meat 13
Beat The Shit Out Of Someone 13
Beatch. 13
Beaten With The Ugly Stick. . 13
"Beats the shit out of me." . . 13
Bestiality 14
Big Backyard. 14
Big Red Dropped In 15
B-I-T-C-H 16
Bitch 16
Bitch On Wheels 16
Bitch Session 16
Bitchin' 17
Bleed The Weasel 17
Blimp 17
Blow Chunks 18
Blue Balls 19
Blue-veined Throbber 19
Boink 19
Bone 19

Boner 20
Boob 20
Booger 20
Boot 20
Booty 21
Booty Call 21
Bottom 21
Boytoy. 22
Break Wind 22
Breast Man 22
Breeder 22
Broad 23
Buffalo Chips. 23
Buick 23
Bullshit 24
Bump And Grind 24
Bump Uglies 25
Bung Hole 25
Buns. 25
Bust Ass 26
Butch 26
Butt Pirate 27
Butt Plug 27
Butt Ugly 27
Butthead. 27
Button. 27
C-U-Next-Tuesday 28
Cajones 29
Call Boy 29
Call Girl 29
Can 29
Candy-ass 29
Canned Fruit 29
Cans. 30
Catch Shit 30
Catcher 30
Cathouse 30
Cha-cha 30
Chick 31
Chicken Hawk 31
Chicken Ranch 31
Chicken-shit 32
Choke The Chicken. 32
Chubby-chaser. 32
Chum 32
Chunder 33
Circle Jerk 33
Closet Case 34
Closet Queen 34
Collar The Cock 35
Come Hell Or High Water . . 36
Cover Your Ass. 37
Cow 37
Coyote Ugly 37
Crabs 38
Crackhead 38

Crap. 38
Crapper 39
Crater-face 40
Crock Of Shit 40
Crop-Dusting 40
Cucumber 41
Cunnilingus 42
Cut One 42
Cut The Cheese 42
Cyclops 42
Daddy 43
Damn 44
Date Rosy Palm And Her
  Five Sisters 44
Decorate The Pavement . . . 45
Deliver Street Pizza 45
Dental Dam 45
Dick 46
Dickie And The Boys 46
Dildo 46
Dipshit 47
Dirtbag 47
Dishonorable Discharge . . . 48
Diving Suit 48
Do It 48
Do The Deed 48
Do The Do 48
Do The Nasty 48
Do The Wild Thing 49
"Does a bear shit in the
  woods?". 49
Dog 49
Doggie-style 50
Dominant 50
Dominatrix. 50
"Don't get your panties in a
  bunch." 50
Don't Have A Snowball's
  Chance In Hell 51
Don't Know Jack Shit 51
Don't Know One's Ass From
  One's Elbow 51
Don't Know Shit From Shinola 51
Dong 52
Double Bag It 52
Douche 52
Douche Bag 52
Dragging Ass 54
Drain The Lizard 54
Drive The Porcelain Bus . . 54
Drop One's Load 54
Drop Some Thunder 54
Drop The Kids Off At The Pool 54
Dumb-ass 55
Dumb-shit 56
Dumper 56

Easy. 57
Eat My Shorts 57
"Eat shit!" 58
Eat Someone Out 58
Eaten By Wolves And Shit
  Over A Cliff 58
80 (Eighty) 58
88 (Eighty-eight). 58
Equipment 59
Eunuch 60
F-ing 61
Fart 63
Fat-head 64
Fatso 64
Feel Like Ass 64
Fell Out Of The Ugly Tree
  And Hit Every Branch On
  The Way Down 64
Flagellation 65
Flat 66
Flatsy Patsy 66
Flesh Peddler 66
Float An Air Biscuit 68
Flog The Bishop 68
Floozy 68
Fluffer 68
For Shit 69
For The Hell Of It 69
Foreplay 69
French Tickler 71
Friend Of Dorothy 71
Friggin' 72
Frigid 72
Frottage 72
Fruit. 72
Fruitcake 72
Fugly 78
Full Of Piss And Vinegar . . 78
Full Of Shit 78
G Spot. 79
Gerbiling. 81
Get A Little Action 81
Get Into Someone's Pants . . 82
Get It On 82
Get It Up 82
Get Laid 82
Get One's Ass in Gear . . . 82
Get One's Shit Together . . . 83
Get Some 83
Get The Lead Out Of One's
  Ass 83
Give A Shit 84
Give Someone Shit. 84
Glory Hole 85
"Go to hell!" 86
"God!" 86

God Damn 86
Golden Shower. 86
Gonads 86
Good Lay 87
Grease the Bayonet 88
Grind 88
Group Grope 89
Grow Some Sack 89
Guns 89
Guppie. 89
Half-assed 90
Hand Job 90
Handballing 91
Happy As A Pig In Shit . . . 91
Hard-ass. 91
Had Hard Miles. 91
Hard On The Eyes 91
Hard-on 91
Hardcore. 92
Haul Ass 92
Have a Bug Up One's Ass . . 92
Have A Nooner 93
Have A Shit Fit 94
Have Diarrhea Of The Mouth . 94
Have No Lead In One's Pencil . 94
Have One's Back Teeth
    Floating 95
Have One's Head Up One's
    Ass 95
Have One's Thumb Up One's
    Ass 96
Have Shit For Brains 96
Have Someone By The Balls . 96
Have Someone By The
    Short Hairs 96
Have Someone's Ass 96
Headlights 97
Hang A Heat Stick 97
Heave 97
Hell 97
Hell On Something 98
Hell-raiser 98
Hell To Pay 98
"Hell's bells!" 98
Helluva 98
Helmet 99
Hershey Highway 100
Hershey Squirts. 100
Highbeams 100
Hippo. 100
Hit In The Face With A Hot
    Bag Of Nickles 100
Ho 101
Hog 101
Holler At The Toilet 101
"Holy shit!" 102
Home Base 102
Honey Pot 102
Hook Shop 102
Hooker 102
Hooters. 103
Horn Dog 103
Horny 104
Hose 104
Hot And Bothered. 104
Hot Shit 104
"Hot Damn!" 104
Hung 105
Hurl 105
In Deep Shit 106
Jack Off 108
Jack-off 108
Jackass 108
Jail Bait 109
Jerk Off 109
Jerk-off 109
Jerkin' The Gherkin 109
"Jesus Christ !" 109
Jesus-freak 110
Jism 110
Johnson 110
Joystick 110
Jugs 110
Jump Someone's Bones . . . 110
Junior 111
Junk 111
"Keep your panties on." . . . 112

Kick Ass 112
Kick-ass 113
Kick Someone's Ass 113
Kiss Ass 113
Kiss-ass 114
Knocked Up. 114
Knockers. 114
La Petite Mort. 115
Lard-ass 116
Laugh At The Lawn 116
Laugh One's Ass Off. . . . 116
Lay A Log. 116
Lay Pipe 116
Les-be-friends 117
Lesbo 117
Let One Fly 118
Like Hell 118
Lip-lock. 118
Lipstick Lesbian 119
Little Shit. 119
Look Like Death Warmed Over 120
Loose. 120
Maggot 122
Make An Anal Announcement 123
Make The Beast With Two
    Backs 123
Man Juice. 123
Man-hater 124
Maracas 124
Mary 124
Massage Parlor 125
Master 125
Matinee 126
Meat 126
Meat And Two Vegetables . . 126
Melons 126
Menage A Trois 126
Mercy Fuck 127
Milf. 127
Milk Bottles 127
Milk The Chicken 127
Missionary Position 127
Money Shot. 128
Monthly Visitor 128
Mosquito Bites 129
Mother 129
Mr. Happy 130
Muscle Mary 131
Nellie. 133
Nipple Clips. 133
"No shit!". 134
Nocturnal Emission 134
Nookie 134
Not To Have A Pot To Piss In 135
Numb-nuts 135
"Oh, hell!" 138
On Someone's Ass 138
One-eyed Monster 138
Open A Can Of Whoop-ass . 138
Overcoat 140
Package 141
Pain In The Ass 141
Party Hat 142
Pat 142
Pecker 142
Peckerhead 142
Peter 144
Peter-eater 144
Piece Of Shit 144
Pimp Slap 145
Pinch A Loaf 145
Piss 146
Piss Away. 146
Piss Hard-on 146
"Piss on that!" 146
Piss-poor. 146
Pissant 146
Pissed Off 146
Pisser 147
Pistol 147
Pitch A Tent 148
Pitcher 148
Pizza-face 148
Play Bouncy-Bouncy 148
Play Doctor 148
Play "Hide The Sausage" . . 149
Play The Skin Flute 149

Play Tonsil Hockey 149
Play With Oneself 149
Pocket Pool 150
Poke 150
Pole 150
Polish The Knob. 150
Poop Chute 152
Pop Someone's Cherry . . . 152
Pot 152
Precum. 154
Puke 155
Pull Shit 155
Punch The Clown 155
Punk-ass 155
Put Out 156
Queer As A Three-Dollar Bill . 158
Rack 159
Rack Salesman 159
Ralph. 160
Ramrod. 160
Rat-bastard. 160
Raw Sex 160
Ridden Hard And Put Away
    Wet 161
Ride Bareback 162
Ride The Red Tide. 162
Rimming 162
Rip Someone A New Asshole 162
Rod 163
Roll The Fuzzy Dice 164
Rub The Rod 164
Rubber 164
Sack 166
Salami 167
Scare The Shit Out Of
    Someone 167
Scared Shitless 167
Schizo 168
Score. 168
Screamer. 168
Screw 169
"Screw off!" 170
Screw Someone Over . . . 170
Screw Someone's Brains Out 170
Screw the Pooch 170
"Screw you!" 171
Screwed 171
Screwed In The Head . . . 171
Second Base 172
Service Station 173
Shag 174
Shake Hands With The
    Governor 174
Shit 174
Shit a Brick 175
Shit-eating Grin. 175
Shit-faced 175
Shit-for-brains 175
"Shit happens." 175
Shit List 175
Shit On Someone 175
Shit Or Get Off The Pot . . 176
Shit Out Of Luck 176
Shit Someone. 176
Shitbox. 176
Shithead 176
Shithouse 176
Shitload 176
Shitter 176
Shitty 177
Shlong 177
Shoot One's Wad 177
Shoot The Shit 177
Shout At One's Shoes . . . 178
Shtup 178
Silent But Deadly 178
Skank 179
Skin Flick 180
Slap The Snake 180
Sleaze 180
Slimeball 181
Smart-ass 182
Someone's Ass Is Grass . . . 184
Son Of A Bitch 184
Spanish Fly 184
Spew 185
Squat 186

Stacked 187
Staff 187
Stick Something Where The
    Sun Don't Shine 188
Stiffy 188
Stinking Drunk 188
Stupid Drunk 190
Submissive 190
Suck 190
Suck A Golf Ball Through A
    Garden Hose 190
Suck Ass 190
Suck Face 190
Suck The Chrome Off A
    Trailer Hitch 191
Swap Spit 192
Switch Hitter 192
T. And A. 193
Ta-ta's 193
Tail. 193
Take A Dump 194
Take A Leak 194
Take A Shit 194
Take A Squirt 194
Take Shit 194
Talk To Huey On The Big
    White Phone 194
Technicolor Yawn 195
Than Shit. 195
The Back Door 195
The Big "O" 195
The Curse 196
The High Hard One 196
The Red Flag's Up. 196
The Runs 196
The Shit 196
"The shit rolls downhill." . . . 197
"The shit's going to hit the
    fan!" 197
The Trots 197
Thing 198
Think One's Shit Doesn't
    Stink 198
Third Base 198
Third Leg 198
Tickle The Tiger. 200
Tight-ass 200
Toot 201
Top 201
Tough Shit 202
Tramp 202
Trannie 202
Treat Someone Like Shit . . 203
Trick 203
Trouser Snake 203
Tub 203
Tune One's Organ. 204
Turd 204
Turned On 204
12-step. 204
Unit 206
Up Shit Creek. 206
Vibrator 209
Water Sports 211
Wet 212
Wet Dream 212
Whack Off 212
Whale 212
Wham Bam, Thank You,
    Ma'am 212
What The Hell 213
Whip The Weenie 213
White Trash 214
Whiz 214
Whore 214
Whorehouse 214
Wiener 214
Willie. 215
Wonder-down-under 216
Woody 216
Yabbos 218
Yak. 218
Yank The Yak 218
York 219
"You bet your sweet ass!" . . 219
Yuke 219
Zit 220

USED WITH EXTREME CAUTION

Abso-fucking-lutely 2
Ass-fuck 5
Ball 9
Bang 11
Beaver. 14
Beaver-eater. 14
"Big fucking deal." 15
Bitch Slap 17
Blow. 18
Blow Job. 18
Box 22
Box Lunch 22
Breast Fuck 22
Bum-fuck 24
Bump Pussy 24
Bush. 25
Bust A Nut 26
Butt Fuck 26
Camel Toe 29
Cherry. 31
Chocolate Speedway 32
Chucklefuck 32
Clit 33
Clusterfuck 34
Cock 34
Cock-block. 34
Cock Ring 35
Cocksucker 35
Cocktease 35
Cooch 36
Cooter. 36
Cornhole. 37
Crack 38
Cream. 40
Cream One's Jeans 40
Cum. 41
Cunt 42

Daisy Chain 44
Deep Throat 45
Dick With Someone 46
Don't Give A Fuck 51
Drag Queen 53
Dry Fuck. 55
Dumb-fuck. 56
Dyke 56
Fag Hag 62
Faggot. 62
Fairy. 62
Finger-fuck 65
Fisting 65
Flamer. 66
Fuck 72
"Fuck a duck!" 73
Fuck Around 73
Fuck Buddy 73
Fuck Like Bunnies 74
"Fuck no!" 74
"Fuck off!" 74
Fuck Someone Over 74
Fuck Someone's Brains Out. . 74
"Fuck that noise!" 74
Fuck-up 75
Fuck Up Someone 75
Fuck Up Something 76
Fuck With Someone 76
Fuck With Something. . . . 76
"Fuck yes!" 76
"Fuck you!" 76
Fucked 76
Fucked In The Ass 76
Fucked In The Head 77
Fucked-up 77
Fucker. 77
Fuckface. 77

Fucking 77
"Fucking A!" 77
Fucknut 77
Fuckstick 78
Fudgepacker. 78
Fur Pie. 78
Furburger 78
Gang Bang. 80
Get A Piece Of Ass 81
Get Off 82
Get One's Rocks Off 82
Get Some Ass 83
Give Head 84
Go Down On Someone . . . 85
Go Down The Dirt Road. . . 85
Gym Queen 89
Hole 101
Homo 102
Hummer 105
Leather Queen 117
Limp-wrist 118
Love Dungeon 121
Love Muscle 121
Man Pussy 124
Manhole Inspector 124
Mindfuck 127
Motherfucker 130
Motherfucking 130
Muff 130
Muff-diver 130
Muffin 130
Munch Box 131
Munch Carpet. 131
Nail 132
Pearl Necklace 142
Pigfuck 145
Pillow-biter 145

Poonani 150
Poontang 150
Prick 154
Pussy. 155
Pussy-whipped 156
Queef 157
Queen 157
Queer 158
Reach Around. 160
Retard 161
Rump Ranger. 164
Screaming Fairy 168
Sissy 178
68 (Sixty-eight). 179
69 (Sixty-nine) 179
Size Queen 179
Slut 181
Snatch 183
Snowball 183
Spit 186
Spunk 186
Strap-on 189
Suck Someone Off 191
Swallow 192
Sympathy Fuck 192
Tap That Ass 195
Teabag 195
The Y. 197
Throw One In Her. 199
Tit Fuck 200
Tits 201
Twat 204
"Up yours!". 207
Vertical Smile. 208
What The Fuck 213

STREET SPANISH 1
THE BEST OF SPANISH SLANG

Entertaining dialogs, word games, drills, crossword puzzles, and word searches will have you understanding the everyday language spoken throughout the many Spanish-speaking countries. Learn the real language used on the street, in homes, offices, stores, and among family and friends!

Book: 233 pages — ISBN: 0471179-701 • US $16.95

This Audio Cassette contains all the dialogues in the book and a selection of exercises from every lesson.
Audio Cassette — ISBN: 1891888-188 • US $12.50

STREET SPANISH 2
THE BEST OF SPANISH SLANG

This entertaining guide will lead you through the imaginative world of popular Spanish idioms, using dialogues, vocabulary lessons, entertaining word drills and games including crossword puzzles, fill-ins, find-a-word charts, and dictations.
Book: 234 pages — ISBN: 0471179-71X • US $16.95

This Audio Cassette contains all the dialogues in the book and a selection of exercises from every lesson.
Audio Cassette — ISBN: 1891888-196 • US $12.50

STREET SPANISH 3
THE BEST OF NAUGHTY SPANISH

Popular expletives and obscenities – those "dirty" words and phrases constantly used in movies, books, and conversations between native speakers. This is the first step-by-step guide of its kind to explore the most common curses, vulgarities, and obscenities used in many Spanish-speaking countries.
Book: 238 pages — ISBN: 0471179-728 • US $16.95

This Audio Cassette contains all the dialogues in the book and a selection of exercises from every lesson.
Audio Cassette — ISBN: 1891888-20X • US $12.50

STREET SPANISH
SLANG DICTIONARY & THESAURUS

This slang dictionary and thesaurus offers Spanish equivalents and usage tips for over 1,000 Spanish terms, including slang, idioms, colloquialisms, and obscenities. It also offers a fun thesaurus featuring Spanish expressions and obscenities destined to make you feel like an insider in no time!

Book: 267 pages — ISBN: 0471168-343 • US $17.95

STREET FRENCH 1
THE BEST OF FRENCH SLANG

Sacré bleu! This fun guide is the first in a series of books that teach how to speak the real language used daily on the street, in homes, offices, stores, and among family and friends. Entertaining dialogues, word games and drills, crossword puzzles, and word searches will have you sounding like a native fast!

Book: 252 pages — ISBN: 0471138-983 • US $16.95

This Audio Cassette contains all the dialogues in the book and a selection of exercises from every lesson.
Audio Cassette — ISBN: 1891888-005 • US $12.50

STREET FRENCH 2
THE BEST OF FRENCH IDIOMS

This fully-illustrated guide explores some of the most popular idioms used in France. This book is packed with word games, dialogues using idioms, crossword puzzles, find-a-word grids, and special tips guaranteed to make you *au jus* ("up-to-date" or, literally, "juiced up") before you know it!

Book: 268 pages — ISBN: 0471138-991 • US $16.95

This Audio Cassette contains all the dialogues in the book and a selection of exercises from every lesson.
Audio Cassette — ISBN: 1891888-013 • US $12.50

STREET FRENCH 3
THE BEST OF NAUGHTY FRENCH

This is the first step-by-step guide of its kind to explore the most common curses, crude terms, and obscenities used in France. Chapters include: dating slang, non-vulgar / vulgar insults and put-downs, name-calling, body parts in slang, sexual slang, bodily functions, plus sounds and smells!

Book: 239 pages — ISBN: 0471138-009 • US $17.95

This Audio Cassette contains all the dialogues in the book and a selection of exercises from every lesson.
Audio Cassette — ISBN: 1891888-021 • US $12.50

STREET FRENCH
SLANG DICTIONARY & THESAURUS

This unique dictionary and thesaurus offers English equivalents and usage tips for over 1,000 French terms, including slang, idioms, colloquialisms, and obscenities. It also offers a fun thesaurus featuring French expressions, obscenities, and slang synonyms for English words and phrases!

Book: 322 pages — ISBN: 0471168-068 • US $17.95

STREET ITALIAN 1
THE BEST OF ITALIAN SLANG

Mamma mia! This fun guide will teach you how to speak the real language used on the street, in homes, offices, stores, and among family & friends. Entertaining dialogues, word games and drills, crossword puzzles, word searches, and will have you sounding like a native in a flash!

Book: 246 pages — ISBN: 0471384-380 • US $15.95

STREET ITALIAN 2
THE BEST OF ITALIAN SLANG

No book on everyday Italian would be complete without presenting popular insults, obscenities, curses, and gestures! This is the first step-by-step guide of its kind to explore this back alley language used is movies, conversations, TV, and virtually everyone!

Book: 246 pages — ISBN: 0471384-399 • US $15.95

ORDER FORM

SLANGMAN®
EDUCATION ESSENTIALS

dba Slangman Publishing
12206 Hillslope Street
Studio City, CA 91604 - USA

INTERNATIONAL:
1-818-769-1914

TOLL FREE (US/Canada):
1-877-SLANGMAN (752-6462)

WORLDWIDE FAX:
1-413-647-1589

EMAIL:
info@slangman.com

Preview chapters and shop online at:
WWW. SLANGMAN .COM

SHIPPING

Domestic Orders

SURFACE MAIL
(Delivery time 5-7 days).
Add $5 shipping/handling for the first item,
$1 for each additional item.

RUSH SERVICE
Available at extra charge. Contact us for details.

International Orders

SURFACE MAIL
(Delivery time 6-8 weeks).
Add $5 shipping/handling for the first item,
$2 for each additional item. Note that shipping to some countries may be more expensive. Contact us for details.

AIRMAIL
Available at extra charge. Contact us for details.

Method of Payment (Check one):

☐ Personal Check or Money Order
   (Must be in U.S. funds and drawn on a U.S. bank.)

☐ VISA   ☐ Master Card   ☐ Discover   ☐ American Express   ☐ JCB

Credit Card Number

Expiration Date

TITLE	ISBN	QTY	PRICE	TOTAL
The Slangman Guide To **STREET SPEAK 1**	Book: 1891888-080		$18.95	
	CDs: 1891888-293		$35.00	
	Cassettes: 1891888-307		$25.00	
The Slangman Guide To **STREET SPEAK 2**	Book: 1891888-064		$21.95	
	CDs: 1891888-315		$35.00	
	Cassettes: 1891888-323		$25.00	
The Slangman Guide To **STREET SPEAK 3**	Book: 1891888-226		$21.95	
	CDs: 1891888-331		$35.00	
	Cassettes: 1891888-34X		$25.00	
The Slangman Guide To **BIZ SPEAK 1**	Book: 1891888-145		$21.95	
	CDs: 1891888-358		$35.00	
	Cassettes: 1891888-366		$25.00	
The Slangman Guide To **BIZ SPEAK 2**	Book: 1891888-153		$21.95	
	CDs: 1891888-374		$35.00	
	Cassettes: 1891888-382		$25.00	
The Slangman Guide To **DIRTY ENGLISH**	Book: 1891888-234		$21.95	
STREET SPANISH 1	Book: 1471179-701		$16.95	
	Cassette: 1891888-188		$12.50	
STREET SPANISH 2	Book: 0471179-71X		$16.95	
	Cassette: 1891888-196		$12.50	
STREET SPANISH 3	Book: 0471179-728		$16.95	
	Cassette: 1891888-20X		$12.50	
STREET SPANISH SLANG DICTIONARY & THESAURUS	Book: 0471168-343		$17.95	
STREET FRENCH 1	Book: 0471138-983		$16.95	
	Cassette: 1891888-005		$12.50	
STREET FRENCH 2	Book: 0471138-991		$16.95	
	Cassette: 1891888-013		$12.50	
STREET FRENCH 3	Book: 0471138-009		$17.95	
	Cassette: 1891888-021		$12.50	
STREET FRENCH SLANG DICTIONARY & THESAURUS	Book: 0471168-068		$17.95	
STREET ITALIAN 1	Book: 0471384-380		$15.95	
STREET ITALIAN 2	Book: 0471384-399		$15.95	
	Total for Merchandise			
Sales Tax *(California residents only add applicable sales tax)*				
	Shipping *(See left)*			
	ORDER TOTAL			

Prices/availability subject to change

Name _____

(School/Company) _____

Street Address _____

City _____ State/Province _____ Postal Code _____

Country _____ Phone _____

Email _____

Signature _____